*The Crimes of Womanhood*

# The Crimes of Womanhood

## Defining Femininity in a Court of Law

A. CHEREE CARLSON

*University of Illinois Press*

URBANA, CHICAGO, AND SPRINGFIELD

First Illinois paperback, 2014
© 2009 by the Board of Trustees
of the University of Illinois
All rights reserved
Manufactured in the United States of America
1 2 3 4 5 C P 5 4 3 2 1
♾ This book is printed on acid-free paper.

The Library of Congress cataloged the cloth edition as follows:
Carlson, A. Cheree
The crimes of womanhood : defining femininity in
a court of law / A. Cheree Carlson.
p.   cm.
Includes bibliographical references and index.
ISBN 978-0-252-03401-5 (cloth : alk. paper)
1. Sex discrimination against women—Law and
legislation—United States—History.
2. Female offenders—Legal status, laws, etc.—
United States—History.
3. Women—United States—Social conditions—History.
4. Femininity in popular culture—United States—History.
5. Femininity—Social aspects—United States—History.
6. Trials—United States—History.
I. Title.
KF4758.C368     2009
345.73'03—dc22     2008027211

PAPERBACK ISBN 978-0-252-08002-9

*To Leonard F. Carlson*
*Sorry it took so long, Daddy.*

# Contents

# Acknowledgments

This book was a long time from start to finish. Were it not for the efforts of many friends and colleagues it would have remained unfinished. My deepest appreciation to all of you, with a special shout-out to:

Michelle Holling, who was there at the start.

Marouf Hassian and Tom Nakayama, who stepped into the breach.

The staff at Rehab without Walls in Phoenix, Arizona, who got me back to work.

And especially to Peter Hom, who stuck with me through the absolute worst.

My thanks also to Laurie Matheson at the University of Illinois Press, Karen Foss, Martha Solomon Watson, and several anonymous readers for their comments and guidance on the manuscript in its various incarnations.

# Introduction

*Womanhood on Trial*

This is a book about stories. More precisely, it is about stories told by white male lawyers to white male juries concerning women of all kinds. One might even consider them "morality tales" recast for their contemporary, and presumably more sophisticated, audiences. In these stories, virtuous women are betrayed by libertines, and innocent men are seduced by fallen women. Insane women threaten the safety of the community and sane women are exploited by greedy physicians. The odd fact that sometimes all these things occur simultaneously to the same characters is mainly due to conflicting goals of the narrators. Lawyers tell stories to win verdicts. Thus, lawyers often find themselves working to construct stories that will make the same characters and plots arrive at very different conclusions.

By now it should be no shock to the student of law that it is possible to define the task of persuading juries as a form of storytelling. Landmark works by luminaries such as James Boyd White have established that the law itself relies on narratives. And it is not merely scholars who have made that leap. Practicing, and practical, lawyers such as Gerry Spence have made the art of storytelling a central part of seminars meant to improve the skills of trial lawyers.

What is less evident in the scholarship is the recognition that, since a story is a rhetorical construction, the stories of law are subject to the same rhetorical rules and strategies as those told everywhere else. In their coherence, in their believability, and in their mutability, the narratives of law are not that different from all the other stories in our culture—from classical novels to comic books.

The stories told in courts of law, of course, are qualitatively different from those of literature. At the very least, they possess more concrete effects upon human behavior. Jurors base verdicts on these stories. Judges write decisions that enter into the narratives of precedent and set the boundaries for future arguments. The press copies them for distribution of moral precepts to the masses. Eventually, elements of the story integrate themselves into the "law" so thoroughly that they become "facts." Facts are hard to dispute and harder to escape.

*stories become "facts"*

Some of this process is conscious. As Wetlaufer notes, any lawyers worth their salt "will make every effort to disguise the fact" that a story is a "creation, and to present it instead as a simple revelation of the objective truth" (1559). Simultaneously, they may construct that story from "objective truths" that were actually derived from other stories once told with similar effort. In this case, no one is consciously aware of the transformation taking place.

It is at this invisible nexus of "truth" and "fiction" that the discipline of rhetoric is at its best. Rhetoric is intimately concerned with the means by which communicators transform their beliefs into believable narratives that will sway audiences. It also provides the tools through which a commonly accepted narrative can be used to create new stories—even stories that will contradict the original. Rhetoric thus aids us in the examination of narratives as tools for both creating the status quo and dismantling social orders.

The field of rhetoric itself has gone through multiple iterations of theories and methods from which to evaluate this endless process. Walter R. Fisher moved to both narrow and broaden the scope of narrative theory. Fisher claimed that narrative was more than just a story; it was, in fact, a perspective one could take toward all claims to "truth." Every attempt to order reality into some instructive whole involves narrative. At the same time that he expanded narrative into every realm of human reasoning, he also narrowed its scope. For Fisher, the best use of narrative analysis was in the arena of public moral argument. The most enduring "facts" created by stories, he claimed, were those moral touchstones that could later serve as the bases for evaluating morals, ethics, and social conventions. These touchstones exist independently of reasoning processes such as the highly formalized rules of law, although they may be used as warrants in that process by trained arguers.

The increased interest in narratives as conveyances of moral values has been heralded as a victory for disenfranchised social entities who have no formal training in, nor access to forums for, the traditional models of argument found in the law. Traditional models of reasoning based upon the classic Aristotelian method require extensive training, which usually is only offered to individuals who can acquire a university education. In order to apply these linear models of thought, one must be familiar with the specific field of argument that supplies the premises upon which to base new contentions. Law is one of the least accessible of those fields. Most legal arguments are based upon premises embedded in centuries of precedents and practices, which are hopelessly arcane to the uninitiated.

Although many fields are similarly difficult to grasp completely, the legal field is one wherein the insiders craft legal standards to which even outsiders must adhere. This becomes a problem when the law is asked to render judgments in what might be considered "moral" arenas, such as practices related to gender or culture. What is a sensible practice to one group might be considered evil by another, and the law often comes down upon one side or the other without making its decision processes understandable to either group. Outsiders cannot easily attack, defend, or ameliorate the new practices that result from those decisions.

Since the moral stakes are equally high for all individuals in a society, a model that automatically excludes the majority of them is inherently oppressive; thus, releasing moral argument from traditional constraints can be viewed as liberating. As a result of this equalizing impetus, the possibilities of using narratives as touchstones to direct and constrain public moral argument have been discussed thoroughly in the discipline of rhetoric. Naturally, this enterprise creates dilemmas of its own. Regardless of the mechanism through which they are derived, many agreed-upon social values exist explicitly to control, constrain, or oppress human behavior in directions preferred by some privileged class. Once we privilege narrative as a creator of social values, we must also hold it responsible for reifying any of those values we deem negative. There is little help for this task within the narratives themselves; no value is without its rhetorical ancestor, and these ancestral narratives can easily be used to alter, manipulate, or reapply those values to fit the judgment desired by majority.

In response to this problem, critics have begun to explore new ways of looking at narratives in the social realm. Celeste Condit began that search by suggesting a new metaphor for narrative itself. Instead of viewing narratives as instantiations of some ideal moral code, she argues, consider them tools used to craft virtue. This way, the critical focus is less on the possible "negative" effects of specific narratives and more on the possibilities they hold for creating "positive" touchstones for moral judgment. William Kirkwood has begun a close look at the techniques available within that craft for creating such possibilities. Critics, he claims, would do well to view narratives as performances that open options for moral action rather than as instantiations of values that close them.

This brings us to the current volume. In the nineteenth century, there was a strong and unquestioned tendency to define American culture as "a republic of virtue" (Hirshman and Larson). Virtue, as an embodiment of all that was morally superior about the United States, was celebrated in song, novels, plays, speeches, and art. It was also argued about, molded, and set in place by the law. The law was not merely upholding the principles of jurisprudence; it served as the arbiter of cultural values. In some cases, it even imposed new societal norms upon individuals who had not yet accepted them.

Given the structure of both American law and society at that time, it was inevitable that these new values would be constructed and imposed by one normative cultural group without much understanding or concern for others. In the nineteenth century, the law was white, male, and middle class. This held true throughout the antebellum period and changed only slowly after the Civil War. One body of citizens that was regularly excluded from this arena was women of all races and classes. The possession of a female body dispossessed one of the right to participate in the crafting of laws controlling that body. Whereas being of a privileged race or class could guarantee some legal preference, that preference came as the gift of men, in the form they decided upon.

Thus, the narratives related to gender and its "virtues" constructed by legal arguers in the United States were purely male. As a result, they were forced to rely upon other narratives, rather than experience, say, as the source of their facts. These narratives were very often extralegal—derived from other narratives that were already circulating in society at the time.

Focusing on this body of narrative makes a well-defined base from which to examine several dynamics. First, cases that involved "unprecedented" legal issues reveal most clearly the adoption of major elements of popular narratives by lawyers. These elements then take on lives of their own. The struggles and strategies of competing lawyers to make these "facts" serve the purpose of their respective goals reveals the power of the new narratives to constrain decision making. Finally, tactics used by a number of rhetors to transform those elements even as they made use of them offer us hope for the possibility of using them to liberate as well as oppress.

## The "Womanhood" Narrative as Trope in the Nineteenth Century

During the nineteenth century, the rise of modern mass publishing in the United States created a number of new avenues for attracting readers. Trial reports achieved special popularity as a form of "light entertainment" in the

United States during this century (Leps 111). So, coincidentally, did literary works aimed at female audiences. Increased availability of both of these spheres of literature to the general public created a matrix of images and symbols in the popular culture that could be transferred from one to the other at any given moment. There was always the possibility that literary images of American culture would eventually make their way into the closing argument of a prosecuting attorney or two. The moments when that possibility was realized provide fascinating windows into the development of our images of American womanhood, as well to what extent those images were present in the minds of ordinary men at the time.

There has been a great deal of work tracing our modern visions of womanhood back to nineteenth-century literature, predominantly popular literature. The questionable premise in these works is that the images created in the fiction and fashion magazines of the time were accurate mirrors of the images called upon by citizens to deal with practical decision making.

It is not at all difficult to trace the antecedents of "womanhood" in the literary realm. The development of this narrative was part of a trend in popular literature toward "feminization" that directly reflected cultural forces in the United States. Americans accepted British culture's sentimental view of women that eventually blossomed into the Victorian ideal of feminine character.

In the United States, however, that character was transformed into a distinctive entity and given the heavy responsibility of guiding the morality of the nation. Wasserstrom asserts that although Britons and Americans had similar views about ideal feminine behavior, only Americans forced woman to "embody her society"; Americans "incarnated the meaning of a whole culture" in the behavior of its women (126). This extreme form of identification led to a fascination with the "proper" female character, for as she went, so, symbolically, went the national character. Society's preoccupation with women and their role in preserving American morality eventually became so widespread that writers as distinct in time and place as de Tocqueville and Oscar Wilde observed the fascination.

This elevation of woman's role stimulated a body of American literature aimed at determining the final form of the feminine character. This trend, beginning as early as the 1820s, saw the rise of what is now called "domestic" writing (Papashivly; Welter). Domestic treatises were first published in the guise of books of household advice which went beyond home economics to character improvement. The genre eventually grew to include fictional pieces whose heroines embodied traits that American women were to emulate.

Narratives celebrating "the woman's sphere" did not blossom, however, until a new generation of authors, primarily women, reached maturity in the 1850s. These new writers quickly showed "a preference for heroines rather than heroes. These girls were designed to represent the whole range of attitudes and ideals . . . that defined civilization in the United States" (Wasserstrom 3). Although male writers helped perfect this definition, the real task fell upon the women writers, whose works would be read by young girls and women.

The "ideal" feminine character quickly became a constraint upon these writers. They were at first expected to make their writing "feminine"; that is, they were expected to create compliant, soft (but of course plucky) female characters to instruct the reader in her proper role. This development led to a sentimental style of writing that set the mold for a pattern of good feminine behavior.

That these narrative templates existed is beyond question. The issue that raised, and still raises, arguments among literary scholars is the extent to which these templates were used in other arenas. Did these cultural narratives have a concrete effect on the lives of those who read them? Were these fictional roles eventually transferred to the women themselves? Some of the earliest forays into that debate responded with a resounding yes.

The classic statement of this argument was made by Barbara Welter in the late 1960s. Welter reviewed novels, women's magazines, religious literature, and gift annuals published between 1820 and 1860, and discovered therein a cluster of virtues that she termed "the Cult of True Womanhood." In her study, Welter claimed that the "cardinal virtues" of femininity in this master narrative consisted of piety, purity, submissiveness, and domesticity (21). The details of these clusters will be addressed later, but for now it is important to note that Welter believed that American women and men derived their behavioral expectations from that literature and used it to guide their evaluations of others. Welter went so far as to state, "If anyone, male or female, dared to tamper with the complex of virtues which made up True Womanhood, he was damned immediately as an enemy of God, of civilization and of the Republic" (21).

Since the 1970s, most researchers in women's history have accepted as a given the existence of the narrative of "True Womanhood" in one form or another that dominated the literary culture of nineteenth-century Americans. Other researchers quickly built upon, modified, and sometimes contradicted Welter's initial premise.

Although they might have agreed that there was a clear cluster of values developing in the popular literature, most of the scholars who came after Welter disagreed with her interpretation (see Roberts). Welter and many other feminists in the early 1970s were heavily influenced by Marxist theory. Thus she saw in "True Womanhood" a clear male conspiracy aimed at keeping women subjugated by creating a separate, and powerless, arena for feminine behavior. Several other writers agreed. Mary Ryan, for example, blamed *Godey's Lady's Book* for the entire concept of "woman's sphere," stating that the periodical "conceived and propagated a whole new scheme of gender differentiation" almost singlehandedly (*Womanhood* 114–15). Francis Cogan proffered a vision of mid-nineteenth-century femininity called "Real Womanhood" that differed in the cardinal virtues (a "real woman," thankfully, had a backbone) but was still derived from literary resources. These studies are interesting and compelling, but they share a tendency to accept fiction as a mirror for political culture in spite of the fact that these literary models rarely bore any resemblance to the circumstances faced by real-life women, at least, not middle- to working-class women, who were arguably in the majority (Vincinus ix).

The trope of the "cult" held powerfully even as the political waters changed in the ensuing decades. As scholars rejected Marxist theory, they also rejected the notion that the gender roles depicted in literature were necessarily negative. The view shifted toward "womanhood" as secret source of empowerment for women; one often promoted by women themselves (Kerber, "Separate Spheres" 17). This trend reached an apotheosis with the publication of Katheryn Sklar's landmark biography of Catherine Beecher. Sklar claimed that Beecher, a teacher and popular author of housekeeping and cookery manuals, used the traditionally feminine sphere of home and hearth as an avenue for female power. Thus, claimed Sklar, the delineation of separate gender norms was actually subversive to the system. Sklar privileged a cult of domesticity over one of true womanhood, which is reasonable given the focus of Beecher's work. Still, she maintained that literary efforts, in this case nonfictional, had concrete and far-reaching effects upon the lives of women.

As the astute reader may have noticed, no scholar denied that gender roles were copiously and rigorously delineated in the novels, plays, gift books, and household manuals of the day. The debate was over the extent to which narratives in literature might concretely affect the lives of women. Perhaps the characters demonstrated no more than wishful thinking on the part of the author. Perhaps readers were perfectly aware of the line between literature and life—then again, perhaps not. There was also debate over whether those effects, if genuine, would be positive or negative.[1]

The debate over what constitutes "real" was predictably unproductive. The literary data was the only unassailable fact. In addition, political pressures in academia had again changed. The entire notion of separate spheres of male and female function, in literature, in politics, and in the social order itself smacked too much of inequality. In the quest to dismantle the hierarchies of the present, many literary scholars scorned recognizing the hierarchies of the past.

Thus, the rise of a postmodern, and more rhetorical, perspective was needed to provide scholars with a new avenue from which to study the pervasive cultural narrative. The first call for this perspective was sounded by an historian, Linda Kerber. She proposed that productive scholarship focused not on women's sphere but on the *language* of women's sphere: how and when it was developed and used in response to changing social "realities" ("Separate Spheres" 21). Thus, whatever the contemporary politics, one could appreciate the cult of womanhood as a rhetorical entity and find in it a mirror for American attitudes about women.

Naturally, rhetoric is more than just a mirror. It is also an intensely practical art of effecting change in one's social world. One thing missing from the scholarly wrangle over womanhood through the 1980s and early 1990s was an appreciation for the literary narratives as rhetorical entities to be appreciated on their own merits as clues to attitudes and potential rules for decision making. As a result, too much effort was spent determining whether the literature was "real" and not enough on determining the "reality" in which they were vital participants. As Kenneth Burke has noted, "Every document bequeathed to us by history must be treated as a *strategy for encompassing a situation . . .* as the *answer or rejoinder* to assertions current in the situation in which it arose" (*Philosophy* 29, emphasis in the original). The narratives celebrating womanhood exist because someone at the time thought that it was important to introduce them into American culture. Whether it was a conservative male fighting off a perceived threat to his power or a woman struggling to delineate her role in a shifting social order, that person was enlisting rhetoric as a tool for achieving that end. Thus, by becoming aware of where "womanhood" rhetoric turns up, in which situations and for what purposes, will reveal much about what our forbearers believed in and fought to maintain.

It will also reveal more clearly the limits to which American males were willing to go in fighting over gender. Ed Black has noted that "groups of people often become distinctive as groups by their habitual patterns of commitment—not by the beliefs they hold, but by the manner in which they hold them and give them expression. Such people do not necessarily share ideas. Rather, they share stylistic proclivities and the qualities of mental life of which those proclivities are tokens" (112).

Black maintains that the fiercest defenses of culture emerge in what he calls the "sentimental style," an emotionally overwrought form that goes to great lengths to dictate not only how people should think but how they should feel about the subject under discussion. Debates about gender invariably drip with pathos, which Black would aver indicates the importance of the issue to those attempting rhetorically to define it.

As Kerber has astutely noted, it is time for scholars "to understand that gender itself is a rhetorical construction" ("Introduction" 5). Communication scholars are uniquely aware of the power of messages to alter perceptions of reality. A study that illuminates the origins of many of these rhetorical tropes will aid us in finding the trajectory of similar debates related to gender in contemporary life. If we truly want to understand the reality of women's lives, we had best consider the rhetoric that provided the foundation for current constructions.

Rhetorical narratives serve as guides that can be used by individuals to aid in day-to-day decision making. An individual might embrace a literary character as a role model. The actions taken in popular dramas might create an expectation that taking similar actions at home will lead to similar ends. Most importantly for the purposes of this volume, a narrative might contain rhetorical characters that are "representative" of certain persons one might encounter in real life. Thus, an individual might be persuaded that certain kinds of behaviors can be predicted for certain kinds of people. This brings us to one important venue for such a rhetorical process—the trial by jury.

## Tropes and Border Crossing

Popular literature is only one arena in which a narrative might manifest, one that is difficult to translate into behavior. We know that the cult of womanhood was ingrained in the reading materials of the educated woman of the day, but we do not know the extent to which it might affect serious decisions made daily in the "real life" worlds of both sexes. The law, on the other hand, is a rhetorical field explicitly concerned with translating narratives into behavior. Those behaviors are then supposed evaluated by "universal" premises that apply equally to all members of the culture. Thus, if a narrative from popular literature were to make its way into legal argumentation, the consequences of accepting it immediately become noticeable.

On the face of it, the literary conventions of womanhood would appear to have been accepted in nineteenth-century discourse on criminal women. Reluctant to study these women directly, historians and social scientists of the era often relied on images in the popular culture to discuss the subject. When they did so, "they cited the same literary sources novelists did—Clytemnestra and Lady Macbeth, for instance—as exemplars of the evil women were capable of" (Morris 3–4). Lawyers were also reluctant to look too closely at accused women. As Hartman discovered in her study of English and French murder trials, the female principals "were almost never presented as the women they were. They assumed multiple identities fashioned both by themselves and others" when presented to both the court and general public (255). Hartman presumed that the "real" face of womanhood was too disturbing to be viewed directly. Thus, like Medusa, woman had to be viewed in a mirror, lest the vision of her true self destroy carefully wrought cultural images.

Obviously, that a lawyer might call upon what he perceived as icons of femininity does not guarantee that the audience will accept his choice. Lady Macbeth might be a believable fiction, but would her characteristics transfer successfully to a real live woman standing in the dock? Luckily for the rhetorician, there is at least one test of the power of a characterization: the verdict. In any case that goes to a jury, at least twelve "peers" of the principals decide which story is more believable.[2] In a nineteenth-century trial, a woman's peers were men. Without direct physical experiences tied to the feminine gender, male jurists had to construct womanhood whole cloth from the narratives of their culture, as formed and directed by lawyers on both sides. The lawyer with the most skillful distillation of these elements could occasionally even turn the tide of a case in the face of compelling physical evidence. Naturally, too many factors enter in to a case to make any sort of causal argument about these narratives in a particular instance. As Oliver has noted, "This is not to say that courtroom speeches that win verdicts are always 'good' and that those that lose are always 'bad.' But more than for most kinds of speaking, the correlation between eloquence and success is very high" (402).

Is there a similar correlation between the appeals to men through images of women? This investigation will show that, in the nineteenth century, such appeals were often successful.

One might not expect males to have much sense of investment in characterizations of female behaviors. In actuality, they were probably heavily invested. The masculine ideal was directly tied to concepts of womanhood. Masculinity was often defined using femininity as a negative example. A more practical consideration is that men dealt daily with women, usually in the bosom of their own families. Maintaining "normal" relations between the sexes would thus add relevance to their decisions. Men, then, would be careful in choosing which stories to accept.

In addition to the direct test of attitudes made visible when male jurors voted on the verdict, trials are also texts that test attitudes in the public realm. The popular media of the period did not merely "report" on a trial; they also molded and transformed the narratives to suit the reading audience of both sexes. The choices made by journalists as to which elements to emphasize and the public debate over decisions made in the court reveal whether narrative elements brought to trial were also compelling on the "outside."

In sum, trials are one arena of discourse where popular culture and life-or-death decisions are merged through the skills of communicators. The resulting narratives reveal much about what it meant to be a "woman" in the nineteenth century.

## Overview of the Selected Cases

An excellent way to explore the power of these icons is to investigate cases where definite decisions were made in arenas where the reasoning process is still relatively available to the researcher. Those trials which became "popular" and attracted wide public attention in the United States have arguably more resonance with important attitudes of their times. This popularity is an underlying element of the cases selected for this volume, as it details the arguments used by men to evaluate the behavior of women.

The trials in this volume are "popular" trials that captured the attention of a wide audience outside the legal system. This level of information dissemination was no easy achievement in an era before broadcast media. From the universe of popular trials, I have selected cases wherein the gender of the defendant/principal was a central feature. This guaranteed that the rhetoric produced would circulate around my main subject. In a nutshell, the rhetoric produced in these venues was literally "voted on" by a duly constituted jury. Because the cases were popular, Americans paid close attention to the arguments and counterarguments. Because they were argued before a jury, we have at least a small amount of empirical evidence as to which arguments were persuasive to males selected from that public. There were no hung juries in these cases. Most importantly, the discussants were not men pontificating at a club or reading a novel. They were making decisions that entered into the legal stream of precedents that would inform the body of law in years to come.

The volume analyzes several crimes that we would still consider serious today, including murder. The nineteenth century, however, had a surprising range of possible "crimes" for women, so there will also be cases one might not expect. Overall, I hope that there is something in this volume to intrigue every reader.

The "crimes" committed by females often mirrored the crimes that were committed by males. However, gender became an important factor in assigning guilt or assessing punishment. The proper character of the middle-class woman was as important in a variety of civil proceedings as it was in criminal cases.

One area of civil law has regularly circulated around issues of competence. This arena was more likely to concern women because women were often viewed as being closer to incompetence than men. For example, the sanity hearings of Packard and Lincoln, one held before and one after the passage of a pivotal Illinois law, will reveal the sometimes surprising views on what makes a woman prone to insanity. Sanity laws in the nineteenth-century Illinois required that any person to be committed must first have a trial by jury. These proceedings are fertile ground for discovering which feminine behaviors could be construed as insane. The first trial and the one that created the precedent occurred in 1864, when Elizabeth P. W. Packard, the wife of a minister, decided to change her religion and was declared insane. Mary Todd Lincoln, the widow of the president of the United States, received two trials under that law. These cases reveal clearly just how narrow was the line that women had to walk—the same womanly virtues that were expected of them could be turned against them at any time.

Mental competence also became an issue in criminal trials, usually when a defendant claimed insanity as a defense of their actions. Mary Harris was tried in 1865 for the murder of her former fiancé when she found he had already married another woman. The narrative of innocence destroyed was potent enough to result in a not guilty verdict, which suggests that at least sometimes men thought that loss of virginity was justifiable grounds for homicide. An interesting aspect of this case was that Harris was a working-class Irish woman; one would expect a jury of those times to be less impressed by her betrayal. Her lawyers, however, labored diligently to transform her person into a mirror of the feminine ideal.

The stereotype of "frail femininity" remained active throughout the nineteenth century, so much so that it was possible for a woman to be served by it even when everyone in the community "knew" she was guilty. Our example is the 1895 trial of Lizzie Borden for allegedly axe murdering her father and step-mother. This is today viewed as a paradigmatic example of a murderer "getting away with it" because men could not be convinced that a woman was capable of a brutal slaying. It is evident, however, that stereotypes of womanhood were what led the police to consider her a suspect in the first place. Thus, gender served as a dual-edged weapon.

It is more difficult to pinpoint just when Ann Lohman (aka Madame Restell) became a criminal. Lohman was a female physician who practiced abortion in New York City. When she began her career in the late 1820s, her work was legal. When she ended it in 1878, abortion was a felony. She was in and out of court for the better part of the century. The rhetoric surrounding her shows that abortion was purely a woman's crime, in both supply and demand.

The final case occurred in 1925, and thus crosses the line into the twentieth century, but it is a perfect climax to the case studies. In it, nearly all of the nineteenth-century views of white middle-class womanhood are reaffirmed and applied to the twentieth-century story of a working-class woman of mixed race. Alice Rhinelander was sued for fraud by her new husband for "passing" as white. The most fascinating aspect of this case was that narratives of race and gender came together in such a way that the jury was moved more by the betrayal of Alice as a woman than the defrauding of Leonard as a white male, and found in Alice's favor. The vision of womanhood forged in the previous century displayed remarkable staying power.

The case studies, taken together, show how dangerous it is to assume traditional gender norms as cultural givens. Even the most powerful cultural premises can be altered rhetorically to fit new circumstances. Sometimes adherence to feminine norms were used as a basis from which to condemn, as well as free, a woman. Sometimes feminine norms jumped racial and economic boundaries. And sometimes one did not have to be a woman at all to benefit or suffer from feminine stereotypes. The cases reveal the power of rhetoric to shape arguments based on those norms, thus affecting how they are used in decision making.

# 1. Narrative Intersections in Popular Trials

In the introduction, I argued that the ideal way to explore the power of literary icons of womanhood is to investigate cases where definite decisions were made, in arenas where the reasoning process is still relatively available to the researcher. Trials are especially good starting points for such an investigation.

In addition to the obvious benefit of having individuals "vote," trials are also mirrors of attitudes in the public realm. Trials serve as "a form of social knowledge in that it is the means by which we hold what we know. It is a symbolic container allowing symbolic material to be collected and affirmed as social goods—that is, as substantive knowledge" (Hariman 21). This "substantive knowledge" is reified well beyond the confines of the courtroom. Published accounts of trials were popular newspaper fare and often inspired debate in other arenas.

All trials do not enter the public imagination on an equal footing. Unless there is local interest, the vast majority of cases proceed unnoticed by press or public. Yet sometimes a case becomes so compelling that it is reported, discussed, and dissected on a larger stage. The names of the principals became familiar to a national audience. Indeed, since the advent of television, even the lawyers often become celebrities. When a trial achieves such status, it becomes known as a "popular" trial. Hariman provides a basic definition: "a popular trial is a judicial proceeding that gains the attention of a general audience, usually through sustained coverage by the mass media" (2).

Those trials that achieve popular status are important on multiple levels. First, the very fact that a trial can hold the attention of a broad audience  indicates that it in some way mirrors "the interests, values, and controversies of society" (Schuetz 2). Thus, we can discover in them which legal issues are of genuine concern to citizens outside the courtroom.

Second, trials are indicators of public attitudes about the moral and cultural implications of those issues. In a clash of social values, trials tell us, through verdicts, which values are as compelling as we in the audience believe them to be. They tell us which forms of knowledge are easily manipulated by discourse and which are contradicted by law.

Finally, popular trials provide additional salience to the outcome of jury deliberations. Although verdicts in all trials are obviously important to the principals, often they are not the subject of public debate and discussion outside of the legal field. The exception is the popular trial. In many cases, a trial might be argued and reargued by the public and the press. The resulting body of new texts offers additional insights on the attitudes of laypeople—occasionally even those who do not participate in the narratives of white masculinity.

## Rhetorical Analysis and Trial Narratives

While it is obvious that the media coverage of a particular case is thoroughly grounded in popular culture, it might not be so clear that the discourse produced *within* a case is also so grounded. Indeed, narratives produced outside the courtroom are often viewed as "contaminating" the process of rational decision making, as witnessed by both lawyers' attempts to discover the potential jurors who have read the least about a case in the newspapers.

The fact, however, that neither lawyers, judges, nor juries enter the courtroom tabula rasa guarantees that material derived from years of exposure to preexisting narratives can, and probably will, be used in creating persuasive appeals. The discipline of rhetoric is perfectly suited for an investigation of how those appeals are constructed and delivered to the target audience.

The rhetorical approach to the study of legal discourse takes as a given that the law is not a static entity but is rather the outcome of the dynamics of discourse. This perspective acknowledges the role of logic and precedents in framing discourse while simultaneously exploring the manner in which those frames are manipulated and altered by skillful rhetoric. The utility of this approach has been proven repeatedly in research on the law and popular trials. Naturally, rhetorical analyses can, and have, been pursued through a variety of specific methods aimed at highlighting elements of discourse appropriate to the goal of the researcher. For example, Schuetz, in *The Logic of Women on Trial,* used a variety of methods focused on the forms of "logic" used to affect decision making in cases about women, and Jamieson concentrated on the effects new forms of media had on the outcome of the Scopes trial (*Eloquence* 31–42).

Since my purpose is to explicate the manner in which images of womanhood were manipulated, with varying degrees of skill, by male rhetors, I will use methods that highlight the manner in which symbolic constructions born in one rhetorical arena could be transformed and inserted into another. Thus, I will use a narrative approach to discourse that is informed by the theory of discourse created by Kenneth Burke.

## Narratives and Decision Making

Rather than analyzing the "reasons" given in the cases, I will review the arguments as though they were narratives produced by storytellers. There is well-established precedent in rhetorical scholarship for this approach, which at times can be more revealing than parsing arguments. It has been argued that "narrative is a major (perhaps the major) form of cultural communication of common-sense notions. It is the mode in which many of our value-judgments are stored and transmitted—rather than being conceptualized or communicated in analytical discourse" (Jackson 61). Narratives are central to criminal trials, which are "organized around storytelling" (Bennett and Feldman 3). Such stories upon which verdicts are based often have little to do with what really happened in a dispute but instead create a reality that the audience may or may not accept.

Obviously, receivers must use some standards to evaluate stories or they could never choose between competing versions of events. The nature of these standards has not been clearly established, as they seem to vary in ways not clearly derived from the legal process. While one jury might adhere to strict legal standards of evidence, another might apparently ignore those standards to judge based on personal prejudice. There have been several attempts to discover some basic universal mechanisms. For example, Fisher's prototypical model of narrative rationality bifurcates the evaluation process. He claims that audiences judge the internal coherence of story elements, such as plot, character, and timing, then proceed to evaluate "narrative fidelity," or whether the story "rings true" with other stories with which they are familiar (*Human Communication*).

At this level, preexisting cultural narratives become important to the process. I believe that the process operates more reciprocally than the categories set by Fisher may indicate; story elements that do not align with preconceived notions are more likely to be dismissed as incoherent than evaluated for plot function. Thus, narratives and their applications are at the heart of the process that Fisher terms "narrative rationality" (47).

A primary narrative element in a case determining criminality is character. A rhetor faced with a woman whose behavior is out of the ordinary might attempt to create a coherent persona for her by casting her in a role as though her life were a narrative to be evaluated. Character is central to this process. Though they begin as the building blocks of stories, characterizations can take on lives of their own, moving between and among other narratives until they become "culturally accepted accurate descriptions of a class" and can be labeled "character-types" (Condit, "Democracy and Civil Rights" 4). Character types function as universals against which we can compare new characterization.

Using universalized characters to evaluate a narrative becomes delicate when the universals are embedded in cultural narratives that have come to define who we are as a society. When drawing a line to include or exclude a character from lawful society, the rhetor must be certain that this line does not threaten the character of the audience. As Fisher notes, if "a story denies a person's self-conception, it does not matter what it says about the world. . . . the only way to bridge the gap . . . is by telling stories that do not negate the self conceptions that people hold of themselves" (*Human Communication* 75).

This fine line between a person's concept of self and other must be manipulated carefully. There is usually enough ambiguity in a particular concept that it can be symbolically manipulated to create strategic points of identification between who we think we are and who the rhetor would like us to believe we are, in order to alter our judgment of the actions of a particular character. These points of ambiguity are a specific focus of Burke's theory of the function of symbolic constructions in rhetorical influence.

## Burkean Concepts and Narratives

Kenneth Burke is one of the most influential rhetorical theorists of the twentieth century. An important focus of his system is the ontological claim that human beings are human precisely because they create, and are created by, complex symbolic structures that alter their perception of the world (*Language* 15). In the broadest terms, Burke's logic proceeds as follows: Human beings create symbols to order reality, but those symbols rarely have any concrete connection to that reality. Since there is no necessary link between symbol and referent, we can use a wide range of symbols to refer to the same referent. Thus, our choice of the precise symbol to use to describe an object can serve as a marker for our attitude toward that object. Burke then makes the claim that our attitude toward something will affect our actions in reference to it. For example, choosing to name defendants in a bombing case either anarchists or freedom fighters will have a material effect upon our judgment of the behavior.

This line of reasoning leads naturally to the proposition that we can find out how a culture views a woman by examining the symbolic structures that attach themselves to her. Such examination also provides important clues to how these symbols might be altered during a trial to redefine her character along the lines preferred by an attorney.

Symbolic structures are usually composed of multiple elements that are not mutually exclusive; a woman might be either working class or middle class, simultaneously parent and child, or excellent at only one of several gender-defined roles. The grey areas between categories are of special interest to Burke. As he notes, when categories blur "so that you cannot know for certain just where one ends and the other begins, you have the characteristic invitation to rhetoric" (*Rhetoric* 25).

Overlapping categories create potential ambiguity. Skilled rhetors know how to capitalize on ambiguity. Rhetoric can thus become a form of alchemy wherein a communicator can transform an element of character from a narrative in one context into an appropriate element from which to draw a conclusion in another. The process requires finding some area of "common ground": "participation in a common ground makes for transformability. At every point where the field covered by any one of these terms overlaps upon the field covered by any other, there is an alchemic opportunity, whereby we can put one philosophy or doctrine of motivation into the alembic, make the appropriate passes, and take out another" (Burke, *Grammar* xix). There are a number of tools available for "making the appropriate passes." Although they differ in practice, they are similar in goal. One finds discussions of a symbolic element within narratives already assimilated into the culture and finds a common ground from which to transform it into an element fitting a new narrative.

Burke's dramatistic theory contains a number of rich heuristic concepts that can be used to unearth the many ways storytellers can achieve these transformations. For the most part, I will discuss the appropriate concept in the chapter where it is applied to its most noticeable effect. There are, however, two narrative tools that were used frequently in a number of contexts: bridging devices and frames. These bear introduction here, for they will appear repeatedly in the analyses.

A common tactic in narrative manipulation is using "bridging devices," or "symbolic structures whereby one 'transcends' a conflict in one way or another" (Burke, *Permanence* 224). A bridging device is a symbol that shares substantive elements of more than one social category, creating those "areas of ambiguity" from which one can transform meaning.

A second means of manipulating narratives is "framing." On the broadest level, a frame is a "more or less organized system of meanings by which a thinking man gauges the historical situation and adopts a role with relation to it" (Burke, *Attitudes* 5). Burke's investigation of frames is particularly suited to this analysis because he delineates the myriad of responses to situations in terms of overarching literary forms, such as tragedy, comedy, satire, and burlesque. The same series of events, framed differently, can lead audiences to radically different evaluations of those events. This concept brings narrative and interpretation together in a productive manner.

In the cases that follow, rhetors of all sorts—lawyers, doctors, scientists, women's rights advocates, and ordinary citizens—will attempt to call upon characterizations of "woman" found in American culture and use them as premises from which to build narratives to attack or defend a particular defendant. Their relative success and failure in these endeavors will reveal which characterizations were "givens," which were subject to debate, and which did not seem to affect the audience at all. They will ultimately form a clear picture of what American audiences, particularly male audiences, thought about the "trials of womanhood."

## 2. Framing Madness in the Sanity Trial of Elizabeth Parsons Ware Packard

Much madness is divinest sense
To a discerning eye;
Much sense the starkest madness.
'Tis the majority
In this, as all, prevails.
Assent, and you are sane;
Demur,—you're straightway dangerous,
And handled with a chain.

—Emily Dickinson

Emily Dickinson, a figure known almost as well for her eccentricity as for her poetry, has encapsulated in these lines a dilemma that plagued both law and medicine in the nineteenth century. At what point does nonconformity cross the line into madness? And when does it become necessary to attach that chain?

This chapter explores that shifting line by analyzing the case of a woman who was actually tried for insanity in Illinois during the latter half of the nineteenth century. Due to an unusual set of circumstances, Elizabeth Parsons Ware Packard, a woman who appeared destined for quiet disappearance, instead was allowed to fight for her freedom. A jury of twelve men was asked to decide whether she was mad despite the fact that hers was not a criminal case; laymen could overturn a medical psychiatrist's opinion as to a person's sanity. In the presentation of arguments attempting to sway the opinions of men as to the state of a woman's mind, we can discover what both physicians and laymen thought it took to make a woman mad. This case is an excellent test of the potential power of preexisting narratives about women in American culture. What icons of womanhood could and could not be violated safely? Which ones were taken as "scientific" criteria for determining insanity?

The Packard case reveals that traditional elements of womanhood can be found operating behind the choice of evidence used by physicians, lawyers, and laymen to judge her. These elements, however, do not always lead to conclusions that we expect from our vision of these virtues. In some cases, too firm a commitment to a traditional virtue was as damning as a violation. What is praiseworthy at one moment is objectionable in the next. Women got no clear-cut guidelines for behavior from traditional feminine norms. An eccentric woman walked a thin line between being considered sane and insane, a line that could shift under her feet.

## The Law Seeks a Discerning Eye

Prior to the nineteenth century, the role of the physician in the court was limited, even in cases involving insanity. The law dealt primarily with the criminally insane, and physicians testified as to the mental competence of the subject well after a crime had been committed. Thus incarceration was, at least in principle, based on an overt break with established law. As the new century progressed, however, the standing of medical science within the community improved. The burgeoning science of psychiatry had successfully constructed a new view that insanity "was a disease, requiring segregation from society and long term medical care" (Himelhoch and Shaffer 343).

Obviously, an insane person was not likely to recognize his or her own illness and voluntarily submit to treatment. The public turned to the law for a way to manage unacceptable behavior. State legislatures obliged by passing statutes to create a new class of citizen who might benefit from involuntary incarceration. The dilemma was that these people were not criminals; though "diseased," they were rarely an actual threat to person or property. The only charitable solution, in the eyes of paternalistic lawmakers, was to make provision for public "asylums" and create rules for determining who would be sent there.

Most commonly, physicians evaluated the mental health of an individual. In most states, if a number of physicians (the number varied) agreed that an individual was insane, involuntary commitment followed. When physicians determined that a cure had been achieved, the person would be released. It was expected that the doctors would always use the strictest medical criteria in making their determinations. The power placed in the hands of physicians was enormous and surprising, given that there was no agreement within the medical community as to the causes, symptoms, and cure of mental illness. The potential for abuse was evident, as the opinion of a small number of "experts" could rob an individual of both reputation and liberty.

Although the commitment process was designed without reference to sex, women found themselves especially vulnerable. The prevailing medical opinion was that women were naturally more likely than men to become insane. Her weak constitution, plagued by a raging hormonal cycle, made every woman a candidate for at least temporary insanity. In addition, a woman unfairly labeled insane had no recourse to legal intervention. A woman's legal existence ended with her marriage, merged with the identity of her husband. He was both her lord and her guardian. As her protector, a husband could even demand a wife be imprisoned for her own good. He could usually find a sympathetic doctor willing to sign the papers.

## The Case of Elizabeth Parsons Ware Packard

This state of affairs persisted nationwide, but in Illinois, things began to change in 1864 when Elizabeth Parsons Ware Packard won a judgment of sanity from a jury in a trial that took place mainly by accident. After her release, Packard became an agitator for the civil rights of mental patients nationwide. In 1867, she succeeded in convincing Illinois lawmakers to guarantee that all mental patients would have the right to a precommitment trial. No person would be imprisoned without the concurrence of a jury. For the next twenty-six years, sanity trials were the law in Illinois. Whether this law operated to the overall benefit or detriment of mental patients was hotly debated, but it removed the definition of insanity from the complete control of the medical community and placed some power in the hands of lawyers and juries. Although a woman's fate was still in the hands of a group composed of males, at least it was a more diverse group, and with a trial, a woman had more chance of drawing public attention to her case.

The trial of Elizabeth Parsons Ware Packard is most unusual in that it took place at all. There was no provision for insanity trials in the Illinois statutes of the time. Packard's day in court was the result of a tactical error by her husband, which allowed her friends to challenge his diagnosis. The ensuing battle was the beginning of a fight that led to the reform of insanity laws in several states.

Illinois state laws regarding insanity were not out of line with those of the rest of the country. As noted earlier, the most common way to deal with the sanity issue was to let members of the medical profession decide who required commitment. Thus, in 1851, Illinois lawmakers followed the lead of other states and ruled that anyone could be involuntarily committed, provided two physicians performed an examination and signed documents declaring the person insane. As shaky as this medical protection was, the process was only guaranteed to adult males, for the Illinois law added a clause concerning exceptions: "Married women and infants, who, in the judgment of the medical superintendent, are evidently insane or distracted, may be entered or detained in the hospital on the request of the husband of the woman or the guardian of the infant, without the evidence of insanity required in other cases" (Packard 54).

If the superintendent of the state hospital agreed, a man could have his wife committed with no examination, no paperwork, and no due process. Even single women were not entirely safe, as their fathers were their legal guardians until marriage. Thus, a woman who lost the positive regard of her male guardian for any reason could find herself locked in an asylum for an unspecified period of time. Once in, she was at the mercy of the superintendent (also male), who could, with a stroke of a pen, either free her or pronounce her incurable. If abuses of the law occurred, it was not difficult to silence the offended party. Elizabeth Packard remained imprisoned under this statute for three years.

In 1860, when Reverend Theophilus Packard had his wife committed, their marriage was on shaky ground. Packard was a strong-willed woman and had never quite been able to adapt to her role of helpmate as required by Reverend Packard's career as a Presbyterian minister. Still, the couple got along tolerably well until 1858, when Packard was exposed to spiritualism. She became fascinated and eventually turned to the study of Swedenborgianism, a mystical philosophy that was at odds with traditional Christianity. Her husband and his congregation were not amenable to her desire to debate religious principles. Thus, Packard petitioned to transfer to the Methodist church, where her ideas were more welcome.

Reverend Packard faced a crisis: a minister who could not keep his own wife from converting risked a major loss of credibility in the community. To prevent this, he had her committed. Early one morning, while Packard was still dressing, Reverend Packard entered the bedroom with two doctors, both members of his congregation. They took her pulse and left. The next thing Packard knew, she was on her way to the Illinois State Hospital. She was treated well at first but later claimed that her continued agitation for her freedom led to confinement in the "maniac" ward. At any rate, she succeeded mainly in irritating the superintendent, Dr. Andrew MacFarland. He was not about to become her ally.

Packard might have remained in the hospital for the rest of her life but for the support of her eldest son. As a minor he could do nothing, but he visited frequently, and the two planned for the day when he turned twenty-one and could file a petition for his mother's freedom. Coincidentally, shortly after the young man reached his majority, Dr. MacFarland released Packard back into her husband's custody. He did not pronounce her cured. Rather, he stated that she was incorrigible and refused to keep her. This seems an odd reaction; after all, asylums were designed to hold just such people. Packard believed she had finally worn him down. A more cynical view is that MacFarland did not want young Packard bringing the case under a judge's scrutiny.

This is when Reverend Packard made his tactical error. He made plans to remove her to an asylum in another state. If his plan had stayed secret, he would have succeeded in spiriting her away. Instead, he left revealing letters lying about. When she discovered them, he told her all, locked her in the nursery and took away her clothes to prevent her escape. Even the windows were nailed shut. Friends who came to visit were told Packard did not want to see anyone.

In a move that would suit any melodrama, Packard managed to write a note explaining her plight and slid it out a gap in the window frame when she saw a stranger pass the house. The note brought a friendly neighbor, who ascertained that she was indeed a prisoner. That neighbor went directly to a judge. Although there was no law preventing Reverend Packard from committing his wife, there was one preventing him from keeping her imprisoned in his house. The judge issued a writ of habeas corpus. Reverend Packard was ordered to appear before Judge Charles C. Starr of the Fifth Circuit Court in Kankakee on charges of false imprisonment. The trial took place July 11–19, 1864. Since Reverend Packard's reason for locking up his wife was that she was mad, the judge decided the real issue in the case was Packard's sanity, and he turned the trial into a sanity trial. A jury would decide whether Packard was in control of her senses.

Each side retained a team of three lawyers. One of Packard's attorneys, J. W. Orr, refused to take the case until his family physician examined her. After this, however, he took her into his own home for the duration of the trial. Packard had to borrow clothing from Mrs. Orr in order to appear in court.

A second Packard attorney, Stephen Moore, chose to keep shorthand records of the proceedings. This account was later published and is now the *sources* only extant account of the trial, as the original records were destroyed in a fire. Other discussions of the case were printed in the newspapers. Debate was also sparked in medical journals, where the Packard case was tried and retried in an arena more sympathetic to medical expertise. Taken together, one gets a picture of what was considered evidence of a woman's sanity.

## Narratives and Frames of Reference

Arguers in the Packard case appeared to consider certain territory sacred. No accuser ever said that Packard was insane because she was a woman, nor did defenders question Reverend Packard's right to control his household.

In most cases, overt behavior was described and then interpreted. These interpretations, however, were clearly based on the same unspoken norms of female character. That these interpretations were so diametrically opposed reveals an important caveat in judging narratives: The evaluation of identical narrative elements depends to a great extent upon the frame of reference imposed upon it by the participants. No matter how strong the norms of True Womanhood might have been, they were still subject to rhetorical manipulation in pursuit of a desired outcome.

The manipulations in this trial serve as excellent examples of how a speaker might use rhetorical framing to impose a narrative form upon a series of events. As explained in the previous chapter, Burke reminds us that all stories are "framed" by the larger cultural genres that surround them. Casting identical events in different frames leads to dramatically different interpretations of the "meaning" of those events.

Two Burkean frames stand out in the clash over the Packard case. Packard's accusers, as well as the greater number of medical professionals who discussed the case, told their story from the perspective of "burlesque." Burlesque "selects the externals of behavior, driving them to a 'logical' conclusion that becomes their 'reduction to absurdity.'" It "deliberately suppresses any consideration of the 'mitigating circumstances' that would put his subject in a better light" (Burke, *Attitudes* 54–55). Substitute "reduction to insanity" for "burlesque" in this description, and it provides an accurate picture of the accusatorial narrative.[1] It is a partisan perspective, relying as it does on a clear "us" versus "them" delineation of character. Packard remains a clear "other." Burlesque is a perfect mode when the business at hand is culling defective individuals from the herd.

Packard's defenders promulgated a more "comic" attitude. Comic perspectives focus upon the social aspects of behavior. It requires people to be as aware of their own behavior as that of others. People are flawed, but the comic reasoner knows that everyone is flawed, "hence it provides the charitable attitude toward people that is required for purposes of persuasion and cooperation" (Burke, *Attitudes* 166). This frame offers more opportunity for an auditor to identify with a character. In the burlesque mode, the accusers assumed the auditors identified with them. In the comic mode, the defense worked to create identification with Packard. This contrast led to radically different interpretations of her character in reference to the norm.

## The Attack

The trial itself did not go well for the accusers from the beginning, in part due to the inconsistencies lent to the narrative by the medical testimony.

Three doctors who had examined Packard prior to her commitment were called to testify. One now stated that she was probably not insane after all. The other two did not agree as to symptoms or the extent of her problem. It might have been laughable had not the "expertise" of these medical men deprived Packard of nearly three years of her life. This mixed testimony was buttressed by a letter written by Andrew MacFarland stating that Packard was incurably insane, as well as testimony from a variety of laypeople upon her behavior. The testimony in this case continued long after the verdict was handed down. The medical community, keenly aware of the blow to its authority, continued to "try" Packard and concluded that she was insane but that the jury was not qualified to realize this. MacFarland was especially diligent in this project, as his reputation as state superintendent of the asylum was at stake. He had wanted to testify at the trial but was out of town at a funeral when the case took its surprising turn toward trying insanity. He offered to return within ten days, but the judge refused to delay the trial. MacFarland was forced to make his points with letters to newspapers and scholarly papers at conventions.

The narrative created by these arguers used traditional values attached to womanhood in a burlesque way. Burlesque is essentially a negative frame of reference in that it usually arises when an individual rejects an aspect of the social order. Often that aspect is "represented" by characters already existing in the narrative. The need to reject these elements sometimes leads to the burlesque focus on the "depiction of very despicable, forlorn and dissipated people," a focus wherein "the writer might very well protect himself by not imagining them with too great intimacy" (Burke, *Attitudes* 53). Burlesque is exaggerated polemic or caricature of an other; its focus stays firmly on the side of the rejector.

This frame is especially suited for the "medical" narrative of insanity. It enables one to assert one's expertise at diagnosing people without risk. Its self-righteousness converts "every 'perhaps' into a 'positively'" (Burke, *Attitudes* 55). When faced with a situation in which the narrators' hegemony was threatened, the burlesque response enables them to assert their superiority symbolically, only at the expense of a single woman's character. The ensuing story made every violation of femininity grounds for commitment.

The primary point of contention at the trial was religion. Packard's desire to convert to a different denomination that better suited her beliefs was a major reason that the reverend had wanted her committed. Ordinarily, religiosity was "associated with female nature" (Berg 79). Welter called this element "piety" and claimed it was "the core of woman's virtue, the source of her strength" (21). Religiosity was a good thing, desirable in a woman. Unfortunately, Packard's religiosity no longer matched that of her husband.

This difference of opinion was magnified by the lens of burlesque into a certain sign of madness. All the accusatory witnesses discussed it. As one doctor explained, "she was what might be called a monomaniac" (Moore 17). Although on cross-examination he admitted that he "did not think it was a bad case," he took her determination as a sign of mental disturbance. The other physicians concurred. The second stated, "I brought up the subject of religion. We discussed that subject for a long time, and then I had not the slightest difficulty concluding that she was hopelessly insane" (Moore 19). Even the witness who changed his mind equivocated that "at the time I thought her to be somewhat deranged on the subject" although "I would not swear now that she was insane" (Moore 21).

Lay witnesses were convinced she was mad mainly due to her behavior in the Sunday school. Packard was bringing Swedenborgian ideas into the classroom. Packard's brother-in-law, Abijah Dole (he was married to the reverend's sister), described a watershed event in terms that stressed her derangement:

> One Sabbath, just at the close of the school, I was behind the desk, and almost like a vision she appeared before me, and requested to deliver or read an address to the school. I was much surprised; I felt so bad, I did not know what to do. [At his point the court report states that he began to cry.] I was willing to gratify her all I could, for I knew she was crazy. . . . I cannot state any of the particulars of the paper. It bore evidence of her insanity. She went on and condemned the church, all in all, and the individuals composing the church, because they did not agree with her. She looked very wild and very much excited. She seemed to be insane. (Moore 23)

No witness could recall exactly what Packard's paper had said, but all knew insanity when they heard it. Obviously, "visions" who appear condemning those who do not agree on religious matters are a very bad sign. Dole was positive in own diagnosis:

> QUESTION: Was it an indication of insanity that she wanted to leave the Presbyterian Church?
> ANSWER: I think it strange that she should ask for letters from the church. She would not leave the church unless she was insane. (Moore 23–24)

Packard's insistence that her opinion be heard in the church and her equal insistence that she be allowed to transfer when it became clear that she was not welcome were signs of Packard's religious monomania.

Monomania was a recognized class of insanity. It was discussed thoroughly by one of the founders of the field of medical jurisprudence, Isaac Ray. "In the simplest form of monomania, the understanding appears to be, and probably is, perfectly sound, on all subjects but those connected with the hallucination" (Ray, *Treatise* 167). Thus it was considered possible to be rational in all other contexts, but to still be insane on one topic. Ray's examples of monomania, however, are extreme: a man who thought he had eels in his gut and demanded surgery; a Jesuit priest who thought he was a cardinal. Even before the trial, MacFarland had no trouble magnifying Packard's religious convictions to these proportions:

> all [Packard's] perversity of conduct arose out of one single delusion; and the delusion was that, in the Trinity, distinctions of sex had to exist; that there could be in the trinity no more than in the family unity of sex [Swedenborgians believed that if God was the Father and Christ the Son, then the Holy Ghost had to be a woman]. . . . It appeared, moreover, unmistakably in her writings that this delusion had possessed her for eighteen years, growing and increasing upon her, and giving origin to all this perversity of conduct, clearly and connectedly as I now see it. Making out a case perfectly consistent with the idea of original intellectual delusion, underlying and producing all the so-called phenomena of moral insanity. (Association of Medical Superintendents)

Thus to be monomaniacal on the subject of religion could lead directly to "moral insanity." The entire discussion of religion shows how easily the burlesque attitude can lead to exaggeration. No one could remember what Packard had actually said, and no one was willing to place what bits they did recall into context. Her religious ideas, eccentric or not, were secondary to the unladylike behaviors she evinced. Thus they were one clear criterion for condemning her to the asylum.

Other reasons for calling Packard insane were related to her failures as a wife, for her behavior toward her husband violated two more womanly virtues. The first, submission, was based on the idea that women need male protectors. A good woman submits to her husband's wishes in all things. This virtue is tied to domesticity, or the importance placed upon a woman's ability to run a household, raise her children, and nurse sick family members. During the trial, lay witnesses were more apt to note that Packard sassed her husband than were the medical men, possibly because neighbors saw more of the couple's interactions. There were grounds in the medical literature of the time, however, to warrant marking resistance as a symptom.

That Packard was not a loving, submissive partner to her spouse was brought up frequently by the accusers. In many cases, the context of her behavior was plainly ignored. When asked what, besides religious mania, "showed marks of insanity," one physician stated, "She found fault particularly that Mr. Packard would not discuss their points of difference on religion in an open, manly way, instead of going around and denouncing her as crazy to her friends and to the church" (Moore 20). Thus her anger at her husband was another strike against her. The doctor did not think that the Reverend's telling the entire neighborhood she was insane was rational grounds for Mrs. Packard's aversion to her husband. Every time she had a disagreement with her husband, it was a potential sign of madness. The reverend's sister remembered several incidents clearly:

> She was very much excited about her son remaining at Marshall [going to seminary]. She was wild. She thought it was very wrong and tyrannical for Mr. Packard not to permit her son to remain there. She said very many things which seemed unnatural. Her voice, manner and ways, all showed she was insane. . . . At another time, at the table, she was talking about religion, when Mr. Packard remonstrated with her; she became angry, and told him she would talk what and when she had a mind to. She rose up from the table, and took her tea cup, and left the room in great violence. (Moore 25–26)

Couples often disagree without one side accusing the other of insanity. In Packard's case, however, every show of temper was liable to exaggeration. When she took offense at being called insane, this served as further evidence of her insanity.

Once again, there was established medical opinion related to this "symptom." Ray noted, "A very common feature of moral mania is a deep perversion of the social affections, whereby the feelings of kindness and attachment that flow from the relations of father, husband, and child are replaced by a perpetual inclination to tease, worry and embitter the existence of others" (Ray, *Treatise* 182). In his description, Ray used words such as "brutal ferocity" and "ungovernable temper." His example was of a man who beat his wife and children and spat in their food. It does not take that much effort for a woman to show perversion. All Packard had to do is evince "a disposition to thwart her husband in little matters and throw checks in his way—questioning the propriety of what he was doing in regard to matters affecting his church" (Association of Medical Superintendents 90). Her feeling was exaggerated by MacFarland to satanic proportions: "Her hatred of her husband had something diabolical about it. Every instinct of her love was banished from her. She was thoroughly demoralized, and corrupted in all her moral sentiments. Yet, the closest study could not discover any intellectual impairments, except when she was sick; then delusion would exhibit itself and then only" (Association of Medical Superintendents 91). Intellectual impairment was not at issue; if it had Packard may never have been committed. It was her lack of proper submission to her husband, a "moral" failing, that helped condemn her.

Even domesticity could be turned into madness. Women were supposed to be good mothers—it was instinctual. Yet Packard's behavior when her child was ill with "brain fever" was taken as a symptom of madness. She was distraught; she wept and was "wild." All Dole, predisposed to find her mad, could say was, "I supposed when I first went into the room that her influence over the child had caused the child to become deranged" (Moore 23). When he later discovered that the child was physically ill, his mistaken attribution did not cause him to question his previous opinion. MacFarland was equally stubborn. Two years after the trial, he still fought against her reforms by attacking her sanity, and noted in a letter to the *New Haven Daily Morning Journal and Courier* that "I had rather see my daughter in her grave than to suffer her one month under Mrs. Packard's influence" (quoted in Himmelhoch and Shaffer 360).

Another element of domesticity was household management. Women were supposed to be in charge of cleaning, cooking, gardening, child rearing, and a host of related chores. As in all areas of femininity, whether one does one's duty is less important than the way in which it is done. Sarah Rumsey was a neighbor who helped out as a "hired girl" for the Packards and had a lot to say about Packard's attitude. For example, "I thought it was evidence of insanity for her to order me into the kitchen; she ought to have known that I was not an ordinary servant" (Moore 29). She admitted that Packard was "very tidy in her habits" and was "very fond of her children" most of the time, but sometimes when she worked, "she was very angry and excited, and showed ill-will" (Moore 29). Keeping a spotless home, tidy garden, and happy children will not keep a woman out of the asylum, not if she lets slip that she is not always happy while doing it.

The last element of femininity, purity, was closely related to sexual innocence. Women were naturally higher minded than men, and one of their functions in society was to save men from themselves (Welter 23–25). Packard's purity was not questioned during the sanity trial, but it eventually became an issue at another kind of hearing—one before the state legislature. After her release from custody, Packard became very successful as an agitator for patient rights. She was the prime mover behind the repeal of the 1851 statute that denied women a hearing and behind a new law requiring every patient to have a sanity trial prior to commitment.

She faced an old foe, MacFarland, on her next project, which was to aid an investigation into the treatment of prisoners at the state asylum. The committee called her to testify. MacFarland attended the hearings and pulled out all the stops in an attempt to prove to the committee that she was still insane. All the old arguments about her religious mania were recalled. Packard was questioned closely by MacFarland's lawyers for six hours before they brought forward their coup de grace—a "love" letter written by Packard to Dr. Mac-Farland while she had been in the asylum. This was a direct attempt to show that she was mad because her purity was questionable.

The letter itself is tame by modern standards, but it was scandalous because both she and MacFarland were married to other people at the time. Her letter clearly showed that she knew better than to actually violate norms of behavior, as when she wrote, "I love your *spirit*, your *manliness*, now, but I must not love your *person*, so long as that love is justly claimed by another woman—your legal wife" (Sapinsley appendix 6). However, the committee took it very seriously; Packard's testimony about how inmates were treated was in danger of compromise because of her questionable purity. Packard explained that she had been incarcerated for over two years when she wrote that letter, and she saw flattering MacFarland's male ego as her last resort. The committee chided Packard for "an indiscreet and foolish letter" (Himelhoch and Shaffer 363). MacFarland's tactic to produce the letter backfired, for in revealing Packard's violation of her feminine role, he also revealed his lack of manly decency: a gentleman does not play with a lady's reputation. He was censured for failing in his gender role more severely than was Packard.

Burke notes that a "frame becomes deceptive when it provides too great plausibility for the writer who would *condemn symptoms* without being able to gauge the *causal pressure* behind the symptoms" (Burke, *Attitudes* 41). The arguments leveled against Packard all had one thing in common—they were bald statements of her behaviors subjected to reductio ad absurdum by the interpretations of the observer. No one testifying questioned why Packard might be behaving oddly, nor were they willing to supply circumstances under which her behavior might be excusable. Within this frame, Packard could not win, since both a lack and an oversupply of feminine virtue were subject to negative construction: the narrative regarding true womanhood became a weapon for controlling and condemning women's behavior. As long as the medical profession adhered strictly to burlesque, no woman was safe.

## The Defense

Packard's defenders, in contrast, assumed a comic frame. This is "neither wholly euphemistic, nor wholly debunking—hence it provides a charitable attitude towards people that is required for purposes of persuasion and co-operation" (Burke, *Attitudes* 166). The defense narrative undercut the accusers' simply by providing balance. Wherever the accusers noted odd behavior, the defenders worked to provide a context for it, either by discussing the circumstance or by creating hints as to Packard's "true" internal state of mind. They accomplished this by both their cross-examinations of witnesses and their choice of new witnesses.

The number of witnesses called matched the prosecution: three physicians and five laypeople. Two of the physicians were community members and one was the doctor summoned by defense attorney Orr to examine Packard. In this case, the physicians were not as useful to the case as the laypeople. Each doctor stated he saw no sign of madness in Packard, but each also admitted that his exposure to her was limited and that he did not know her well. The lawyers focused on community members who had day-to-day dealings with Packard.

The first accusation to be refuted was Packard's religious monomania. The lawyers were not foolish enough to deny Packard's faith, nor did they defend that faith in itself. Swedenborgianism, with its emphasis on spiritualism, was highly suspect in conservative Christian communities. Instead, the defense selected aspects of the faith that were innocuous, or even shared by mainstream religions, and showed that Packard's beliefs were not so odd. Then they compared the extent of her faith to that of others, so that she looked no worse than eccentric. Orr's physician, Dr. Duncanson, was called to explain that Packard's religion, understood in its context, was a sane one:

> There are thousands of persons who believe just as she does. Many of her ideas and doctrines are embraced in Swedenborgianism. . . . The best and most learned men of both Europe and this country, are advocates of these doctrines, in one shape or the other; and some bigots and men with minds of small calibre may call these great minds insane; but that does not make them insane. An insane mind is a diseased mind. These minds are the perfection of intellectual powers, healthy, strong, vigorous, and just the reverse of diseased minds, or insane. (Moore 37)

Simply by explaining what the beliefs *were* that made her argue so hotly, the defense removes Packard from the category of insanity and allies her with "the perfection of intellectual powers." Just in case there was still question, the defense also asked that Mrs. Packard's infamous "Sunday School" letter be read. This was the letter whose content no accusatory witness could recall although all of them were certain it bore signs of insanity. Over protestations from Reverend Packard's lawyers, Packard herself was allowed to read the letter aloud to the jury. It was in no way incoherent or deranged. The effect of Packard reading her own perfectly sane words aloud was a tremendous blow to the accusers. The jury had heard only secondhand testimony that she was insane. They now had firsthand experience of her behaving sanely.

Once her theology had been defended, her religious "extremism" was placed in context. The physician who termed her a "monomaniac" on religious matters, under cross-examination, was forced to admit that he would have to put "Henry Ward Beecher, Spurgeon, Horace Greely, and like persons" in the same category (Moore 18). Each of these men was a powerful leader, not a lunatic. Her beliefs were also placed in relief against less stellar company. When cross-examining Abijah Dole, the lawyers explored the nature of his beliefs:

QUES: Do you believe literally that Jonah was swallowed by a whale, and remained in its belly three days, and was then cast up?
ANS: I do.
QUES: Do you believe literally that Elijah went direct [sic] up to Heaven in a chariot of fire—that the chariot had wheels, and seats. And was drawn by horses?
ANS: I do—for with God all things are possible.
QUES: Do you believe Mrs. Packard was insane, and is insane?
ANS: I do. (Moore 24)

In comparison, Dole's belief in heavenly chariots seems as mad as Packard's that women embody the Holy Ghost. Yet Dole walked free while Packard was imprisoned.

Packard's second symptom was that she had an aversion to her husband and did not submit to his will. Again, this was defused by stressing the context of her behavior. Sybil Dole had made an especially damning claim that Packard had once referred to her husband as an "unfruitful work of darkness" and stormed from the dining room. Dole was recalled by the defense:

QUESTION: Did you deem that evidence of insanity?
ANSWER: I did.
QUES: She called Mr. Packard the unfruitful work of darkness?
ANS: I suppose so.
QUES: Did she also include you?
ANS: She might have done so.
QUES: This was about the time that her husband was plotting to kidnap her, was it not?
ANS: It was just before she was removed to the Asylum.
QUES: He had been charging her with insanity, had he not, at the table?
ANS: He had. (Moore 30)

Given the circumstances, what woman would not have gotten angry at her husband? He called her insane at the diner table, in front of a witness. The defense strategy of calling the commitment a "kidnaping" was also interesting, for it undercut the reverend's claim that he was simply exercising his rights as a husband. No one has a right to kidnap another.

The kidnaping motif was carried forward in the testimony of two of Packard's neighbors who visited her after her return from the asylum. They attested to treatment that clearly revealed that Reverend Packard was no loving husband abused by his wife. One woman noted that after the writ of habeas corpus was served, she was "let into the room by Mr. Packard; she had no fire in it; we sat there in the cold. Mr. Packard had a handful of keys, and unlocked the door and let me in. . . . Before this, Mrs. Hanford and myself went there to see her; he would not let us see her; he shook his hand at me, and threatened to put me out" (Moore 36).

This was hardly the behavior of a kindly husband, to leave his wife locked in a cold room with no fire. He behaved in as agitated a manner as his wife had earlier. He was also extreme in his precautions to prevent her escape. Another visitor found that "the son refused me admission. The window was fastened with nails on the inside, and by two screws, passing through the lower part of the upper sash, and the upper part of the lower sash, from the outside" (Moore, 36). He took her clothes away; the clothing she wore to court had to be borrowed.

Given his treatment of her, Packard's desperation and her accusations that her husband was evil seemed much less strange. In fact, one of the women who had visited admitted suggesting that Packard seek a divorce. Packard said she did not want a divorce, only protection from her husband's cruelty (Moore 36). Thus she occupied a high moral ground, for she showed her reverence for the sacred institution of marriage despite her husband's abuse.

The defense countered the attacks on Packard's domestic affection by creating a powerfully positive image of her role as a mother. Every accuser was asked how Packard was with the children, and all had to admit that she loved them and was never known to be unkind to them. Even Dole, under cross-examination, had to back down on this topic. He had earlier described Packard as "wild" when she cared for the child with brain fever; now he admitted that her reaction was probably because she had been up all night nursing the child (Moore 23).

An especially telling moment in the courtroom occurred off the stand. It was so perfectly timed that one has to wonder how spontaneous it was. About halfway though the prosecution, it was Sybil Dole's turn to testify. In order to attend, she had to bring with her one of Packard's children, the very same girl whose brain fever had so worried Packard:

> in passing by the table occupied by Mrs. Packard and her counsel, the child stopped, went up to her mother, kissed and hugged her, and was clinging to her with childlike fervor, when it was observed by Mrs. Dole, who snatched the child up—and bid it "come away from that woman"; adding, "She is not

fit to take care of you—I have you in my charge"; and thereupon led her away. The court-room was crowded to its utmost, and not a mother's heart there but what was touched, and scarce a dry eye was seen. Quite a stir was made, but the sheriff soon restored order. (Moore 25)

Though it was not part of the "official" record, Moore included a description of the episode in the name of "accuracy" (he did not mention that the child was fourteen years old). The jury was male and thus perhaps less likely to be touched, but the image had been planted: the child clinging to her loving mother, the two snatched apart by the sister of Reverend Packard. Packard may have "failed" her husband, but she never failed her children.

The matter of Packard's domestic economy was also addressed. As mentioned earlier, even the Reverend's witnesses were forced to admit that she kept a clean house. Her failing on that front was that she was huffy and angry while doing her chores. The defense noted that the family had for quite a while employed a French woman as a servant. Reverend Packard fired her without consulting his wife. Sarah Rumsey informed her of the fact when she entered the house to help out, which might explain Packard's sharp admonition that she go to the kitchen immediately (Moore 28–29). She had also seemed particularly agitated while doing the yard work. However, she had been trying for a while to get Reverend Packard to clean up the yard, and he refused (Moore 29).

Each of Packard's questionable behaviors, when put in context, became actions that the jury could identify with. Who had never espoused ideas that others thought were wrongheaded? Who wouldn't become agitated if someone told the whole neighborhood he or she was insane? How could one stay up all night with a sick child and not look disheveled? In this construction, Packard's behavior was perfectly normal, if not always wise. The comic frame allowed a different use for the narrative of True Womanhood. In this context, the feminine norms for behavior were violated but with good reason. Packard's behavior was warranted. It was this charitable view that the jury found compelling. Whatever their view of her behavior, they came to the conclusion that her motives did not arise from madness.

It took the jury only seven minutes to find Packard sane. It took nearly fifty years for the medical profession to get over her blow to their ego. As late as 1913, at least one psychiatrist was still trying to prove her insane, although he used more contemporary terms. He called her paranoiac, was certain that she was menopausal, and claimed that she was the worst enemy a really ill person could have had (Dewey). He argued sanity trials had been a bad idea but seemed much more concerned with attacking Packard than the law.

## Conclusions

The results in the Packard case reveal an important consideration in the evaluation of narratives. As well as laying out elements of plot and character for analysis, one must consider the overall frame of reference from which the narrator constructs the story. This framing can completely alter the audience's ensuing interpretation of the other elements. In Packard's case, the comic frame created a more compelling mode for the lay audience. It created identification with her character rather than a burlesque parody of her behavior. This identification helped the defense. As Fisher has noted, the "operative principle of narrative rationality is identification rather than deliberation" (Fisher, *Human Communication* 66). The jury wasted little time returning a verdict: they quickly laid the interpretation of one set of witnesses against the other and found they preferred the defense. After having been reminded that they themselves had probably occasionally behaved in a similar manner, this was the only course that would not violate their senses of self.

The medical arguers were unable to recognize even the existence of a charitable viewpoint, even when adapting the discussion to a lay audience was vital to their cause. This hampered them later when they attempted to reassert their hegemony. They were unable to persuade voters or legislators to resist Packard's campaign to reform commitment and investigate asylum management. The burlesque frame required them to see themselves as separate from their audience; so separate that they on occasion they could not even speak to it.

Hindsight makes it easy to condemn an arguer for not recognizing that alternate perspectives exist. There is evidence, however, that the medical community itself became aware of this and, in some cases, began to adjust toward a more charitable perspective. For example, Ray's theories recognized a form of insanity wherein a wife becomes overwhelmingly averse to having sexual intercourse with her husband. He noted that this behavior, even if unaccompanied by further symptoms, is still pathological (Ray, *Treatise* 121).

A later physician revisited this topic and agreed with Ray in principle. He added, however, that one had to judge the behavior in context—sometimes women suffer from painful intercourse, or she could have just found out that her husband was cheating on her (Storer 121). Thus, although a violation of womanly submission was still a bad sign, it was not always a sign that the woman was insane. Storer was, within limits, willing to use comic identification in his diagnosis.

This new consciousness is still no guarantee of a different outcome, thus still making evaluation difficult. A later accuser of Packard made an attempt to add context to his charge. Regarding her "love letter," he, unlike MacFarland years before, stated that moral laxity is not a clear sign of insanity. In her case, however, since her life lacked any further evidence that she was lacking in morals, the letter had to mean that "disorder of the mind seems the more probable explanation" (Dewey 581). In the minefield of womanhood, even a pure moral life can be used against you.

This case also illustrates the no-win situation faced by nineteenth-century women who weren't quite passive enough. If she lived up to the norms of femininity required by the "true woman" narrative, she was safe only so long as a new storyteller did not impose a new frame of reference that rendered her character suspect. If that storyteller has power, say if he is a doctor, lawyer, minister, or judge, that new interpretation could destroy her "real" life. A careful woman would keep a watchful eye, keep her head down, and never question why her character had to be so narrowly defined in the first place—for in that direction lies madness.

# 3. The Mad Doctors Meet McNaughton: The Battle for Narrative Supremacy in the Trial of Mary Harris

> The doctor, like the poor, we always have with us. Like bad luck
> (and very much like it), he is everywhere.
> —Richard Harris, *Hints on Advocacy*

The narrative elements of a popular trial can be manipulated by either side in an attempt to persuade juries that a particular woman is a criminal or a victim. The Packard case is a simple example. It is easy for the modern reader to dismiss the antiquated notion that failing to obey one's husband is either a crime or a sure indication of madness. But it is also easy to dismiss the case on another basis. The judge in the case deliberately refused to delay the trial until an "expert" on insanity could arrive to testify. Thus, the rhetors and their audience were both comprised of laymen. Perhaps, the reader could say, the lack of any knowledge of the medical "facts" on all sides gave the popular concept of "womanhood" more persuasive influence that it might normally have had. Indeed, the medical profession's insistence that Packard was insane despite the trial would indicate that at least one group remained unconvinced.

So far, then, it has been demonstrated that popular images of women's roles can sway ordinary, untrained reasoners. Although juries will likely never be comprised of experts, one still wonders what kind of narrative transformations can be wrought by trained professionals with "facts" at their fingertips. Thus it might be instructive to look at a case where "experts" are battling each other.

Communication research has been slow to adapt narrative methods in the study of legal rhetoric, perhaps due to an overall hesitancy with the concept of narrative itself. Although narrative has long been studied within rhetoric as a form of support for arguments within a particular case, the notion that argument itself can be subsumed by narrative is more problematic (Fisher). Judges and advocates, well trained in the premises and precedents of their profession, work within a tightly defined framework to create legal arguments that are inaccessible to individuals not equally trained. An attempt to reduce this rhetoric to "mere" storytelling is a daunting task. Human beings, however, are exposed to the common cultural narratives that surround their daily lives, no matter what their profession. When lawyers cross from the public sphere to the legal sphere, they do not shed that culture. It is inevitable that public moral narratives will meet and interact with traditional legal opinions, sometimes altering both forever. As Ferguson notes, "The cultural work of interpretation in courtroom analysis lies, therefore, in the relation *between* legal and nonlegal narratives" (84).

The word "between" is instructive, because it implies that there are only two universes, the legal, populated by trained lawyers, and the nonlegal, populated by everyone else. In fact, the nexus of stories that come together in a legal case might involve multiple narrative universes that on the surface would appear to have little to do with one another. The previous chapter demonstrated that the stories about the feminine character produced by popular culture can influence a lawyer's weapons of argument. These popular images, however, also have influenced the development of stories in a second professional realm that is ostensibly logical, scientific, and completely within the "rational world" model of persuasion: the profession of medicine.

The relationship between the popular view of womanhood and the professional practice of physicians has been well documented (Smith-Rosenberg; Showalter). In addition, the medical profession had to deal with popular notions of the character of physicians, which impinged upon their power and social standing in the community (Mohr). These narrative elements, already present to some extent in American courtrooms, become especially salient when a physician is called upon to enter the legal wrangling over a case. Suddenly three narrative universes are interacting. The stock plot lines, characters, and morals from each are molded by the concerned rhetors into narratives that will be accepted by all participants. The stories that result are then carried back into their respective fields.

I will take a critical look at this important relationship through the analysis of a landmark criminal trial that marks a major turning point in the battle for supremacy between two professional groups that were highly suspect at the time: lawyers and doctors. In 1865, a fierce battle over who had the right to determine the guilt or innocence of Miss Mary Harris became the center of a professional turf battle still fought to this day: who determines whether a criminal is "not guilty by reason of insanity," the law or medicine?

Ostensibly, the jury made this decision—but not until after it was pummeled with expert testimony from both sides. When faced with two sets of esoteric knowledge, each claiming supremacy in knowledge of criminal insanity, each calling for the opposite verdict, each bolstered by rousing rhetoric, what the jury eventually had were two narratives about the reliability of the standards of two argument fields. Their decision in the Harris case reveals much about the role of narrativity in legal argument. It also reveals how narratives can be used successfully by a disenfranchised group to garner public legitimacy, for neither side was especially well respected by the public at this moment in time.

After a brief discussion of the facts of the case, it will be placed within the context of the public perception of doctors and lawyers in the nineteenth century. Analysis of the competing tales of guilt and innocence constructed by rhetors from both professions reveals how the more skillful professional tale was able to win the day.

## The Case of Mary Harris

The life of Mary Harris did not have a promising beginning. She was born into a poor, Irish Catholic family in the small town of Burlington, Iowa. The family had put nine-year-old Mary to work at a local milliner's shop in order to make ends meet. As a result, she had little education and could only hope that the milliner would teach her the trade. While working in the front of the shop, she attracted the attention of Adoniram Judson Burroughs, a young man in his twenties who owned a store down the street. Judson, as he was called by his family, had been thrown out of his church over some disagreement. He found the little girl a more sympathetic listener to his tale of woe than others in the community.

Burroughs eventually formed romantic intentions toward her and intimated that when she grew up he would marry her. Her parents opposed this, apparently not because he was a grown man but because he was a Baptist. For three years he "courted" her, provided her with some education, and groomed her to mix with genteel society. Then his business failed and he was forced to move to Chicago, where his brother lived, to find new opportunities.

After the move, Burroughs wrote Harris regularly expressing his love. He continued until she turned eighteen, at which time he asked her to join him in Chicago. Harris and her friends understood this proposition as a proposal of marriage, although lawyers for the prosecution later disputed this assumption. It was, as events transpired, not exactly a proposal. Burroughs said he wanted to marry but not until he had secured a living. He tried, and failed, to get a commission in the Union army. In the meantime, Mary was hired as a bookkeeper at a Chicago millinery owned by two sisters who were also of Irish descent.

During this period, the couple's public behavior was scandalous enough that word reached Burroughs's brother, John, a minister who was president of the Chicago Theological Seminary. A government job in Washington, D.C., miraculously became available, and Judson Burroughs moved again. He left Harris in Chicago. Harris spent the subsequent months reading the letters Burroughs continued to write and anticipating her wedding. On September 8, 1863, however, she received an odd letter. Unsigned, it purported to be from a male admirer who was anxious to make her acquaintance. He requested that she come to a certain address at a certain date. She was confused; the handwriting looked like her lover's, but it apparently was not from him. She showed the letter to one of her employers, who also thought the handwriting looked like that in the previous letters. The employer, Louisa Devlin, suggested that a reply be sent stating that although she was interested, she was unavailable at that date. The women would alert the postal clerk, wait until the letter was collected at the post office, and then question him about who had come for it. This was accomplished, and the clerk described a man "very like" Burroughs, wearing a ring "very like" one Harris had given him. They brought the clerk a photograph from which he made an identification. Harris was even more confused when Louisa Devlin reported that the address turned out to be a local house of prostitution. When Mary received another letter offering an alternate date, she and Jane Devlin went to the house together and, staying on the front porch, questioned the owner about who was waiting there. The woman identified Burroughs from the photograph. She said he had been there, but when he saw that Harris was not alone he had gone out the back door.[1]

Now thoroughly alarmed, Harris went to see Reverend John Burroughs. She took all the letters with her. The reverend identified the love letters as having been written by his brother but said the two anonymous letters were definitely not his handwriting. He also told Harris that Burroughs was not even in Chicago at the time the letters were mailed. She went home reassured. Then she saw in the papers a wedding announcement. The very day of her interview with John Burroughs (or, as he claimed, the day before),[2] he had officiated at the Chicago wedding of Judson Burroughs to another woman.

Harris was distraught, and she became hysterical and quarrelsome. She lost weight and began wandering aimlessly at night. When Jane Devlin said she never wanted to hear Judson's name again, Harris flew at her with a knife and had to be wrestled down by Louisa. Harris struck a woman in the shop over some imagined slur and tore an expensive quilt to shreds. The Devlins called a doctor, who said that Harris was having menstrual troubles and prescribed rest. Harris consulted a lawyer about a breach of promise lawsuit, but he said she had to pursue it in Washington, where Burroughs now resided, so she did not proceed. Several months passed, during which the Devlins decided to relocate to Wisconsin, taking Harris with them. She went, but her bouts of "odd" behavior continued. In January 1865, she borrowed money from the Devlins and went to Washington to take up her lawsuit. The Devlins did not know that, along with legal documents, she had a gun in her purse. She went straight to Burroughs's office and inquired for him. She was asked to wait, and so she sat down. When Burroughs came into the hall, she pulled out her gun and shot him twice.

Witnesses reported that she was completely calm during the attack, but that afterward she screamed and tore at her hair. Upon her arrest, she apparently told conflicting stories: telling one man Burroughs had "ruined" her but telling another that she was still "pure." While in prison, she was visited by several physicians who noted various levels of "hysterical" behavior. When she came up for trial, her lawyers entered a plea of not guilty by reason of insanity.

It was not going to be an easy case. The fact that Harris, jilted in September 1863, did not commit the murder until January 1865 precluded a plea on manslaughter charges because too much time had passed for it to be a "crime of passion." A guilty verdict on the greater charge automatically carried the death penalty.[3] There was no physical evidence that Judson Burroughs had ever promised marriage, only hearsay based upon hints in the letters and the assumptions of her friends. Witnesses were also problematic. All of the witnesses to their romantic relationship lived in either Burlington or Chicago. In those days, a trip of that distance was no casual affair, and Harris had no money to help defray expenses. Witnesses were deposed, but one cannot cross-examine a deposition in front of the jury.

John Burroughs was more than willing to come to Washington and swear in court that the assignation letters were not in his brother's handwriting. He also came up with funds to pay hostile witnesses their fare to Washington. The only person who knew whether Judson Burroughs was the man in the brothel, the madam, refused to give a deposition unless she was paid to do so. John Burroughs refused to pay, and Harris couldn't. The madam disappeared before she could be served a subpoena. The postal clerk had joined the Union army; in the postwar confusion the War Department could not find him.

Thus Harris did not have concrete evidence, besides the love letters, that

Burroughs had wronged her. The final nail in her apparent coffin was a radical change of precedent. When Harris was arrested, no woman had ever been executed in the District of Columbia. By the time she was tried, another Mary, Mary Surratt, had been tried, convicted, and condemned for conspiracy in the murder of Abraham Lincoln. Although Surratt was hung by a military tribunal rather than a civilian court, the ice had been broken. Womanhood was no shield from execution in the District of Columbia.

Although she had little money, Harris was extremely lucky in the quality of her personality. She made such a good impression upon other women that they became firm supporters. The Devlin sisters, for example, closed up their shop in Wisconsin and traveled to Washington to testify on her behalf—no small sacrifice for self-supporting women. Two other female friends also made the journey. Two local Washington women who did not even know her volunteered to run errands for her.

Perhaps her most important friend was Joseph Bradley, her defense council. Bradley practiced both law and medicine. He had been asked by the court-appointed attorney to observe her in jail and offer his medical opinion on her mental state. He became so intrigued by her case that he volunteered to join her defense for free. He was instrumental in obtaining a great deal of additional pro bono labor. More importantly, he was able to martial an impressive array of medical experts on the subject of insanity.[4]

## Doctors and the Law

That Bradley could practice two professions simultaneously was not unusual in 1865. Until about 1870, state bar associations did not require extensive formal education; instead "lawyers selected and sponsored young men on the basis of a personal assessment of their character and talent" (Johnson 24). Since passing the bar rarely required a specialized formal education, a man like Bradley could easily pursue a law career while attending medical school. It also meant, however, that professional lawyers varied widely in their level of education, ethics, and honesty. With no formalized standards, lawyers were socialized (or not) by their peers. The quality of the resulting advocate was often in spite of, rather than because of, his training. The resulting variance meant that lawyering was not automatically viewed by the public as a legitimate profession. Still, in the courtroom, the lawyer's voice was *the* voice of the law, and thus the privileged voice.

The practice of medicine was not much more respectable in the public's estimation. Medical schools were completely unregulated, so there was no guarantee that a physician was competent. Even the definition of "competence" was debatable. The nineteenth and early twentieth centuries were marked by "competition between homeopaths, botanical practitioners, and a host of other medical sects," each claiming that theirs was the "true" science (Geller et al. 4). Although the American Medical Association had been established in 1847 and had published a code of ethics, there was still no nationally recognized standard for licensing doctors.[5] The Civil War had forcefully demonstrated the seriousness of the problem; soldiers were as likely to die in the hospital as on the battlefield. As a result, the physician's voice sometimes was not even privileged in questions of medical knowledge let alone in other arenas, such as the law.

There was a way for persons outside the field of law to exert limited influence. Since many criminal proceedings relied on evidence evaluated by experts in other professions, the voices of these witnesses were also heard. The most frequent expert witnesses, and by far the most troublesome, were physicians. Physicians considered applying their expertise to legal questions a natural component of the justice system, not an invasion of lawyers' "turf." The most egregious example of this was a two-volume work *Elements of Medical Jurisprudence*, published by two physicians, Theodric Beck and John Beck, in 1835. It was the culmination of a decade of Theodric Beck's efforts to legitimize forensic medicine. The book included discussions on topics such as detecting poisons. The subtext of the work was that doctors needed to know about these things because lawyers could not do the job properly. Lawyers usually responded by noting that most physicians were quacks; none of them understood the law sufficiently.

Nowhere was the battle between the two professions revealed more clearly than on the issue of insanity. The law recognized insanity as a mitigating circumstance in criminal cases but only under a strictly defined set of criteria— criteria that bore little resemblance to burgeoning medical theories.

To be fair, it must be noted that physicians had staked out their turf first. Doctors had, from ancient times, claimed special knowledge of all bodily ills including those affecting the personality and behavior of the patient. Although the nature of that knowledge changed as scientific methods developed, *ownership* of the expertise stayed in medical hands. Doctors used this ownership to gain importance in the legal field as well as their own. At first, they were consulted mainly in cases involving competence, as when heirs battled over the legalities of wills or when relatives desired to commit a loved one to an asylum.

As time passed, however, the doctors began to make their way into criminal trials as well. Since many disturbed individuals went on to commit crimes, it was natural that enough patients would wind up in court to create a demand for specialized medical experts. In the United States, physicians worked diligently to cement that authority. In 1817, Thomas Blatchford published *An Inaugural Dissertation on Feigned Diseases*, a treatise aimed at determining whether a person was faking insanity to dodge punishment for criminal behavior. This work became a medical standard and codified "much of what would be called state of the art by mid century" (Geller et al. 8). Blatchford laid the foundations for medical determination of "moral" insanity.

A few years later, in 1823, T. R. Beck incorporated insanity into his first edition of *Elements of Medical Jurisprudence*, making it a standard element in the new field of medical jurisprudence. The book was a great success, going through several editions in both the United States and England. It was followed by a host of imitators, all of which found it necessary to discuss feigned insanity at some point. The crowning achievement of the medical literature was the 1838 publication of Isaac Ray's *A Treatise on the Medical Jurisprudence of Insanity*. "This work became a classic almost from the moment of its appearance, and would draw the medical world's attention to America" (Robinson 287 fn71). This book left the determination of sanity to physicians. If an insanity plea was entered in the courtroom, a physician would be called in, basically to tell the jury which way to vote.

This circumstance, which lent so much authority to physicians, changed forever in 1843. In London, an Englishman named Daniel McNaughton came to believe that the prime minister was conspiring against him. He planned to foil this plot by assassinating the minister and succeeded in killing Edward Drummond, a personal secretary. As usual, physicians were called in, including an American expert in absentia, Isaac Ray (Robinson 166). The jury found McNaughton "not guilty by reason of insanity." The public outcry over this verdict prompted Queen Victoria to demand that the courts devise a *legal* standard for determining sanity, doubtless to prevent any repeats of such a verdict.

The result was the famous "McNaughton rule," which stated that in order to be found not guilty "it must be clearly proved that at the time of committing the act, the party accused was laboring under such a defect of reason, from disease of the mind, as not to know the nature and quality of the act he was doing; or if he did know it, that he did not know he was doing what was wrong" (Freedman 162).

The McNaughton rule quickly became the legal standard on both sides of the Atlantic. From that moment, physicians were hamstrung. No matter what their opinion concerning the actual sanity of a defendant, they were reduced to arguing over the legal standard. That standard flew in the face of established medical opinion, which had recognized that a state such as monomania or paranoia could drive people to commit crimes despite knowing that their acts were illegal. Also struck down was the still-controversial concept of "moral insanity," wherein people of otherwise perfect rationality were incapable of controlling specific behaviors that society found abhorrent.

The dismantling of moral insanity in the social fabric of the United States would have been a boon to most females, who suffered under the judgment of male physicians quick to attribute undesirable feminine behavior to mental disease. It has been clearly demonstrated that women were overrepresented in mental institutions—and not always because they were a physical threat to others or to themselves (Showalter). A stricter guideline might have saved a few of these women from institutionalization.

However, the threat to medical primogeniture in criminal cases made physicians more determined to keep control of the definition of insanity in other fields of argument. In 1844, they got organized. The newly formed Association of Medical Superintendents of American Institutions for the Insane (precursor to the American Psychiatric Association) became the central organization for physicians with an interest in mental diseases. They held conventions, sponsored public lectures, and published a professional journal, the *American Journal of Insanity* (Freedman 153). The new specialty in psychiatric medicine was on its way to legitimacy.

These endeavors were not met with respect by lawyers, who referred to their opponents as "mad doctors"—pun intended. People such as Joseph Bradley, who practiced in both professions, were exceedingly rare. Bradley found himself in a difficult position. Based on the standards of medicine, his new client had been insane. Under the legal definition, however, she was competent. Bradley clearly understood that his case would rise or fall based upon which definition was accepted by the jury, and he gathered a collection of physicians to assault the legal citadel once more. The tension between the two professions over the question of legal insanity peaked in the case of Mary Harris.

## The Trial

The case did not initially attract much attention. There were other events competing for public attention at the time: the mustering out of troops from the Civil War, the assassination of Abraham Lincoln, and the trials and executions of the conspirators. As details began to emerge in the local press, however, the case became the sensation of July 1865. The *Washington Evening Star* began to print the salacious details. The *New York Times*, which had initially buried on page 8 a report lifted from a Virginia newspaper, decided to send their own stenographer to Washington and began running the story on page 1.

Each day, the crowd in the courtroom got larger. On the last day, it was standing room only. The case of the beautiful young woman who had avenged her own dishonor fascinated the public, and they read her story avidly. Whether they were aware of it or not, they were also reading the story of how physicians' vision of female insanity ran head-on into the law's supposedly "gender-free" vision.

The battle over Mary Harris was characterized by two different arguments: about the defendant and about the witnesses. The main exigence was the goal of the defense to prove that their client was not guilty by reason of insanity, despite the strictures of McNaughton. This generated a set of arguments around the nature of "womanly" frailties and whether the accused suffered from those frailties. The second major discussion evolved from the prosecution's attempt to minimize the effect of medical witnesses. The battle over "expert" witnesses was one for authority, between medical professionals and the law in cases related to insanity.

These arguments overlapped and blended, demonstrating in a superlative way what Kenneth Burke refers to as the "alchemy" of symbols. Although narratives may appear to be unique on the surface, any distinctions between them are artificial in that a rhetor has decided to combine the symbols of that narrative in a particular manner. "Let one of these crusted distinctions return to its source, and in this alchemic center it may be remade, again becoming molten liquid, and may enter into new combinations, whereat it may again be thrown forth as a new crust, a different distinction" (*A Grammar* xix). The new narrative again appears unique, but it is still the result of mixing old symbolic devices and putting them together in a new manner.

Bradley was a lawyer, but he was also a physician. He wanted to free his client, but he also wanted to highlight the weaknesses of McNaughton and reestablish medical expertise in determining insanity. In pursuing those goals, Bradley and his fellow doctors called upon established narratives in American discourse. The first was the popular narrative regarding the value of a woman's honor and the complete ruin that dishonor could bring. This theme appeared repeatedly in popular plays and novels; no doubt the jury was familiar with these. The second narrative was based upon the established medical theory that women were more prone to hysteria during menstruation. Since this theory might have been unfamiliar to the all-male jury, Bradley made sure to provide extensive testimony. Together these theories created a matrix that bolstered the much more controversial narrative of moral insanity, where knowing right from wrong was not the issue.

Each base narrative alone was not a complete cause of madness, but the combination created a situation wherein murder was a natural, albeit tragic, outcome. Later, this new combination took on a life of its own in the medical literature, and a violent insanity that could strike only women became an official psychiatric diagnosis.

Despite the "gender-free" nature of the laws concerning homicide, District Attorney Carrington immediately centered the discussion upon the defendant's sex, most likely in an attempt to defuse any sympathy the jury might have felt for the pretty young woman.[6]

> I stand here today to plead the cause of woman—gentle, lovely, virtuous woman, associated in our minds, from earliest infancy, with all that is good, amiable and attractive. Woman, more than man, is interested in the preservation of peace and order, and in the enforcement of the law. To consign an innocent woman to a false doom would be horrible, indeed! To allow a great crime to go unrebuked, because the guilty agent happened to be a woman, would be an act of cowardice, a criminal imbecility. (6)

After reminding the jury that they should not let their natural sympathy for womanhood affect their reason, he got down to the heart of his case, which was that Harris did not fit the legal definition of insanity because she had a rational motive, and this "is utterly incompatible with the idea of insanity. If it appear, therefore, from the evidence, that this homicide was committed in a spirit of revenge—to avenge some wrong—it is a death blow to the plea of insanity" (7). The defendant's sex is thus an instant denial of the insanity plea. A woman's honor is sacred; thus avenging the defilement is a perfectly rational motive for murder. If she had a rational motive, then she was not insane under the law.

Surprisingly, the defense took special pains at first to deny that issues of gender were pertinent in this case. In fact, Bradley's opening remarks were "I have nothing to say to you, gentlemen of the jury, on behalf of the prisoner as a young lady, or even as a woman, nor have I any appeal to make to you on the ground of chivalry or of manhood. Those questions are outside of the present inquiry" (10). Instead, the defense claimed that the question of insanity was a medical issue, not a legal one. After establishing his own expertise as a doctor with twenty years of experience, Bradley assiduously catalogued the physical symptoms he observed in Harris. He also implied that he kept track of the "intervals" of clarity versus "occasions in which she was undoubtedly insane. She was insane from moral causes, aggravated by disease of the body. This is our defense. A pure, virtuous, chaste, delicate little girl, not more than twenty years of age at this time, whose frame is wasting and whose spirits are gone, whose heart is broken, in a paroxysm of insanity has slain the man who has brought upon her all this suffering" (17).

Here was the heart of the defense: Harris was the victim of a strange new syndrome combining the well-known and accepted physical fact of women's "periodic" hysteria with the new theory of "moral" insanity. It neatly dealt with the problem of why it took Harris so long to strike at Burroughs if she wasn't plotting revenge. Bradley claimed that Harris was telling the truth when she said that she did not intend to kill Burroughs despite what he did to her. But fate dictated that she would next meet him when she was having a menstrual period. The combination of the two factors completely swamped her reason. Bradley knew that as Harris's attorney his medical opinion would be suspect, so he promised other "medical witnesses of the highest character." There was no need for chivalry to defend Harris; she had science behind her.

Of course, once the defense claimed that such a thing as moral insanity existed, their entire argument revolved around romantic notions of femininity that moved well away from the unbiased "science" of medicine. In order to prove that a moral insult sufficient to cause insanity had taken place, the defense had to establish that seduction and abandonment was one of the worst things for a woman to suffer, and that Mary Harris had suffered it. Thus, the cauldron in which the rhetorical alchemy was to take place was ready. Romantic narratives about "good" and "bad" women mixed with the scientific narrative of female physiology. The combination was tossed in with the legal standard of insanity to create a new vision that the defense hoped would be used by the jury to find Harris not guilty.

The wrangling over whether Mary Harris was a "good" girl or a "bad" woman continued throughout the initial examination of witnesses. The prosecution attempted to paint Harris as a character unlikely to receive a moral shock. She was a sturdy working-class Irish girl, after all, not a delicate flower from society.[7] In addition, it was clear—to the prosecution anyway—that she was exaggerating the extent of Burroughs's commitment to her and hers to him.

The first witnesses called were employed at the treasury building where the shooting took place. They were questioned about her demeanor at the time of the shooting, and they testified that she "very deliberately" took aim at Burroughs and even carefully lined up a second shot when he tried to run away. She was "perfectly cool and self-possessed" (20). In addition, Harris apparently told one witness that Burroughs had never actually seduced her. As he tactfully put it, "I asked her if Mr. Burroughs had done her any other injury than the violation of his engagement. She exclaimed, with a great deal of emphasis, that he had not. I put the question to her, 'Are you a virtuous girl?' 'Yes, as God is my witness,' was her answer" (24). Although her affections might have been toyed with, it wasn't clear that more than her pride was damaged.

The defense tried to weaken this impression by cross-examining witnesses who had seen Harris after the shooting to prove that after the shock wore off she had been distraught. Hughes even asked one witness whether Harris looked insane to him. This led to a lengthy discussion over whether laymen should be allowed to offer opinions on insanity. The court ruled that this witness, at least, should not. Importantly, the rationale for the decision was not because he wasn't a doctor but because he had only just met the defendant and had no basis for judgment. Other witnesses would be allowed their opinions if they were familiar with Harris. The judge was apparently not predisposed to grant physicians expertise.

At the core of the prosecution's argument against Harris's purity was her relationship with the Devlins. At first, Carrington and Wilson were subtle in developing this argument. During cross-examination of Louisa Devlin, for example, Wilson asked how often the women attended church, whether Harris entertained any other males at the boardinghouse, and whether Harris frequented the theater. He then increased the pressure.[8] If the Devlins noticed that Harris was acting oddly, why did they not inform her father? When she bought a pistol, why did they not threaten to discharge her? Carrington asked questions about the millinery, questions that seemed innocuous but that Louisa refused to answer. Was Harris the only clerk? How many women were employed at the shop? How did the Devlins know that the house referred to in the letter had a "bad" reputation? The import of these questions became clear later:

> What sort of millinery establishment was it? I wanted to find out, and in the most courteous and respectful manner, for no one is more courteous to a lady than myself, I asked her how many young ladies she had in her employment. She threw herself back on her dignity and said, "that is my business and none of yours." There is Mary Harris in a millinery establishment, the character of which the proprietress is ashamed to describe. (165)
>
> Who is Louisa Devlin? When asked about her business, her color would come and go. By her own admission, she went to an assignation-house on Quincy Street on a fool's errand. [Here he was interrupted by Bradley who reminded him that Louisa did no such thing.] Jane Devlin did. . . . notwithstanding the eulogium pronounced upon [Louisa], I say she is a woman without delicacy, without refinement, and without sensibility, for during this trial she has sat here giggling while her friend was on trial for her life, as though she were on a debauch in Quincy street, Chicago, at the house of Ellen Mills. (170)

Ellen Mills was the madam who had disappeared before the trial. Carrington's innuendo was that the Devlins were selling more than hats in their millinery, and that any young woman who associated with them was far from innocent. Two single women supporting themselves and a female friend without a male protector? There was clearly only one way they managed that!

This tactic backfired, however. Bradley exploded at the manner in which the Devlins were being treated, and Judge Wylie fully concurred, stating that it was unsuitable "in regard to a female witness, who is here, to all appearances, without a protector" (170). Although Wylie followed this immediately by telling the jury that his censure of Carrington should in no way be taken as an opinion regarding the case as a whole, they were still present for this show of masculine chivalry. The gist of the discussion, that women needed protection, was surely going to help Harris.

Such displays were also clear signs that one underlying premise of the defense's case was going to be accepted: any "good" woman who had been seduced and abandoned would suffer a deep moral shock. It would take some doing to define Harris as a good woman, but if they were successful in that, the rest would follow. Their task was difficult because the standard narrative of feminine purity was clearly designed for the middle-class woman. A working-class Irish girl with questionable relationships did not automatically fit this construct. Thus, the defense made sure to recast her character so as to make her worthy.

Bradley recognized Harris's roots as a detriment, and worked diligently to alter the jury's view. He admitted that as she was "of Irish descent" she "had few advantages of early education and moral culture" (10). On the other hand, she was so young when Burroughs took an interest in her that her character was still malleable:

> He was a man of education and knowledge of the world, her senior at that time of more than double her years. He had during the acquaintance between them, cultivated her intellect, and assisted in refining her manners, and thus she became fitted for, and was admitted into, the best society of Burlington. From that time forth, . . . she was received as the friend of ladies of the highest character and repute, well known in that town. Her associations were with the children of these ladies, principally among married ladies, and of persons older than herself. (10)

Harris was not naturally vulnerable, but she *became* vulnerable because she spent her youth among genteel people. It was Burroughs himself who molded Harris into a woman of high morals and pure instincts. That made

him all the more culpable in his own murder. This theme of innocence betrayed was touched upon throughout the rest of the trial. There were deft
touches during cross-examination. The defense consistently asked witnesses
to describe her although no one contested that Harris pulled the trigger—it
was not an effort to challenge the identity of the shooter. These questions
were not limited to her behavior, as might be expected in an insanity case,
but also her appearance. Harris, for example, "wore her hair in curls. I believe
around the whole of her head; certainly around her face" in a feminine touch
noted by more than one witness (20). She was a "little girl," a "child," "not
more than twenty"—her youth and femininity were constantly brought up.

Once Harris was defined as a working-class woman with a genteel mind, it
was left to Hughes to decorate the first closing argument with the traditional
story of innocence betrayed. In his narrative, Burroughs was the villain and
Harris the instrument of God's vengeance:

> Who is to punish the betrayer of female honor? Who is to punish the serpent
> that with his slimy track pursues from early girlhood to budding womanhood
> the unfortunate girl, separates her from her friends, her family, and leaves her
> alone and isolated, without father or brother to defend or protect her, then
> throws her heartlessly upon the world? Who is to punish him? . . . There is a
> just God, however, who administers justice in such cases, and he chose as the
> instrument of his justice, in this particular case, the poor unfortunate girl whose
> life had been forever blighted. That little girl, (pointing to the prisoner,) with
> that little hand poised the pistol . . . He took away her reason, and she stands
> here today secure from human justice. That overruling Providence, without
> whose consent not even a sparrow falls, brought punishment to the door of
> the deceased—brought it by the hand of her that he had ruined, and placed
> her in a position where she shall answer to Him alone for what she has done,
> and not to human laws. (125)

Thus the groundwork for the first narrative is laid. No treasure is more
valuable to a genteel woman than her virtue. Harris was certain to suffer the
deepest moral shock when Burroughs rejected her. Since the poor woman
had no close relatives to look out for her (the Devlins did not count), she
had nowhere to go for guidance. Obviously, this blow alone, though disas-
trous, would not make a woman a killer, but if she were also suffering from
a menstrual disorder, the combination would be fatal. It was up to Bradley
and his collection of medical men to provide the "scientific" proof that this
syndrome existed.

There were two medical witnesses who were central to the creation of this
second narrative. The first was Charles H. Nichols, the superintendent of

the local "government hospital for the insane" and a nationally recognized proponent of Isaac Ray's theory of moral insanity. The second was Bradley himself. Bradley not only examined the other medical witnesses but called himself as a witness.[9] Naturally, the prosecution had witnesses who were just as convinced that moral insanity was a sham illness. As the trial progressed, the former were referred to as "mad doctors" and the latter as "common sense" doctors. Interestingly, even the common sense doctors allowed that a woman could easily become hysterical during menstruation; they just did not believe that it could render one homicidal.

The groundwork was laid by calling Calvin Fitch, the Chicago physician whom the Devlins had called when Harris began acting strangely. He had visited her five times in the months after she had discovered Burrough's marriage. Ostensibly called to confirm that Harris suffered from "severe congestive dysmenorrhea," he was soon asked to speculate on Harris's sanity based only upon what he had seen of police testimony and written reports. Fitch noted that he saw no signs of insanity in Harris at the time, but that was because he was not informed about her recent rejection. Had he known, he would have looked more carefully: "We know that among the moral causes of insanity, disappointed affection is one of the most frequent; and we know that among physical causes, uterine irritation is one of the most frequent. The combination of the two causes we should naturally expect to produce a very much greater effect than either would alone" (51). Although Bradley tried, he could not get Fitch to comment on her probable mental state at the time of the crime. Still, Fitch admitted that two possible causes for insanity existed simultaneously. The prosecution settled here for noting that Fitch was not a specialist in insanity. Since he willingly admitted that a few fifteen-minute consultations were not enough to determine a patient's sanity, he was not a threat.

The threat came from the physicians who had seen Harris in prison. Bradley and Nichols were both convinced that Harris suffered from a special form of moral insanity that could, by definition, only affect females. Bradley's testimony took the form of a monologue. Hughes was primed to ask him whether he "took any notes" during his visits to Harris. Bradley then read those verbatim. His litany of symptoms provides an interesting look into the science of psychology at the time considered relevant: nervous excitement, rapid pulse, dilated pupils, sudden mood swings, a high tolerance for cold, and a recurring fever that left her head "so hot as to be uncomfortable to the hand" despite an open window that admitted the winter wind—"her hands were cold; the top of her head seemed to send off steam" (63–65). He peppered his discussion with descriptions of their meetings, aimed at constructing her character in the best possible way. When she was in a sane phase, she was angelic. She was aware that she had orphaned Burrough's child, and she was distraught about that. She was still a virgin, and her only show of violent temper came when she was informed of a newspaper story that implied otherwise. When her mind was clear, she was sweet and tender and full of gaiety.

One interesting addition to the story was an episode that could only have been told to show that she was also patriotic. On one day Bradley was due to visit, there was a special review of troops returning from the war. She asked him to leave because "our *western men* are to pass today, and I'll tell you at another time what I wanted to say. I wish you would see our western men" (68). All those virtues, and loyal to the Union, too!

Only after this lengthy paean to feminine character did Hughes interrupt to ask Bradley's opinion of her sanity. This answer was considerably briefer, as his testimony was meant as a precursor to the expert witness:

> I have no hesitation in saying . . . that in certain conditions of the system her mind is so far affected, not by nervous condition alone, but by moral causes, that when a fact or substance is suddenly presented to her mind, connected with these moral causes, or during this state of excitement of her mind, that she is incapable of thinking and acting in regard to that subject with reason or discretion; and that she is subject to certain impulses which control her will in reference to the same matter; and that is what I understand to be paroxysmal insanity from moral causes. (69)

The mental cause did not even have to be genuine. If Harris erred in thinking Burroughs was going to marry her, it was not important. "Whether delusion or actual fact, the effect upon the mind would be the same" (69). It was unfortunate that Harris met Burroughs at a moment when she would be unable to control herself.[10] Bradley finished by admitting that he was no specialist but that one would be testifying. He often hedged his "medical" opinions even as he presented them as authoritative. He knew insanity because he had seen it, not because he'd been trained in a specialty. This left the door open for the defense to ask laymen their opinion of Harris. For example, once Bradley had explained that dilated pupils were a sign of insanity, the defense asked their lay witnesses whether they noticed anything about Harris's eyes. The warden at the jail especially noticed that her eye was "entirely suffused." "In fact," he said, "it did not look like an eye at all" (71). He was so struck by it that he made a note of the date of the encounter. The warden recognized that something was wrong even without medical expertise.

Bradley's testimony was clearly intended to tie Harris's character as a good and pure woman to the more technical testimony of Nichols, who would state that a pure woman was at special risk for moral insanity. Nichols was a strong believer in moral insanity and a firm opponent of the "raving maniac" criterion for legal insanity. As such, he made an excellent witness for the defense. Nichols had been called in by court-appointed lawyers to look at Harris in his capacity as asylum superintendent. He was asked before the current defense team came on board, and he formed his opinion over the course of five visits. Thus he was free of the taint of "paid expert" who would draw conclusions based upon a cursory examination. In fact, he admitted that he did not think Harris was insane at first. It was not until a later visit that he noticed signs of escalating hysteria. He then suspected some form of periodic disorder and proceeded to collect evidence that his suspicion was correct. Nichols shared Bradley's high opinion of Harris's general intelligence and demeanor. He noted that the good ladies of Burlington had done an excellent job of counteracting her lack of "advantages of much moral or mental training." In his opinion, however, it was just this superior sort of female who was "peculiarly susceptible" to insanity (74). The dilemma this placed the average woman in was clear; in order to escape the lower classes, she had to improve herself, but once uplifted she was "susceptible" to new diseases that could knock her back down. This particular disease was caused by a combination of dysmenorrhea and "disappointment in love; this great shock to her delicate moral sensibilities" (74). Interestingly, Nichols noted that the second factor could also render a male insane, although not nearly as often: "I am under the impression that disappointment in love is a more frequent cause of insanity among women than men" (75). Only a woman, of course, faced the confluence of two overwhelming factors and was thus more likely to succumb to violence.

Although Nichols seconded Bradley's diagnosis, his real contribution to the defense rested in his firm opposition to the McNaughton rule. The jury might be sympathetic to Harris because of her mental anguish, but their legal charge stipulated that the criterion for insanity was an inability to tell right from wrong. The prosecution made much of that criterion. If Harris was sane enough to buy a gun, wait for the right time, travel to a new city, and stalk her victim, then she was sane enough to know she was doing wrong. If her motive arose from having been jilted, that is a rational motive, and having a rational motive precluded insanity. The existence of a disease, if there were one, was no excuse at all. Thus the testimony of a physician was immaterial to the legal issue.

Nichols was obviously called to dismantle that criterion in the eyes of the jury so that they might be more likely to nullify the charge. After ascertaining that Harris was symptomatic, Voorhees changed course and specifically asked, "State whether a knowledge of right and wrong is any longer considered as a test of insanity" (74). Nichols replied, "I do not consider a knowledge of right and wrong, in the abstract, as a test of insanity; nor even a knowledge of right and wrong in respect to any criminal act that may be committed by an insane person" (74). He archly added that physicians had *never* believed it "though the views of your profession [law] have never been as clearly defined as those of mine" (75). Physicians, on the other hand, recognized the "insane impulse" where a person is driven "suddenly to commit an act that he is unable to restrain himself from committing" (75). Nichols clearly believed that under that criterion, Harris was insane.

Nichols could not be shaken from that opinion although the prosecution tried hard during the cross-examination. Carrington asked Nichols whether he really thought a person could do all the very clever things that Harris had prior to the shooting and not know right from wrong, but Nichols refused to be drawn upon that criterion and stuck to his own: "I will say, in reply to that, that no amount of premeditation and preparation to commit a homicide, in my judgment, precludes the idea that that homicide was an insane act. I, however, deem it equally due to the truth of science to say, that if there was evidence of premeditation and preparation, a much closer scrutiny should be made in respect to the existence or non-existence of insanity, if insanity is presumed to exist" (77). The requirement for closer scrutiny had been met by his own investigation as a trained doctor, thus reinforcing the need to put medical experts on the case before determining legal insanity. Nichols answered any similar queries in the same manner. Carrington eventually shifted to undermining the extent of Nichols's observations and questioning whether he had been influenced by other witnesses' interpretations of Harris's behavior.

Naturally, the prosecution was ready with physicians of their own who were not aligned with Nichols's school of thought. Their testimony, however, was not nearly as interesting as the reaction of the defense to their being called at all. The discussion was summarized by the court reporter. When John May, a general practitioner, was called, the defense team immediately raised numerous objections. Voorhees "had a great deal of respect for the witness . . . but before he was a competent witness it should be ascertained whether or not he made that branch of study a specialty" (97). Carrington replied that "any educated physician was a proper witness on a question of insanity" (98).

At this point, it was no longer simply a question of whether doctors were better judges than laypeople, but whether only certain kinds of doctors should be held up as experts. The so-called commonsense doctors were being shunted aside by their brethren on the defense. The judge, unwilling to make such a call himself, finally settled for allowing the testimony while warning the prosecution that it might have to be stricken later if it was decided that May was not an expert. May was then allowed to state that, lacking a complete medical history, he would not, given the evidence, call Harris insane. His testimony was a subtle attack upon Nichols, who had not investigated the patient's history prior to the crime.

Several other doctors were called although the defense, having made their point, stopped objecting to every single one. Naturally, these doctors were not convinced of Harris's insanity, although most of them had not met her and based their opinions upon testimony already provided. The defense shifted to the tactic of presenting hypothetical cases upon cross-examination. Given these hypothetical scenarios, the witness was asked whether a woman might go mad. The witnesses usually admitted that a woman could indeed go insane. These answers did not escape the accepted medical narrative that linked womanhood with mental disease. Thus even the prosecution's witnesses had to allow that Harris fit the medical model.

It did not hurt, either, that every hypothetical case reminded the jury about how cruelly Burroughs had treated Harris, for Bradley took great care to state the case in heartrending detail to every witness. He began one line of questioning with, "A little girl not more than ten or eleven years of age . . . attracts the attention of a man almost old enough to be her father," and went on in enough detail to fill four pages with the tale of the girl with the "broken spirit" (101–5). Bradley's questions were usually much longer than the witnesses' answers. The two narratives, that of innocent girlhood betrayed and that of the medical model of female insanity, were neatly laid out in the course of the trial. These were then woven together through the lens of gender. Issues of gender were woven throughout the case, and not simply in the obvious places. Although the prosecution stuck to its guns and hammered at the doctors with the legal definition of insanity, as an insurance policy Carrington continued to attempt to undermine the character of Harris so as to render her theoretically insensible to moral shock. In the end, he had a great deal of trouble doing so because of gender expectations. Carrington was male, and he was of that class of males who had created the icon of genteel womanhood. He was not tactful enough to make his point without crossing the line of "gentlemanly" behavior. Every time he attempted to discredit a witness, the defense was able to make him look churlish.

It did not help that his main witnesses were male, either. The defense seemed able to insult their character at will. One important witness, for example, was John Burroughs, brother of the deceased. One would think that a minister and seminary president would be unassailable, but the defense effectively turned him into a monster.

Burroughs was called to deny that the bordello letters were in his brother's handwriting and to bolster the prosecution claim that the engagement and jilting were a product of Harris's wishful thinking. Carrington implied that Harris visited Burroughs to extort money for a breach of contract, hardly the behavior of an innocent woman. Bradley, on the other hand, accused Burroughs of actively interfering in the case by paying for witnesses. Although Bradley never directly said Burroughs suborned witnesses, he came as close as he could. Further, he allied Burroughs with his brother as a partner in the jilting.

The gender bias was very clear here: when Carrington objected to this character assassination, the judge did sustain the objection, but that was all. When Carrington attempted to use similar tactics on the Misses Devlin, as noted earlier, the judge censured the prosecution. One could insult a male witness, but not a female.

It is not clear that the prosecution could have done much to shake the defense's picture of innocence, regardless of gender bias. Since Burlington witnesses were in agreement that Burroughs began his relationship with Harris when she was nine, anyone would have been hard pressed to prove that she was the schemer. Once the judge squashed Carrington's efforts to make Louisa Devlin the secret mastermind of a blackmail plot, there was not much more that could be done. Their only real hope was that the jury would reject the testimony of the "mad doctors" and thus ignore the defense's hints about jury nullification.

The closing arguments in the trial strongly resembled the opening ones. Once more, the defense, while claiming that gender was not an issue, took pains to draw upon every gallant instinct of the male jury. Once more, the prosecution, ostensibly representing a gender-free legal standard, tried to use "true womanhood" as a weapon against Harris's character.

In the first closing argument, Wilson attempted to lead the jury back to the legal definition:

> [Their] defence is insanity—a refuge always sought in cases where other refuge there is none. And it is this defence that you are to examine—to examine not as a school of philosophers, not as a society of metaphysicians, not as a board of trustees considering an application for admission into an insane asylum, but as men of honesty and common sense, needing not the theories and speculations of the books, but having the instructions of the Court, and in them a guiding star, a chart, a compass and rudder by which you may find and follow

that rightful law, whose aim it is, in all the fluctuations of interest, in all the vicissitudes of fortune, to punish guilt, whether in high or low, whether in rich or poor, whether in man or woman.[11]

In the gender-free universe of the law, insanity was the McNaughton rule, women were no more likely to be insane than men, and avenging a woman's honor was no better an excuse for killing than any other form of vengeance.

The defense, on the other hand, wanted to steer the jury toward a different standard. Hughes took up the challenge by giving the jury a precedent for jury nullification of the law. He noted what he believed was a flaw in the system:

> There are those things, gentlemen, in this world, that are more precious than life, and especially is female honor and female character; yet, according to the law as it is found in the books, if Mr. Burroughs had imperiled the life of Miss Harris, she would have been perfectly justifiable, while she was perfectly sane, in taking his life; but having destroyed her honor, her happiness, and made life to her a desert waste, without hope, had she taken his life in her sane moments, she would have rendered herself liable to punishment. This is a defect in our law; yet so it is written . . . (133)

This jury was not the first to face such a dilemma. Wilson gave them a little course in legal history, the point of which was that "human justice, as it moves on, modifies and changes these stern features of the law in their actual demonstration, so as to make the law, instead of being an instrument of oppression and injustice, the safeguard of the citizen and the deliverer of those who are unjustly accused" (134). He first pointed out that McNaughton itself was a change from the traditional definition of insanity. He then discussed a case regarding bridges on the Mississippi. Forbidden when commerce traveled mainly by boat, the advent of new roads and railroads demanded them, and the law was ignored. He next noted that circumstances occasionally "arise when, to convict a party who has suffered a great wrong . . . is so shocking, and so repugnant to human nature, that there must be found some evidence by which to administer the law in a milder spirit than the strict letter of it as laid down in the books" (136). Harris was one of those wronged souls. Sometimes, a jury is better off recalling the *spirit* rather than the *letter* of the law.

Of course, the defense was giving the jury a scientific reason for a not guilty verdict, not only just a moral reason. The legal definition of sanity was simply wrong if the many physicians who testified were to be trusted. The changing medical definition of insanity warranted reconsideration of the law, lest a poor mad woman be put to death. Wilson closed by hinting that failure to initiate the reform process might halt it all together.

The argument left Voorhees free to argue that Harris was mad under the new, medical, standard. In setting that standard, he quoted frequently from Isaac Ray, the famous opponent of McNaughton. He claimed that the prosecution, once

> utterly borne down and crushed by the evidence of Dr. Nichols, the gentlemen who represent the Government boldly and without a blush declare that the opinions of men, who, like him, have given their lives to the study of the mind in all its various and mysterious phases, are less reliable in the discovery of insanity than the opinions of those who have bestowed no particular attention on this great and difficult subject. The cry of "mad doctors" has been raised, and we have heard an appeal against them in favor of what were styled "common sense doctors." (159)

In deciding a case resting on medical issues, who should the jury trust, the lawyers or the doctors? Voorhees had his opinion:

> I submit to you and to the candid judgment of the country, that if Mary Harris can be convicted under the evidence, if Dr. Nichols can be broken down in this court, not by contradiction, but by declamatory appeals to prejudice, and, if finally, the unbroken chain of scientific testimony can be put aside as naught, then the great and settled principles of medical jurisprudence are a delusion and a snare, and the infirmities of the intellect occasioned by misfortune constitute no defense for violent and irrational conduct. (161)

Along the way, Voorhees peppered the discussion with a detailed retelling of the wrongs perpetrated upon Harris. No more hypothetical cases: the emotional details of Harris's life were rehearsed under her own name. This perfectly blended the medical model with the popular narrative of what happens to an innocent woman betrayed by a cad. The mad woman in literature was not only an archetype for the popular minds; medical men often found themselves referring to literature for their descriptions of insanity (Small, Wiesenthal). Thus the science of one field was easy fodder for the sentiment of the other. Voorhees painted a vivid portrait in the sentimental colors of literary visions of the madwoman. Ophelia herself could not have been more pitiful: "At times she sinks in long and gloomy spells of abstracted silence. She gazes steadily on space and distance, all unconscious of surrounding objects. . . . At other times she starts up singing in plaintive strains, the broken fragments of some melancholy song, which tells of disappointed love. When the witness heard her murmuring 'I loved him, but he doubted me,' she heard the universal wail of woman's broken heart and wandering mind" (157).

Poor Mary Harris, seduced and betrayed, perfectly fit the popular notion of madness. This model, intertwined with the medical testimony, created a persuasive image of shattered womanhood. How could the court possibly come up with any punishment fitting the crime? She had already met the proverbial "fate worse than death" and had to live with that disgrace for the rest of her life. Voorhees called the prosecution's case a matter of vengeance, not justice, and told the jury that it was up to them to administer true justice by showing mercy.

> She has suffered more already than the king of terrors in his most frightful form can inflict. If she had been broken in the wheel, her limbs disjointed, and her flesh torn in piecemeal by the most fiendish skill of the executioner, her tortures would have been merciful compared to the racking which sunders into fragments the immortal mind. There is no arrow in death's full quiver that can give this young breast a new sensation of agony. . . . Restore her by your verdict to the soothing influence of friends, of home. Let her go and lay her aching head on the maternal bosom of that Church which for eighteen centuries has tenderly ministered to her children in distress. Let her go and seek, in the love and mercy of the Father of us all, consolation for the cruelty and inhumanity of man. (161)

Voorhees brought the two powerful narratives together in an equally powerful rationale for acquittal. If the jury was persuaded that the medical definition of insanity rang more "true" than the legal one, then the battle was nearly over. The prosecution had only one more chance to turn the tide.

The prosecutor had not given up on his attempts to darken the character of Harris and her associates, although at this point he had learned to couch his digs as asides and "joking" digs at the defense, chiding them for their overt sentimentality. He clearly thought that Bradley and Hughes were overacting and could not resist reminding them (and the jury) of the fact: "Appeals have been made to your sympathies; and that is all, as I will show. Sympathy! sympathy! sympathy! and nothing else, and with unusual zeal and eloquence" (163). He even at one point accused them of crying on cue (174). He found humor in Bradley's double role, as well, for it reminded of him of a joke about a lawyer who advertised "Fees moderate, except where evidence is furnished" (177). Bradley was frequently moved to snipe back; it is telling that the record does not show the judge censuring him for that. Such byplay was apparently the order of the moment.

Still, Carrington did not forget his main duty, which was to convince the jury that Harris could not be considered insane under the law. Carrington was obviously aware of the power of the literary image of Ophelia that had been subtly drawn by the defense. His riposte was to call upon another image of a madwoman: Lady Macbeth. In his narrative, Harris never truly loved Burroughs with that "holy" affection romanticized by the defense. She loved for the sake of material gain, and, when thwarted in that goal, she killed in cold hatred.

> Prompted not by "insane impulse" but by hatred she comes to the city of Washington to institute a suit for breach of promise of marriage. [She went to the office and waited until closing time.] There was time for passion to subside and reason to resume its sway. There was time for "insane impulse" to pass away, and the power of volition to return. He passes by. She fires at him deliberately. He falls; she fires a second time, aiming directly at his head. . . . She wanted revenge, and would have it at the risk of her life. She showed no emotion until the bleeding, mangled corpse of her victim is brought into her presence. And this is evidence of insanity. This is evidence, gentlemen of the jury, of sanity. It is woman's nature speaking out. When Lady Macbeth was reproving her husband for his irresolution, she said "I had done the deed, but the grey-haired Duncan resembled my father as he slept." Proud, cruel, ambitious woman. Still she was a woman. So, Mary Harris, having accomplished her purpose, and when she sees before her the bleeding evidence of her guilt, suffers the pangs of remorse. This is sanity. . . . Now gentlemen, that is the case, and what do you call it? Science, as the learned counsel understands it, calls it "insane impulse." Science, as I understand it, and as I think you understand it, gentlemen of the jury, calls it murder. (171)

Carrington referred to Lady Macbeth often. His point was that all the behaviors observed by Bradley and Nichols could be explained as easily by remorse as by madness. In the literary example, it was remorse that drove the woman mad—*after* the crime. Surely it was no different for Harris. No matter how distraught she was afterwards, if she was thinking clearly at the moment she fired the shot, she was guilty.

Carrington's second line of argument was that ignoring the law for Harris would set a dangerous precedent, as well as make Washington, D.C., a national laughingstock.

> It is throwing open the doors wide to violence and crime, and I ask, "What man in the community is safe, if a jury so far mistake the law as to acquit this woman upon the ground of 'insane impulse'?" By such an absurd verdict, you say to every wicked woman in the city of Washington, kill a man for revenge if you please, and then take care to tear your hair, cry, and cut up a few antics, and we will call it insane impulse, and thus we will not only approve, but applaud the act. (172)

This appeal to an all-male jury was interesting. Carrington envisions a city where men are under continual threat from rejected women, as though they were lined up and waiting. He clearly expects this darker vision of woman to resonate with this audience.

Finally, he reminds the jury not to let physicians usurp the power of the jury. He notes the custom in cases "when the defense of insanity is made, to examine the prisoner carefully yourselves, and form your opinion from a personal inspection and examination of the accused" (177–78). In this case, doctors are usurping that custom. One might as well put Nichols in the jury box. For Carrington, privileging the expert witness violated the entire principle behind having a trial in the first place. It was, in effect, allowing physicians to dictate the law, much as they had apparently done prior to the McNaughton trial. He called upon the jury to uphold their duty and convict Harris.

Such appeals to civic pride apparently fell upon deaf ears. The jury retired for about five minutes, then returned with a verdict of "not guilty." The announcement was met with pandemonium, all positive. Bradley kissed Harris (or she kissed him, depending upon the newspaper) and took her to a waiting carriage, where she was returned to the custody of her parents in Burlington. A small notice in the *New York Times* noted that proceeds of the sales of the official transcript were being donated to a fund to defray travel expenses ("Your Small Change Wanted"). The Devlin sisters moved to Baltimore and reopened their shop ("Mary Harris Goes Home").

The defense had struck a powerful blow, not merely for their client but for the medical profession. Given the choice of using the legal definition of insanity and the medical definition, the jury sided with the mad doctors. Whether they did so out of respect for science or out of emotional response to a pretty young woman cannot be known for sure, but the defense was wise enough to blend appeals to both. The accepted narrative that woman's only "jewel" was her innocence was not merely an emotional appeal but also formed the premise for the argument that a woman could receive a "moral shock" from seduction. The accepted medical narrative that women were halfway to madness every twenty-eight or so days blended seamlessly with that premise of an additional "shock" to the system. The resulting third narrative—that "paroxysmal insanity" combined with "moral shock" could indeed lead to murder—was then easy to sell to the jury. Once the jury was convinced that the third narrative was a reasonable alternative to the legal standard, it was simply a matter of reminding them that they were free to reject the latter if the former was more "just."

## Aftershocks

Although the trial was officially over, the arguments generated by the case continued in the medical community for years. This victory, however limited, spurred physicians to reignite the debate over ownership of criminal insanity. Through letters to newspapers and talks at conventions, physicians reaffirmed that detection of insanity was purely a medical matter. Although they generously allowed that not all moral lapses were due to insanity, the bulk of them did not believe the courts should try to determine which ones were. As one physician put it in a letter to the *New York Times,* "Now, sir, these legal instructions on insanity are nothing but imaginary conceptions, having no foundation in nature. They present an inescapable confusion of legal criminality mixed up with doubtful speculations on moral freedom. . . . Physical and mental symptoms are the only test of mental disease" (Parigot).

Such arguments apparently had little success, as the McNaughton rule was not substantially altered for decades and the "right-wrong" test of insanity remains a standard in many states today (Robinson 183; Rosenberg 1968). The law was not about to give up its authority.

The leading figure in medical jurisprudence at the time, Isaac Ray, when commenting on the case, was not shy about calling the law's treatment of insanity a clear danger to society. He first flatly denied that the McNaughton rule was at all useful in determining sanity: "That this [rationality] should be considered incompatible with insanity, only indicates how imperfect are the prevalent notions respecting this disease. It needs but little observation of the insane to see that they often act from rational motives. Strike an insane man, and he will be very likely to strike back. . . . [The response] may be disproportionate, cruel and felonious, and therein consists the manifestation of the disease" ("Insanity of Women" 268). Ray was as concerned with the disposition of the person as he was with the verdict. He was appalled that Harris was remanded to the custody of her parents instead of that of a doctor, apparently because there was no law concerning the disposal of such individuals: "And thus a woman, having committed a capital crime, under the influence of insanity, is let again loose upon the community, to repeat the act whenever the occasion may be offered" ("Insanity of Women" 265). He urged Congress to change the law so that all states would have to hospitalize such individuals until a doctor pronounced them recovered.

A more important battle, for future female patients at any rate, was waged within the profession. The medical profession was itself divided over the "true" causes and symptoms of insanity. As Geller notes, "The debate pitted the alienists, functional theorists who had primarily viewed mental illness from a psycho-social perspective, against the neurologists, who saw the etiology of mental illness in the brain and nervous system" (Geller et al. 4). The two groups were frequently at odds with each other, as evidenced by some contradictory testimony during the case. In the trial of Mary Harris, a physician had successfully transcended two schools of thought on the nature of insanity by combining the psychosocial narrative of woman's natural purity and delicate sensibility with the physiological narrative of her susceptibility to menstrual disorders. It was a perfect union that enabled the doctors, divided over principles of medicine, to meet on the common ground of a woman's body. Here, at least, they could all agree.

The testimony of the "mad doctors," especially Nichols, was soon incorporated into the "official" criminal insanity narrative. After the trial, no less a person than Isaac Ray made a speech before the annual convention of the Association of Medical Superintendents of American Institutions for the Insane.[12] Its title, "The Insanity of Women Produced by Desertion or Seduction," is a strong clue to the tenor of his discussion. Ray believed that the Harris trial provided an opportunity "to call attention to a class of cases of which this may be considered as a fair representative" (266). This new classification concerned women made insane by a combination of "a strong moral shock and an irritable condition of the nervous system" (267–68). Ray noted that the latter was an established fact: "[T]he thoughtful inquirer cannot fail to perceive the peculiar influence of those organs which play so large a part of the female economy . . . With woman it is but a step from extreme nervous susceptibility to downright hysteria, and from that to overt insanity" (267).

The argument he advanced was that this step over the line could be caused by an assault on a woman's honor, either through seduction or desertion. He noted that he had noticed several murder cases with the following commonalities:

> In all, there has been a grievous disappointment or outrage. . . . a strong and sudden revulsion of feeling, in which love and confidence were succeeded by deadliest hate. . . . more or less mental disturbance [was] exhibited, not so much in the form of delusion as in that of paroxysmal fury and uncontrollable criminal impulse. . . . an entire abandonment of every interest and feeling not connected with the single purpose of revenge . . . [and] the person gives herself up to justice, glories in the bloody deed, and is careless of the future. (266)

These cases had heretofore been regarded as simple revenge killings. What Ray saw was possibly a new mental disease. "What we are greatly in need of now, is a collection of these cases, accurately reported" (269). Ray called upon his fellows to make note of similar cases and research them so that the syndrome could be used in medical jurisprudence.

Jurors who acquit such unfortunates are thus "not the fruit of a morbid sentimentalism, or a fashionable indulgence, to crime" but a "true humanity enlightened by true science" (269). Although Ray's stated purpose was to create "scientific" standards by which physicians could help courts determine whether a woman was insane, he apparently missed the fact that his definition of "moral shock" was firmly grounded in cultural narratives regarding woman's naturally pure and delicate sensibilities.

For example, one of the factors Ray seems to think would help save such unfortunate women was "a larger religious element in her education." A healthy dose of a "submissive, Christian spirit" might prevent a potential killer from snapping (273). His sentimentalism, while perhaps not "morbid," was sentimentalism nonetheless.

He was also sentimental in his belief in the infallibility of physicians. The most obvious problem with the moral insanity defense was that it gave murderous females an extra opportunity to feign madness as a way to escape justice. Ray seemed to believe that a well-trained doctor would be able to tell the difference—and that no physician would fabricate a diagnosis for money. His detractors, even in the present day, are quick to point out cases where physicians failed the court on both counts. Interestingly, some have even chosen Mary Harris as a paradigm case of feigning that led to a miscarriage of justice (Geller et al.). This is odd, because subsequent events proved that, in this case at least, Nichols had been correct with his diagnosis. By 1867, Mary Harris had been committed to an asylum in Washington, D.C., and she spent the next fifteen years bouncing in and out of mental hospitals. She apparently really was suffering from some reoccurring disorder.[13]

Whether genuine or not, this new kind of female insanity was soon popular with lawyers defending female clients (Spiegel and Suskind). The general line was that a combination of moral shock and periodic hysteria produced an "irresistible impulse" that could rob the gentlest soul of her reason. Interestingly, this so-called PMS defense is still occasionally used and still follows the criteria concocted by Ray. As one writer in the 1980s noted, periodic insanity turns up as a plea "only when women have attacked their boyfriends, husbands, or children" (Jacoby 222). Only intimates, it seems, can render the requisite shock to the system.

Physicians, on the other hand, eventually abandoned the concept of moral insanity and preferred to attribute unsocialized behavior to character deficiencies—by the end of the century, the "common sense" doctors had won.

The tables, ironically, had turned: defense lawyers adopted a narrative that physicians eventually rejected.

The popularity of the narrative of periodic hysteria in public discourse, on the other hand, has not dimmed, even with the advent of "modern" science. Although the terminology has changed, from paroxysmal insanity to premenstrual syndrome, the narrative that casts women as periodically insane still surfaces in the popular culture. For example, Eli Lilly and Co. inaugurated an advertising campaign for the twenty-first century by producing commercials showing a wide demographic of females crying for no reason and lashing out at others during their menstrual periods. The "cure" in this case was Serafem, a pill containing a form of Prozac. A news release from MIT quotes Dr. Judith Wurtman, member of the research team who tested the drug: "A mother who is sometimes placid and sometimes a raving maniac makes a child wonder about the stability of his world. Prozac offers real utility where women need to have stability of judgment and behavior." Although Wurtman has a PhD in cell biology rather than an MD, Isaac Ray probably would have agreed with her assessment (Wright; Bloom). Mary Harris, it would appear, still has sisters.

# 4. "True Womanhood" and Perfect Madness: The Sanity Trial of Mary Todd Lincoln

> We, the undersigned jurors in the case of Mary Todd Lincoln,
> having heard the evidence in the case, are satisfied that said Mary
> Todd Lincoln is insane, and is a fit person to be sent to a state
> hospital for the insane.
> —Jury verdict, reached in ten minutes

If one were to use the jury decisions we have seen so far, it could be inferred that in the nineteenth century, women of gentle birth were expected to be demure, picture-perfect icons of domesticity. To violate social norms was to face penalties ranging from social ostracism to legal action. Women who stood out too far from the crowd were often ruined socially, slandered by the press, or, worst of all, declared insane and locked away. This could lead one to believe that women who stay with the prescribed limits would be safe. Surely there was no reason to prosecute a woman unless she actually committed a crime?

In reality, women who did toe the feminine line were not much safer, for their existences depended upon the good will of paternal protectors who may or may not have agreed upon where that line was to be drawn. Women in this era walked a cultural minefield without the benefit of a map. Modern researchers have attempted to assemble such maps to proper behavior—much too late, of course, to help the women who had to live by them. What these maps have accomplished, however, is to remind us that no norm is without its rhetorical ancestor and that these ancestral narratives can easily be manipulated to alter, manipulate, or reapply those norms to fit the judgment desired by society. These cultural narratives provided the map for women of the day, but they also could be used to alter the terrain in midjourney.

Luckily, as women themselves began to examine the outlines of their territory, they began to see the possibilities for alteration themselves. Although gender expectations could constrain a woman, a woman with enough skill could use those same expectations to constrain male behavior in relation to those expectations. She might even be able to manipulate those expectations in order to liberate.

Let us now examine a case wherein the art of rhetoric successfully altered a public interpretation of behaviors that were ostensibly so constrained by public narratives that no new interpretation was possible. Mary Todd Lincoln was the epitome of nineteenth-century genteel womanhood. The narratives created by the rhetors of the time were very clear as to how all womanly virtues were to be used to judge behavior. Under the strict interpretation of these narratives, Lincoln was labeled as insane. Yet through the rhetorical artistry of a strong woman named Myra Bradwell, these narratives were used in such a way that new interpretations became possible. These new interpretations were compelling to enough people that the initial judgment was reversed, and Lincoln was once again called sane. The basic elements of the narrative were not altered, but ownership of the story itself was subtly shifted so that the use of those elements was entrusted to the group most likely to be affected by them: women.

Lincoln was a woman who adhered to feminine norms too well. These norms, interpreted once by male rhetors and once by a female rhetor, were used to produce radically different portraits of her mental state. The rhetoric surrounding her case demonstrates how even a traditionally oppressive narrative may be manipulated to serve a libratory purpose.

## Commitment Laws in Illinois

The fact that Mary Todd Lincoln was even given a sanity hearing was due to the activities of Elizabeth Parsons Ware Packard. After her escape from her husband, Packard launched a legislative campaign to stiffen the criteria used to commit individuals to insane asylums. One of the new steps added to the process was a trial much like the one she was accidentally afforded. No resident of Illinois could be locked away without a formal, public hearing.

The victory of Elizabeth Packard was an unprecedented abridgment of the power of physicians in the process of commitment. Where previously the word and signature of one "expert" could determine a patient's entire future, it now took the approval of a judge and jury, untrained in medical literature, before the dark label of "insane" could be applied to a patient. There were, of course, two sides to this change. On one hand, the danger that a dishonest family member could kidnap a person was eliminated. On the other hand, there was a new danger that a persuasive rhetor could persuade a jury to abet the same action. In addition, that rhetoric might persuade a jury to free a patient who really was a danger to herself and others.

Another problem with the process was related not to justice but to a clearly moral social concern: a trial's violation of privacy. It was no longer possible for a family to hide a loved one's illness. As one visitor from London remarked, "The best feelings of all right minded persons are outraged by seeing presented in court the depraved and unnatural acts and speech of otherwise reputable men and women" (Dewey 582).

One wonders what Mary Todd Lincoln thought of the matter and what aspect was more painful: the trial or that her remaining son wanted her committed. And it was the publicity of the trial that enabled her friends to win her freedom. Lincoln, more than most, had reason to recognize the power of the press.

That Lincoln suffered from some form of mental disorder during the latter part of her life is obvious. Most biographers acknowledge that but then disagree over whether her problems warranted commitment. Obviously, the passage of years has made it impossible to determine whether she was any more disturbed than many neurotic individuals who never had their sanity questioned. This determination is made doubly difficult by the fact that all the evidence offered was secondhand, a web woven of discourse describing and evaluating her behaviors.

One element that stands out is that Lincoln was considered a very "feminine" woman in all ways. Every one of her "insane" behaviors can be seem as a logical extension of too strict an adherence to nineteenth-century norms of womanhood. Lincoln's symptoms might have arisen from some chemical imbalance, but her diagnosis arose from society's need to draw the line between charming feminine frailty and embarrassing incompetence.

## The Case of the Sentimental Woman

All her life, Lincoln's behavior came under close scrutiny. Reared as a pampered Kentucky belle, young Miss Todd thoroughly learned her feminine role and did not hesitate to enact it. She knew that her success in life depended upon selecting the proper husband: "Matrimony had been the goal of her young womanhood, as was meet and proper; it was the goal of every girl she grew up with" (Evans 163). The first time she violated expectations was when she selected a no-account hayseed lawyer named Abraham Lincoln over other suitors both better looking and with better prospects. Having made that decision, however, she dedicated herself to the noblest goal of antebellum womanhood: living her life through the lives of her husband and children. This devotion left her vulnerable and without internal resources after a combination of historical factors and personal tragedies robbed her of all she had lived for. She had always been "high-strung," but in her later years, she faced a series of difficulties that would strain the sanity of even the most level-headed of women.

When Abraham Lincoln became president of the United States in 1861, Mary Lincoln achieved the pinnacle of wifely success. She had much to be proud of, but the toll her husband's prominence took on her personal life was immense. The first thing she lost was her husband's attention; on the eve of the Civil War, Abraham Lincoln did not have time to cater to the needs of his demanding wife.

Second, she lost her close family connections. As first lady, Lincoln was privy to information about the war effort. The newspapers almost immediately seized upon her Kentucky background to brand her a Confederate spy (Evans 183). When she tried to enjoy a visit from her sister, the papers created a conspiracy. She had to steeply curtail her contact with family for the duration of the war, another step toward the total isolation she later felt. Making new friends was difficult, again partly because of her no-win situation; nothing she did was reviewed positively by Washington social circles. When she tried to economize during wartime by cutting back on state dinner parties, she was castigated for violating social tradition. When she obtained funding from Congress to refurbish the White House, she was hounded for spending money on foolishness while the army went hungry.

Her relative isolation left her unprepared for the next blow: the death of her youngest son, William. She sank into a month-long depression during which she could barely function. Only the intervention of her husband snapped her out of it—he reminded her that he might be forced to send her to the government hospital for the insane (Neely and McMurtry 3). Still, she continued to wear black for nearly three years. With most of her relationships severed, Lincoln recovered by throwing herself into the one activity that had never failed to cheer her: shopping. She soon established for herself a reputation as a spendthrift that was to haunt her for the rest of her life. She went over budget on the White House restoration and became fearful of showing her husband her monthly bills. He discovered her difficulties and reined her in for a time. A little attention, even negative, was obviously therapeutic. Later, lacking a husband, she would not be so lucky.

On April 14, 1865, Mary Lincoln faced the cruelest blow. Her husband was assassinated while sitting beside her at Ford's Theater. She was so prostrate with grief that she could not even attend the funeral. Adding insult to injury,

Congress refused to grant her a pension, and took a year to get around to paying her husband's back salary. Abraham Lincoln had left a sizeable estate but no will, so settlement required extensive and costly court action. Mary Lincoln, an indulged wife who never had to deal with finances, was certain she would end up in the poorhouse. Although Congress did eventually approve the pension in 1870, in the ensuing years Lincoln's fear of penury eventually added to her odd behavior.

All Lincoln had left to live for was her children. The elder, Robert, had already started his own family, but she kept the younger, Tad, at her side at all times. This comfort ended abruptly with Tad's death in 1871. She was by then estranged from Robert over an unexplained disagreement with his wife. Cut loose from the anchors to which she had bound her life, she proceeded into the decline that led to her commitment trial in 1875.

On the afternoon of May 19, 1875, Mary Lincoln received a visitor at her Chicago hotel. The gentleman, who turned out to be the prosecuting attorney for her case, told her that her son Robert wanted to see her at the courthouse downtown. She was not informed that he wanted to literally see her "in court" until she arrived there. Robert Lincoln had filed the papers requesting her commitment that morning, and by two o'clock that afternoon, judge, jury, and lawyers were assembled. Her court-appointed lawyer, Isaac N. Arnold, had been a friend of Abraham Lincoln's. Arnold asked Robert to replace him, for he already believed Mary Lincoln was insane. He was persuaded to stay. What followed was a parody of a trial. Several witnesses, including Robert, were called to testify to Lincoln's insanity; none were called in her defense. Arnold went through the motions but obviously had neither the time nor the inclination to prepare a case.

Mary Lincoln was adjudged insane and arrangements were made to send her to a sanitarium in Batavia, Illinois, the next day. That evening, she was inexplicably allowed by her servants to leave her apartment, and she attempted a desperate act. She went to a corner druggist and requested laudanum as a sleep aid and went home and drank the entire bottle. Luckily, the druggist had suspected something was amiss and given her a harmless substance. It is ironic that Lincoln would perform her most clearly "insane" act only after having been labeled insane, for it showed that she was keenly aware of her circumstances. Her only remaining child wanted to lock her away. The woman who defined her entire life through her family had finally failed completely and no longer wanted to live.

It should be made clear that Robert Lincoln was not sending his mother to some stereotypic "madhouse" where she would be mistreated. Bellevue Place in Batavia was an expensive private hospital for female patients. Apparently all of the inmates were genteel ladies with relatively minor conditions. Lincoln had her own room and was allowed to walk freely upon the grounds as long as someone accompanied her. Her son visited her once a week without fail and even once brought her granddaughter along. Still, it was a prison. Although her door was open during the day, at night it was locked and the key was kept by an attendant. Lincoln acquiesced to confinement at first, but then she repeatedly asked that she be released into the custody of her sister. When neither her son nor her doctor would entertain that possibility, Lincoln decided that she needed to contact outside allies. The "rescue" of Mary Lincoln began when she managed to smuggle a letter out of the sanitarium. It was not very difficult. She asked the doctor for permission to write to her sister and then snuck in an additional note for a female friend. The female friend was no ordinary woman but the infamous Myra Bradwell.

Bradwell was already known throughout Illinois as a troublesome agitator for women's rights. She had passed the state bar in 1869, but the state of Illinois forbade Bradwell to practice law because she was a woman. Bradwell and her husband (who was a judge) fought this decision all the way to the Supreme Court and lost (*Bradwell v. Illinois*). The Court agreed that it was unnatural for a woman to practice so masculine a profession: "The paramount destiny and mission of woman are to fulfill the noble and benign offices of wife and mother. This is the law of the Creator. And the rules of civil society must be adapted to the general constitution of things, and cannot be based upon exceptional cases" (*Bradwell v. Illinois* 142).

This decision slowed Bradwell but did not silence her. She proceeded to publish a legal newsletter that was widely read and tirelessly pursued the cause of woman's suffrage.[1] Her reputation might have been why Lincoln chose her; how many other lawyers were so versed in the intersection of womanhood and the law? Bradwell was appalled to learn that Lincoln had been so quickly and brutally robbed of her liberty, and she immediately went to visit. Not surprisingly, she came to the opposite conclusion from the all-male jury. She launched a campaign to get a second hearing.

Some historians, such as Neely and McMurtry, claim that Robert truly believed that his mother was incompetent and only rushed the trial in an attempt to avoid negative publicity. If this attribution is correct, then Robert must have been bitterly disappointed by actual events. Reporters on the courthouse beat rushed to publicize the trial, reprinting the negative testimony word for word. And the irregularities in the trial itself opened the door for his mother's defenders to use the power of the press to harry him into freeing her. The resultant welter of medical and popular opinion reveals much about society's views about women and insanity.[2] This chapter will examine both the first jury trial and the second hearing won for Lincoln by Bradwell, as well as the "trial by public opinion" that Bradwell orchestrated.

## Gender Expectations: "Rotten With Perfection"

The narratives used in Lincoln's case exemplify the rhetorical concept of "symbolic perfection." Stories are linguistic constructions and are thus created and maintained through the manipulation of symbols. What storytellers might not be aware of is the possibility that these symbols are also manipulating *them*. Kenneth Burke links this manipulation to the Classical concept of teleology, the notion that all things contain an internal purpose, a striving to reach perfection, whatever form that perfection may be. Teleology, cast as some form of "purpose," informs many theories related to physical phenomena (for example, evolution). Burke extends this idea of perfection to symbols, which sometimes are not linked to any solid forms at all. As he noted when creating his own symbolic construction of humanity, symbols contain their own inherent teleologies, which constrain the further use and development of language. These symbols lead us to create more symbols, constantly refined and purified, then reinserted into the narrative. Because a symbol does not have to be directly linked to a physical form, a linguistic construction can be absolutely perfect. This becomes a problem when people attempt to apply the standards of that construction to "real world" circumstances.

Take, for example, a political philosophy such as capitalism, which in the symbolic realm of theory will lead to a perfect economic paradise. Once the theory is applied to the untidy realm of limited resources and competing interests, however, it becomes apparent that this "perfection" is impossible to attain in real terms. The human tendency seems to be to keep trying to make the real world match the symbols rather than vice versa, which Burke claims leads to a multitude of tragic circumstances because the goal is always unobtainable. Burke concluded that the human race, manipulated by symbols, had become "rotten with perfection" (*Language* 211). Although Burke's favorite examples usually involved economic theories, one can see his principles operating in narratives related to gender. Gender is a linguistically created concept unrelated to physical sex. One can be "masculine" or "feminine" regardless of one's genetic composition. The concept of "true womanhood" likewise created a set of defining characteristics that were divorced from the physical requirements of the daily life of the white middle-class woman. The social order had begun a symbolic construction of genteel dependency, but the teleology of the narrative demanded that eventually that all those logical character elements must reach a symbolically perfect form. No woman living in the real world could hope to achieve feminine perfection, nor would doing so be guaranteed to make her life equally perfect. Males, on the other hand, might like to contemplate the perfectly dependent, loving, innocent, domestic feminine role model, but it was quite another thing to live with such a woman.

The inherent teleology of "true womanhood" would not be immediately evident to a male audience for a number of reasons, not the least of which was the fact that many women were financially unable to live by those standards unless they married wealthy men. There weren't too many "perfected" women around. Still, that teleology set up the social constraints that set the characters of traditional women such as Lincoln. As it stood, a woman was bound to strive for true womanhood and bound to fail. In order to rescue such women, the narrative had to be altered so as to embrace other possibilities for successful femininity.

We have seen that the narratives used to "praise" a woman can also be used to "blame" her: to call her normal or to call her mad. This chapter argues that the difference in Lincoln's case rested upon how aware the rhetors were of the teleology of the narrative. In this case, those who dwelt within the narrative were able to see the consequences of the story as the outsiders were telling it. Myra Bradwell opened the story enough to provide for an alternative ending. Lincoln's problem was, ironically, that she was too successful: she was a perfect model of nineteenth-century sentimental womanhood.

## The Attack

The case against Mary Todd Lincoln illustrates that many elements of the nineteenth-century definition of womanly virtue could also provide levers with which to unseat a woman's reason. Barker-Benfield has noted that most descriptions of the insane found in nineteenth-century literature look remarkably like descriptions of "normal" women: dependent, unable to govern themselves, indifferent to society, and so forth (52). Thus, the definition of similar behaviors as sane or insane was subject to debate. As Lincoln's mental state deteriorated, her behavior became exaggerated, often to bizarre extremes, yet her actions could all be viewed as natural extensions behaviors expected of a woman of the time. The question before the jury in both of Lincoln's trials was whether her emotional and financial problems went far enough beyond the norm to warrant locking her away.

An important factor in Lincoln's commitment was testimony from various persons that she suffered from delusions. These delusions were indeed serious, yet they were grounded in elements of her character that in other circumstances would be seen as laudable, for they arose from woman's natural religious and maternal instincts.

First, women were considered to be more spiritual than men; a belief in God was "the core of woman's virtue, the source of her strength" (Welter 21). Second, women had primary responsibility for nurturing children, and were expected to love them unreservedly (Welter 38). These two expectations came together in a religious movement that reached a peak in the late nineteenth century, spiritualism. Spiritualism stressed the reality of life after death and the ability of certain "mediums" to communicate with those on the other side. It offered certainty of the existence of God as well as assurance for bereaved persons that their loved ones were not gone. It was extremely popular. In 1871 the *American Booksellers Guide* reported that fifty thousand spiritualist books and an equal number of pamphlets were sold every year (Braude 26). Many of the brightest minds of the age were attracted to spiritualism.

The Lincolns were also fascinated by spiritualism. Mary Lincoln brought mediums to the White House for séances throughout the war. While Abraham listened to advice from spirits purporting to represent the likes of Daniel Webster, Mary hoped for messages from her son William (Maynard).[3] Lincoln found in spiritualism an outlet for her grief and, incidentally, a socially acceptable manner in which to practice religiosity without having to surrender authority to any established church.

Within the medical community, however, spiritualism was seen as a dangerous practice that threatened the sanity of the impressionable women who studied it. One leading psychiatrist wrote a treatise on the threat entitled *Spiritualism and Allied Causes and Conditions of Nervous Derangement* (Hammond). He believed that belief in spiritualism could be interpreted as a sign of mental instability. Mediums tended to be female, and as he claimed, the subjects of one or more "hysteroid affections" (49). In other words, religiosity is a good thing unless the religion is at odds with masculine control of women's spirituality. Several witnesses at the trial offered evidence that Lincoln was a victim of "strange imaginings" ("Clouded Reason" 1). One physician, William Danforth, testified that she came to him in 1873 for treatment of violent headaches, saying that "an Indian was removing the bones from her face and pulling wires out of her eyes" (1). Treatment continued for several weeks, during which she claimed to have been in communication with her dead husband and "imagined that she heard raps on the table conveying the time of her death, and would sit and ask questions and repeat the answers the table would give" (1). She even tried to "prove" her spiritual contact to the doctor by having him put questions into a glass on the table. After the séance, the glass was cracked. Lincoln took this as evidence of contact. The doctor did not.

Although these actions sound strange by today's standards, talking to the dead and "table rapping" were two standard spiritualist practices. Headaches were, in fact, common. Hammond noted that most of the "hysterics" he had seen associated their "hallucinations" with headaches (257). Even Lincoln's choice of metaphor for her headache was interesting: many mediums claimed to channel Native American spirits who would "take over" their bodies. Nettie Colburn, the White House medium, had channeled an "Indian princess" named "Pinkie." This obviously colored Lincoln's description. The text makes it unclear whether Lincoln believed an actual spirit was at work in her head or whether this was simply a graphic way of explaining her pain to Danforth. Either way, the rest of her behavior, though odd, was not unduly strange—for a spiritualist. Two years later, he found her much improved on that particular delusion, but she did mention in conversation that she believed someone had tried to poison her coffee in Florida. For that reason, he decided she was indeed insane, although on "general topics, her conversation was rational" (1).

This testimony was the only medical opinion offered by someone who had had extensive contact with Lincoln. Although indicating that Lincoln was in some manner disturbed, it hardly qualified her for commitment. Other testimony by physicians who had less contact is contradictory. Dr. Nathan S. Davis "saw nothing in her to indicate unsoundness of mind"; rather, she was "eccentric and suffered from nervousness" ("Clouded Reason" 1). He did state that he did not think it wise for her to be left alone. Dr. Hosmer Johnson, on the other hand, said she was clearly "deranged" (1). Dr. Charles Smith, who knew Lincoln by way of being attending physician at Tad's last illness, said that after listening to the evidence presented at the trial, he was "of the opinion that her mind was not sound" (1). In other words, the medical men provided their opinions about her behavior but were not able to agree about her "rationality." It was the testimony of laypeople, most notably Robert Lincoln, that was the most damning. The second delusion plaguing Lincoln arose directly from her maternal instincts. In 1875, she became convinced that Robert was ill. She was continually wiring him for assurances and asking others to check on him. Ralph Isham testified that she abruptly abandoned a vacation in Florida to rush home and check on Robert even though there was no reason to believe he was ill. Her concern was extreme but not outside the boundaries of good motherhood. In fact, the nursing of sick children is one of the paramount duties of womankind. There were certainly enough illnesses in those days to require such duties. Welter points out that "nursing the sick, especially sick males, not only made a woman feel useful and accomplished, but increased her influence" (32). Lincoln herself had lost three children to illness and thus had direct experience with both the threat of illness and the power a mother could exert over a sick child. Robert, however, was grown up, and found her concern bothersome. It was time consuming, for only personal reassurance and his presence seemed to calm her. His testimony concerning her behavior at a Chicago hotel is extensive and shows how "mothering" can cross the line. Each night after his arrival at the hotel, Lincoln would knock on his door to check on him and to ask if she could sleep in his room. This stopped after a few nights when Robert told her that if she persisted he would move out of the hotel. Coincidently, after he forbade these visits, Robert noted a serious deterioration in his mother's behavior. She attempted to leave the hotel "but slightly dressed," and when he "tried to induce her to return to her room," she "regarded my interference as impertinent, and declined to leave the elevator, but I put my arms about her and gently forced her. She screamed 'You are going to murder me'" (1).

From there things rapidly went downhill between them, and her motherly concern vanished into a welter of fears for her own safety. Robert testified extensively as to her increasing paranoia. She began to imagine that there were men following her who wished to do her harm. As Samuel Turner, a hotel employee, testified, she was certain a strange man was hanging about the elevator with intent to molest her. Turner looked but saw no one.

No one thought these delusions sane—nor would anyone who did not know that Robert had hired a Pinkerton detective to secretly follow his mother, for her own safety. He even testified to this action in court, but Lincoln's defense did not pursue the fact that this particular delusion had been grounded in reality.

Although the court case focused on some bizarre actions related to her increasing paranoia, none of these episodes was as well documented and described as her problems with money. In her years of widowhood, she had taken up shopping with a vengeance. In the eyes of the men around her, a "shopping mania" was an irrefutable sign of her madness. For this facet of the case, there were many witnesses in addition to Robert, mostly shopkeepers, salesmen, and clerks.

In her desire to shop, Lincoln was, once again, indulging in a socially sanctioned behavior to an unsanctioned extent. Consumerism had become an important pastime of middle-class women living in the city. As keeper of a happy, comfortable home, a woman was required at the least to decorate, which in the Victorian era meant either buying or making a remarkable number of items. She was also expected to dress well, to serve as an ornament and as a walking advertisement of her husband's success. "As for women, conspicuous consumption, whether on the level of the most marginal or on that of Fifth Avenue, occupied them closer to the heart. . . . The career of the

woman whose busyness is shopping had begun. Man earns, woman spends"
(Meyer qtd. in Barker-Benfield 57).

Lincoln's problem was that she spent far more than necessary on items
that, as a reclusive widow, she would never use. The list is impressive: $600
lace curtains, although she lived in a hotel at the time; three watches totaling
$450; $200 for soaps and perfumes. A jeweler testified that she made several
expensive and "reckless" purchases at his shop. The hotel housekeeper testified that the closet was full of unopened packages Lincoln had purchased.
These were all items that Robert assured his listeners she had no need of,
except perhaps the several trunks she bought in which to pack her purchases.
Lincoln had long been known for reckless shopping binges alternating with
periods of equally intense stinginess. She never bought one pair of gloves if
there were six to be had, yet she bargained hard for a discount on the six for
buying in quantity. Then she would go home and lament to all who would
listen that she was near bankruptcy and could not pay the bills. This was
untrue, for there was usually money to pay the bills, but she often had to
be dunned before she would pay. Perhaps this was a residue from the years
immediately following her husband's death, when she was indeed seriously
in debt but had no access to either his estate or his pension. Lincoln's mania
over money indicated a serious problem, yet, as several authors have pointed
out, for all her histrionics, she never actually spent into the principle of her
accounts.

This behavior was serious enough that she eventually could have met with
financial disaster, but it does not explain why Robert opted to commit his
mother to an asylum rather than applying for conservatorship of her funds
and putting her on an allowance. That this option was available is evidenced
by private correspondence between Robert and David Davis. Their reason for
rejecting it is perhaps most revealing of why a woman might be committed.
Davis noted that merely appointing a conservator "without the confinement,
will not answer the purpose" of the proceedings, which was to stop Lincoln
before she did something that embarrassed the family in public (Neely and
McMurtry 13–14).

The underlying concern with Lincoln's unruly spending was not financial
but social. This concern was never voiced publicly at the trial. Thus, the real
crux of the case was never revealed. The prosecution's stance during the trial
was that Lincoln would be committed because her insane behavior made
her a danger to herself. The truth was that she was committed because her
behavior made her a danger to her family's reputation.

The case against Mary Lincoln was developed mostly through evidence
provided by laypeople: her son and the various hotel personnel and shop-

keepers of Chicago. This served the immediate purpose of the accusers well, for the lay testimony was much more dramatic. It was also exclusively male testimony. The entire interpretation of Lincoln's crossing into "perfected" femininity was in the hands of narrators who did not have to live within the story. Masculine narrators had set the standard for female behavior without thinking through the implications for society if all women actually behaved like pious, ignorant, domestic, and dependent children. The teleology of the narrative was destined to create a large number of Mary Lincolns. The particular rhetors in her case decided that the more appropriate label for this extreme femininity was "insanity."

## The Defense

The manner in which the first insanity hearing was constructed was designed to privilege the masculine voice, mainly in the person of Robert Lincoln. At the same time, however, it made it much easier for Myra Bradwell to come to the rescue. Since Lincoln was committed on the basis of the opinions of ordinary people, she could be freed on that same basis. If male depictions of the feminine character could condemn Lincoln, female intervention could save her.

Bradwell was a master of publicity and was able to create a public image of Lincoln that was powerful enough to force Robert and his allies to back down. She did it by wresting control of the story from the masculine, to the feminine realm. Women embodied "true womanhood" while men could only talk about it. Bradwell used this advantage to gain control of the narrative and open its possibilities so that insanity and committal did not have to be the only ending.

Bradwell's strategy was to use the power of the press to force a retrial. She wrote and published letters that told the story from a new point of view. She maneuvered reporters into printing stories and interviews, and encouraged others to write letters to newspapers. Wisely, she did not directly attack the verdict of the court. Instead, she played upon the theme that men did not understand a woman's needs well enough to make the best decision. In her visit to Batavia, she stated to the owner, Dr. Patterson, that "Mrs. Lincoln was not quite right," but she questioned the wisdom of institutionalizing a woman who probably only needed "to be at home" and have "tender loving care" (patient record, reproduced in Ross 31). Bradwell's goal was to have Lincoln released into the custody of her sister, so that family could care for her.

Bradwell's narrative also played into feminine stereotypes, but in this case it was Lincoln's sister, Elizabeth Todd Edwards, whose womanly virtue would save the day. In Bradwell's version of the story, Lincoln was a sensitive woman made ill by the harsh realities of the world. That world, represented now by the legal and medical establishment, was guilty of keeping her ill. She was a woman temporarily driven over the edge by circumstances that would do the same to any woman. Now she was better, and needed to be in the bosom of her family, cared for tenderly by her sister, in order to recover further.

Other than her statement to the doctor at Batavia, Bradwell did not clutter her narrative with discussion of Lincoln's borderline state. In an interview she arranged with the *Chicago Times*, she baldly stated, "She is no more insane than I am" (Wilkie 5). Since there were probably readers who knew of Bradwell's feminism and would take that as a condemnation, she arranged for the reporter to visit Lincoln, where he concurred that there was "not a sign of weakness or any abnormal manifestations of mind visible" (Wilkie 5). Given this, one might wonder why she was in the asylum in the first place; the explanation is the delicacy of her system: "She had been suffering somewhat from fever, and her nervous system was somewhat shattered. She was prostrated, and any eccentricities she might have manifested then, if any, she attributed to this fact" (5). Thus Bradwell was free to attack the wisdom of keeping Lincoln in Batavia without having to sling mud at the only living son of Abraham Lincoln.

Bradwell continually contrasted the prison-like atmosphere of Batavia with the healthful influence of home and family. An asylum is controlled by men, harsh to what they do not understand. Home is controlled by women, who naturally know how to care for the sick. An article in the *Bloomington Courier* described her first visit to Batavia, where she discovered that an institution could render any woman insane:

> I have no hesitation in saying that, if it should be my fortune to be placed in such asylum, with the feeling within me that my friends placed me there with the desire to be rid of the trouble or care of me, or for some other end in view, or if I really believed they placed me there fully thinking me insane, and I saw no way out, and that speedily, it would take but a few days to make a raving maniac of me. . . . soon, very soon, would all interest in life cease, and if death did not end the darkness that moved over me, the seal of insanity would surely be written upon my brain, and all that remained of life would go out in that hour. (Friedman, *America's First* 54)

Bradwell promoted identification with the suffering innocent. Lincoln was trapped in a "masculine" setting. The male doctors judged her without understanding her delicate nature. They barred the windows, controlled her mail, kept friends from visiting and generally deprived her of those things a woman naturally craves. If Lincoln was not soon rescued, she might well become permanently insane.

On the other hand, the home provided by Elizabeth Edwards would be a perfect haven. As Bradwell noted, "Mrs. Edwards is a lady of fine feelings and cultivation. She has a beautiful home, surrounded by lawns and flowers" (Wilkie 5). There, Lincoln would have the freedom to stroll among flowers, to see her family, and to live in a real home. Since women are naturally able to care for the sick, Edwards would give her sister much better care than any doctor. This description played perfectly into the nineteenth-century worship of the family and the notion that woman was naturally better off at home than anywhere else, even a professional sanitarium. Various Illinois newspapers were soon inundated by letters and stories from laypeople who agreed with this vision and wanted Lincoln freed.

Dr. Patterson, whose establishment was under fire, gave in to the pressure of the press and told Robert Lincoln that it probably would not hurt if Lincoln were released into her sister's care. Lincoln responded by hiring a new doctor who believed Mary Lincoln was insane (without having examined her personally) and wrote a letter to that effect. But for some reason, Robert changed his mind and did not use this letter. He finally gave in and on September 10, 1875, Mrs. Edwards took her sister home.

Although Lincoln remained her exasperating self during her nine-month stay with the Edwards family, she behaved well enough that Robert was persuaded to give up conservatorship of her affairs. In a new hearing held in June 1876, Mr. Edwards testified, "She has not spent all that she was allowed to spend during the last year, and we all think she is in condition to take care of her own affairs" ("Mrs. President Lincoln"). Her ability to not spend money constituted her "restoration to reason and property" and made her once more a sane woman. Once in control of her affairs, she hired a financial conservator, deposited her bonds with him, and drew an allowance. Thus, while she never did stop spending wildly, she was prevented from hurting herself financially. She never forgave Robert for what she perceived as his betrayal and remained estranged from him until her death.

## Conclusion

The result of the trial of Mary Todd Lincoln reveals an important consideration in evaluation of "feminine" behavior. It was clear that the arguers in these cases believed strongly in the traditional values of domesticity, fragility, and motherhood. These people took such presuppositions as gospel and used them as premises for their arguments. One cannot assume, however, that whether a woman did or did not fit the norms will determine whether she will be called sane or insane. If a woman fitted *too* well, she was in danger of crossing an invisible line. A masculine interpretation could draw that line at a point where it was impossible for a woman to achieve a balance. The logical outcome of a story that cast women as weak could only be women who were weaker still. Nevertheless, the medical interpretation of true womanhood indicated that all feminine tendencies were potential indicators for insanity. Behaviors, and the medical interpretation of those behaviors, were considered the only indicators of mental state. It did not matter why such behaviors were exhibited, only that they were.

As Bradwell demonstrated, the narratives provided materials for creating standards, but a new narrative performance could open up the possibility for using different standards. Bradwell did not question the values themselves; she instead created a context that celebrated these feminine tendencies as healthy. The main way to do this was to change the gender of the storyteller. Bradwell argued that the ownership of the narrative of womanhood belonged to women. She proceeded to retell the story of Lincoln in a manner that deflected the narrative from dependency to nurturance. This created identification between a woman and *her* audience. Bradwell then contextualized Lincoln's behavior in ways that made it understandable.

After having been reminded that they themselves might face similar problems, the audience was more willing to err on the side of the woman. In the hands of a new rhetor, an old story took enough of a new twist to set Lincoln free. Bradwell did not have to dismantle the values held dear by the majority; all she had to do was "perform" them in a slightly different way. Once female performers were allowed to control the story, there was hope that it could become a new tale, one that could empower women instead of condemn them.

# 5. Womanhood as Asset and Liability: Lizzie Andrew Borden

Lizzie Borden took an axe,
Gave her mother forty whacks.
When she saw what she had done,
Gave her father forty one.

—Traditional rhyme

Nearly every study of the Borden case includes this verse, and there is no reason for this chapter to stray from convention. That this bit of schoolyard doggerel can still occasionally be heard on the playground attests to the staying power of the legend of this woman. That it got the details completely wrong attests to the power of a narrative to survive despite its contradiction of the facts.

The presupposition of the rhyme is that Lizzie was guilty. A common presupposition of later research on her trial is that she "got off" because she was a woman. Both assumptions oversimplify the complex interplay of social forces that converged in Fall River, Massachusetts, in 1892 and the period that followed. While it is true that Lizzie's gender was probably an asset at her trial, it was not the only reason she was acquitted. In fact, gender norms were also used by the prosecution to make her look guilty. The basic qualities of femininity, as narrative elements, could be used to either end. It took the interaction of these with certain elements of class and social standing to make the pendulum swing in Borden's favor.

Like any unsolved violent crime, the Borden case has inspired endless speculation. Did Lizzie do it? If not, then who? What was the motive? What happened to the weapon? These questions have been rehashed endlessly. The theories that have been produced are interesting in themselves for their variety. Fingers have mainly been pointed at Lizzie Borden, who supposedly acted through greed or jealous hatred of her stepmother. Other writers have accused her sister, Emma; the servant, Bridget; Lizzie's rumored lover; and a purported illegitimate child of her father who resembled the archetypal wild-eyed stranger.

It is not the goal of this chapter to reexamine these issues; what "really" happened is not pertinent here. Rather, the focus is on the rhetorical use of gender-related narratives to persuade the community of guilt or innocence. Gender was indeed an important theme during Lizzie Borden's trial, but it was not the only theme used by the defense and it was probably not the only narrative used by the jury to free her.

The narratives created in this case are also interesting because they illustrate the many ways in which rhetors attempt to mold pieces of empirical reality into meaningful wholes. The Borden case was mounted and argued almost entirely on the basis of circumstantial evidence: There was no direct evidence pointing to the guilt of any individual. There were no witnesses. There was no confession. There was not even a "smoking axe." Someone had killed two people, that much was clear. The web of secondhand evidence only indicated possible killers, and the field was narrowed through human deduction. As a result, the only way to discover what "really" happened was to construct a symbolic reality that would be compelling to the audience being asked to judge the evidence. That determination would have very real consequences for the "guilty" party—the death penalty.

Of course, on the broadest level, all "reality" is circumstantial. No human being can observe every moment in the universe firsthand. The final form of that picture depends entirely upon how a persuader can arrange that clutter into a meaningful whole. The trial of Lizzie Borden shows us two opposing forces, each offering diametrically opposed explanations of the same circumstantial evidence. By examining these explanations, we can learn a lot about the methods through which realities come to exist.

## The Case of Lizzie Andrew Borden

In 1892, Fall River was a prosperous industrial town of about 75,000 people. Although there were new immigrants working in the cotton mills, for the most part residents were native to New England. Immigrants and Yankees lived in segregated communities that rarely mixed, a fact that was to have a noticeable effect on the search for suspects. The community was still small enough that people paid close attention to their neighbors. They knew each other, and each others' business, fairly well. Yet there was apparently no hint as to what was about to happen to one of the most prominent families in town.

The Borden family might be described as Fall River nouveau riche. The family founder had apparently been a fish peddler, but his son, Andrew, parlayed an undertaking establishment into a large fortune. He was president of one bank and on the board of directors of another. He owned farms in the country and at least three houses in town. Despite this fortune, the Borden family continued to live in their original home, a modest house on a street that was well past its prime. This and similar frugalities had earned Andrew a reputation as a miser. His wife and daughters, on the other hand, were pillars of society and pursued a respectable round of meetings at Sunday schools, ladies clubs, and temperance leagues.

However, matters at home were more complicated than their public behavior would indicate. The Borden household consisted of five adults.[1] Andrew, the patriarch, was seventy years old. With him lived his second wife, Abby, aged sixty-four, his daughters Emma (forty-two) and Lizzie (thirty-two), and their maid-of all-work, Bridget Sullivan (twenty-six). Abby had joined the family when Lizzie was barely three. Although there is no evidence that she was a "wicked stepmother," the girls disliked her. Neither called her mother; in fact, Lizzie referred to her as "Mrs. Borden." Whenever Andrew gave Abby anything, the younger women would launch arguments about how giving property to a stranger would deprive his own daughters of their patrimony. The Borden household was not peaceful. The house itself was also unusual. It had originally been designed as a duplex, and the Bordens had never remodeled the upstairs. The second floor had no hallways and the doors were locked in such a way that the daughters' bedrooms and the guestroom could only be reached by the front stairs while the parents' bedroom and servants' quarters (on the third floor) could only be reached by the back stairs. The two "households" were increasingly segregated.

What Bridget Sullivan thought about these arrangements is unknown. She had been with the family for three years as a general servant. Her position is best illustrated by the fact that the Borden daughters called her "Maggie," which was the name of the previous maid. All Irish servants, apparently, were interchangeable. She was sometimes even referred to in the press as Maggie, which only added to the general confusion surrounding the situation.

This less-than-typical family life came to an end in July 1892. Early that month, Emma and Lizzie departed on extended visits to friends in another town, but Lizzie cut short her trip and returned alone. Upon her return, she began acting strangely. She first tried to purchase a known poison, but was turned away by the druggist. She claimed she needed it to clean her fur coat. She also paid a sudden visit to a neighbor and confided that she feared someone had been watching the house. Lizzie told her that she was convinced the family was in danger.

On August 3, the brother of Andrew's first wife came to town for business reasons and persuaded Andrew to let him occupy the guestroom. Later writers would make much of the suspicious coincidence of the arrival of Lizzie's blood uncle and subsequent events.

On August 4, Bridget became ill after breakfast and had to rush outside, overcome by vomiting. This did not prevent Abby from ordering her to wash all the outside windows. The men left the house on their respective business errands. While Bridget washed windows, the two other women were alone inside together for about an hour and a half. When Bridget was finished, she entered just in time to hear a knock on the door. It was Andrew Borden, back from downtown. As Bridget let him in, she heard Lizzie laugh from the top of the front stairs. She said Lizzie came downstairs and announced that Abby had been called away to visit a sick neighbor. This was the first of several contradictions between Lizzie and Bridget. Lizzie claimed at the inquest that she had said Abby had gone to the market. Whatever the story, Bridget took advantage of the mistress's absence to sneak up to her room to lie down. She was eventually aroused by Lizzie's cry of murder.

Lizzie's story was that after her father returned, she went out to the barn—to get iron to mend a screen, or to get iron to make fishing sinkers, or to eat a pear, or to actually carve sinkers—her story varied. She was outside for about a half an hour. Then she heard a scream, or a groan, or a suspicious noise, or no noise at all, and came inside. She found her father lying on the couch, murdered. She called to Bridget, and then hell broke loose.

Bridget was sent across the street to fetch help. When help arrived, Lizzie stated that she thought she had heard Abby return a while ago. Searchers went upstairs and found her in the guestroom, dead. Andrew had been struck with some sharp object twelve times with such ferocity that his face was gone. Abby's head had been hacked to pieces by nineteen blows from the same weapon. They had obviously been overtaken by some insanely strong, violent killer.

But who could that be? The Bordens were fanatical about keeping the house locked, although Lizzie admitted that the side door had been left open while she was in the barn. Forensic evidence later showed that Abby had died first, about an hour and a half before Andrew.[2] She was in the guestroom and the only way out was down the front stairs. What madman could kill Abby, successfully hide from the two other women for over an hour in that tiny house, leap out again to kill Andrew, and escape undetected?

In the ensuing days, rumor ran rampant, but no suspects were arrested. The visiting uncle was an immediate suspect, but witnesses placed him well away from the scene at the time of the crime. Bridget was also suspected, but she was saved by her own "bad habits"—she had snuck away from her work to gossip with the neighbor's Irish maid at the time of Abby's death.[3] Neighbors began to report having seen all manner of "strange" men loitering about the area.

The newspapers printed every rumor and speculation imaginable, except the possibility that the killer might not have been a man. The media clearly supported the stereotype that no woman would have that physical strength, let alone muster that amount of fury. Thus, the eventual arrest of Lizzie herself came as a double shock, for the accused was both ungrateful child and frail female. At this juncture, various narratives began to spin off in the press. Depending upon the politics of the venue, Lizzie's sex became advantage or disadvantage in the quest to prove her innocence.

## Rank and Its Privileges

When one examines the trial itself, there is little doubt that a great deal was going on that had little to do with gender and a great deal to do with class and social connections. Fall River was a close-knit community, and the Bordens were prominent members. The judge at the first hearing had known the family, and was distressed to the point of tears at having to remand Lizzie to trial. The district attorney, Hosea Knowlton, had known Andrew Borden. Knowlton was called upon to lead the prosecution despite the relationship to the family. Another family acquaintance was Judge Albert Mason, whose duty as chief justice was to pick the panel of judges to preside at the trial. He promptly chose himself.

In addition, he selected Justin Dewey, a choice that raised a few eyebrows. Dewey had been appointed to the bench by then-governor George Robinson, who now happened to be the lead attorney on Borden's defense team.[4] Robinson had also served on an important judiciary committee with Mason. The political ties between the defense and two of the judges might not have biased the court, but it certainly left the door open for such accusations.

Thus the prosecution was at a disadvantage before the trial had even begun. This might not have mattered in a routine case, but since the evidence against Borden was almost entirely circumstantial, the prestige of the arguers was of no little importance. Every circumstance could be either a sign of guilt or a simple coincidence, depending upon the argument built from it—and the experienced, enthusiastic arguers were on the defense team.

## The Challenge of Circumstantial Evidence

In reconstructing the narrative of this trial, I will use another Burkean construct, the *dramatisic pentad*. Burke developed the pentad to serve as a "grammar" from which a critic could build tools to examine any instance of rhetoric. He grounded this in the most basic elements required of a good narrative. Scene, act, agent, agency, and purpose are the five minimal elements that must be present in order for an audience to find a story believable. The casual reader may be inclined to view this as a sort of "who did what where" description of a plot. But as a linguistic grammar does infinitely more than explain that a sentence requires both verb and subject, the pentad reveals much more than basic plotline.[5]

The five key elements are not merely plot elements; rather, they serve as a shorthand for all the possible ways to create emphasis upon a particular interpretation of reality. An interpretation of any given situation will naturally contain all five elements because of our tendency to symbolize everything into dramatic form. Humans want stories, and wise speakers work hard to construct them. A speaker creating a dramatic interpretation of a situation may choose to emphasize certain of the pentadic terms and de-emphasize others. These rhetorical manipulations alter the overall meaning given to a particular drama. The effect is sometimes subtle, but sometimes the entire meaning of the tale told can be altered by altering a single facet. Since an actor's motives affect the nature of his or her act, since there is a right and wrong time for taking action, since the tools available in a scene constrain one's plans—for all these reasons, a change in one area can ripple out to alter all five elements.

The pentad thus provides excellent tools with which to examine the role of the arguer in molding circumstantial evidence. By its very nature, circumstantial evidence does not provide enough information to create a complete narrative. For one thing, there is a glaring gap in the element of agent. Without a specific person whose character can be built upon, one cannot easily speculate on the purpose. This guts the narrative of a motivating force, leaving the rest of the elements "hanging" in a seemingly meaningless jumble. The incomplete narrative is especially threatening in a murder case. If there is no killer, justice cannot bring closure. If there is no discernable reason for the crime, then one is cast adrift with the knowledge that random violence could indeed strike anyone in the community.

The narrator's artistry, then, is to assemble the facts that do exist, and use them in an enthymematic fashion to indicate how to "fill the blanks." One might try to persuade the audience that limitations on the scene offer opportunity to only one agent. Another might attempt to construct a purpose that only one person could hold. The first narrative would be no more or less true than the second. The deciding factor is how believable the audience finds the resulting drama.

## Gender and the Pentad

Gender issues were a constant undercurrent during the trial. The prosecution knew this would be the case and attempted to defuse them from the beginning:

> Today a woman of good social position, of hitherto unquestioned character, a member of a Christian church and active in its good works, the own daughter of one of the victims, is at the bar of this Court, accused by the Grand Jury of this County of these crimes.
>
> There is no language, gentlemen, at my command, which can better measure the solemn importance of the inquiry which you are about to begin, than this simple statement of fact. For the sake of these crimes and for the sake of these accusations, every man may well pause at the threshold of this trial and carefully search his understanding and conscience for any vestige of prejudgment, and, finding it, cast it aside as an unclean thing. (1: 47)[6]

Having said this, however, Moody almost immediately used depictions of Lizzie's family life that could only be taken as signs of guilt if the defendant was female. The jury, warned that gender should not be used to find Borden innocent, was encouraged to use it to find her suspicious. Moody promised that future witnesses would testify to various details of the story, but made the effort to include remarks that showed that Borden's relationship to her family was "unnatural": "You cannot fail, I think, to be impressed in this respect with what will appear as to the method of living of this family. It will appear later on in the evidence that, although they occupied the same household, there was built up between them by locks and bolts and bars, almost an impassable wall" (1: 51).

In this case, scene begins literally, with the odd floor plan of the Borden home. The prosecution took it as meaningful that the house was so arranged that the elder and younger family members lived separate lives. Soon, those physical arrangements were cast as a mirror for a matching "spiritual" separation. "Scene" in the prosecution narrative was "family." And the Borden family embodied many elements that could tempt a daughter to murder. Moody set the stage for that transformation by repeating, verbatim, words that a witness would testify to later. When Abby Borden was once mentioned to Lizzie as her "mother,"

I know of nothing that will appear in this case more significant of the feeling that existed between Mrs Borden and the prisoner than a little incident which occurred not long after the discovery of these homicides. When one of the officers of the law, while the father and the stepmother lay at the very place where they had fallen under the blows of the assassin, was seeking information from the prisoner, he said, "When did you last see your mother?" "She is not my mother. She is my stepmother. My mother is dead." (1: 50–51)

Later testimony would fill out the portrait begun by Moody. Underlying this line of argument was the subtle expectation of the proper role between mother and daughter. The first Mrs. Borden had died when Lizzie Borden was not quite three years old. Abby Borden had been the only mother she had known. Yet she was able to speak of hating her, even as she lay dead. This showed disrespect for both motherhood and the dignity of the dead. Here, implied Moody, was a clear sign that Borden was not "natural."

The prosecution called two witnesses to testify that Borden detested her stepmother. A dressmaker quoted her calling Abby Borden "a mean good-for-nothing thing": "I said: 'Oh Lizzie, you don't mean that?' And she said: 'Yes, I don't have much to do with her; I stay in my room most of the time.' And I said: 'You come down to your meals, don't you?' And she said: 'Yes, but we don't eat with them if we can help it'" (2: 1169). A second witness who had traveled to Europe with Borden in 1890 claimed she made a similar statement about an unhappy home. The prosecution argued that they were trying to show that Borden's alienation was long-standing, but this witness's testimony was stricken on the grounds that it had been too "remote" in time from the crime. Bridget Sullivan, among the many details she was asked to recall, was asked about relations and testified that the family did not eat meals together. She also stated that the women took care of their own rooms and that the stepmother never cleaned the daughters' rooms and vice versa. Even defense witnesses were cross-examined about the family. Most notably, Emma Borden was asked about both the arrangement of the house and her sister's odd way of addressing her stepmother. Knowlton went to great lengths to pinpoint the exact moment that Lizzie Borden stopped calling Abby Borden "mother." It appears that Andrew Borden made his wife a present of half-interest in a house where her sister was living. This expenditure apparently caused jealousy.

Q: Did that make some trouble in the family?
A: Yes.
Q: Between whom?
A: Between my father and Mrs. Borden, and my sister and I.

Q: And also between you and your sister and your stepmother?

A: I never said anything to her about it.

Q: If you will observe the question, I did not ask you that; it is a very natural answer, I find no fault with it. Did it make any trouble between your stepmother and Lizzie and you?

A: Yes, sir. (2: 1556)

Andrew Borden was troubled enough that he bought another property and gave it to his daughters as a peace offering. Whether it was a successful one was hard for Knowlton to learn.

Q: And do you say that the relations were entirely cordial between Lizzie and your stepmother after that event?

A: Yes, I do.

Q: Have you ever said differently?

A: I think not.

Q: Did your sister change the form of address to her mother at that time?

A: I can't tell you whether it was at that time or not.

Q: She formerly called her "Mother," didn't she?

A: Yes, sir.

Q: She ceased to call her "Mother," didn't she, practically?

A: Yes, sir.

Q: And wasn't it about at that time that she ceased to call her "Mother"?

A: I don't remember.

Q: Wasn't it five or six years ago?

A: It was some time ago.

Q: What address did she give her after that time?

A: "Mrs. Borden."

Q: And up to the time when she changed she had called her "Mother"?

A: Mostly.

Q: From her childhood?

A: Yes, sir.

Q: And don't you recall that was sometime in connection with the transaction in relation to the house?

A: No, sir, I do not know when it was. (2: 1557–58)

Emma had been much less vague at the inquest, so Knowlton had her testimony there read in court, in the guise of refreshing her memory. "I will read another question: 'That, however, did not heal the breach, whatever breach there was? The giving the property to you did not entirely heal the feeling?' Answer: 'No sir'" (2: 1562). Emma responded that she only meant that it had not healed her own feelings and did not include her sister's in that reply.

Knowlton chased after the topic a bit but was wise enough not to badger the witness, who, after all, was one of the victims in this crime. He had gotten enough for his purposes, however. He now had a bridge between Borden's ill will toward her stepmother and a potential character flaw. Borden was at odds with her family over a piece of property. She allowed simple greed to interfere with family harmony.

Knowlton would use this in his argument for purpose: Borden killed out of greed. He would later argue that she had become aware that Abby as a potential rival for her inheritance and wanted her out of the way. She was greedy enough to reject the woman she had called mother since childhood over half a house. Once she was capable of breaking that sacred feminine bond, she was probably capable of anything. In his closing remarks, Knowlton hammered the scenario home for the jury:

> We must now go into this establishment and see what manner of family this was. It is said that there is a skeleton in the household of every man, but the Borden skeleton—if there was one—was fairly well locked up from view. . . . But there was a skeleton of which we have seen the grinning eye balls and the dangling limbs. It is useless to tell you that there was peace and harmony in that family. We know better. . . . That correction of Mr. Fleet at the very moment the poor woman who had reared that girl lay dead within ten feet of her voice was not merely accidental. It went down deep into the springs of human nature. . . . Mrs. Borden was the only mother she had ever known, and she had given to this girl her mother's love and had given her this love when a child when it was not her own and she had not gone through the pains of child birth, because it was her husband's daughter. And then a quarrel—what a quarrel! A man worth more than a quarter of a million of dollars wants to give his wife—his faithful wife who has served him thirty years for her board and clothes, who has done his work, who has kept his house, who has reared his children . . . a little homestead where her sister lives. How wicked to have found fault with it. How petty to have found fault with it. Nay, if it was a man sitting in that dock instead of a woman, I would characterize it in more opprobrious terms than those. (2: 1774–76)

The prosecution built a narrative that led into what Burke would call a "scene/agent" ratio between pentadic elements. This ratio deals with the relationship between person and place. Given a certain scene, one expects to find a certain type of personality abiding there. The main thrust of such an emphasis is that the scene requires agents who are its "dialectical counterpart" (Burke, *Grammar*, 9). In other words, for a narrative to function, the scene demands a certain type of character, one that matches the surrounding circumstances. There was the father, wealthy, but with a reputation as a skinflint. There were the daughters, arguing with him over property. In a family full of conflict over material things, a woman might come to value material things more than her family.

The defense was aware that this strategy was potentially damaging—after all, only two agents stood to inherit from the deaths, and one of them, Emma, had an alibi. Thus they took pains during the cross-examination to create a less-tense vision of family relations. Robinson took special care in questioning Bridget Sullivan, since she was the only outsider living in the house. His manner of leading up to the issue was quite clever; since he did not know what she would say, he circled the subject instead of asking direct questions.

Q: How long had you been at the house living there?
A: Two years and nine months.
Q: Did you have any trouble there in the family?
A: No, sir.
Q: Not at all?
A: No, sir.
Q: A pleasant place to live?
A: Yes, sir, I liked the place.
Q: And for aught you know, they liked you?
A: As far as I know, yes.
Q: Treated you well?
A: Yes, sir, they did.
Q: It was a pleasant family to be in?
A: I don't know how the family was; I got along all right.
Q: You never saw anything out of the way?
A: No, sir.
Q: You never saw any conflict in the family?
A: No, sir.
Q: Never saw the least,—any quarreling or anything of that kind?
A: No, sir, I did not.
Q: And during the whole time that you were there? You were there two and a half years, I think you said?
A: Yes, sir, two years and nine months.
[ . . . ].
Q: How was it this Thursday morning after they came downstairs?
A: I don't remember.
Q: Didn't they talk in the sitting room?
A: I heard her talk as she came along.
Q: Who spoke?
A: Miss Lizzie and Mrs. Borden.
Q: Talking in the sitting room?
A: Mrs. Borden asked some question and she answered very civilly. I don't know what it was.

Q: Who answered civilly?

A: Miss Lizzie answered.

Q: Answered properly, all right?

A: Yes, sir.

Q: When you heard them talking, they were talking calmly, the same as anybody else?

A: Yes, sir.

Q: There was not, so far as you knew, any trouble that morning?

A: No, sir, I did not see any trouble with the family. (1: 254–57)

Since there was a possibility that Sullivan had seen quarrels, he began by asking her about whether it was a good situation *for her*. Thus, if relationships were remarkably bad, he could stop. He then spent some time asking about the family in general. Only when it was fairly certain that things had gone smoothly did he ask about Borden's demeanor on the day of the crime. Even though Knowlton couldn't get Sullivan to state that the women were friendly, he got her to admit that they did not fight. Lizzie Borden was polite and civil, if not exactly affectionate.

Her affections, it appeared, were saved for her father. Jennings made sure to question Emma Borden on how well those two got along. She testified to an especially sentimental token of love—a ring that Lizzie had given Andrew fifteen years earlier. He wore it constantly—in fact, it was the only piece of jewelry he ever wore. He was buried with it. He apparently did not even own a wedding ring as a token for Abby, but Lizzie's ring he kept religiously (2: 1530).

This narrative was taken as a sign that father and daughter were close. Even if Borden had hated her stepmother, how on earth could she have brought herself to kill her father? Borden's proper filial love was her alibi for the second killing, and weakened the claim that she would have committed the first. Since the scenic narrative of a family in conflict came mainly from sources outside the family circle, while the narrative of love and devotion came from within, the defense could hope that the latter would have more credibility.

The prosecution pursued the link between Borden's reconstructed character and her violation of roles. They had used the link between scene and agent to construct a scenario that allowed for an upper-class woman to be a potential criminal. Once they had painted her as an unwomanly character, for being greedy and disrespectful of the dead, they called witnesses to prove that her actions mirrored that character. This represents a move to the "agent/ act" combination: narratives expect certain kinds of behaviors from certain kinds of people. Again, assumptions based on traditional views of Borden's class and gender would not work in the prosecution's favor. One did not expect a female to be an axe murderer.

The only way to counter this was to show that there was a difference between being female and being a "woman." Thus, Knowlton took pains to inform the jury that Borden did not act womanly immediately after the murders. Women are supposedly emotional by nature, and Lizzie Borden had just been thrust into a situation that would reduce any normal woman to tears. Borden was not only not tearful, she was remarkably calm and collected. The prosecution was dismantling the image of Borden as too feminine to kill. The defense was aware of this strategy and attempted to block it at every turn, as seen in this exchange:

Q [BY KNOWLTON]: Mr. Harrington, without characterizing, can you describe her appearance and manner during this conversation?

MR ROBINSON: Wait a moment—what she did and what she said.

MASON, C. J. [THE CHIEF JUSTICE]: If the witness observes the question carefully he may answer it.

MR ROBINSON: Your honor very properly says if he discriminates carefully he may answer properly. The difficulty is he may give his judgment upon her state of mind from what he saw; that is the difficulty with it.

MASON, C.J.: The question does not call for it, and the witness appears intelligent. Having his attention called to it that he is to do nothing but to answer the question, he may answer it.

[After some byplay, the question was reread to the witness.]

A: She was cool—

MR ROBINSON: Wait.

MR MOODY: Well, that is the difficulty.

THE WITNESS: Well, it is rather a difficult thing to get at, sir.

MR MOODY: By leading a little, perhaps I can get at it.

MR ROBINSON: It should be stricken out, it is not a completed answer.

MR. KNOWLTON: It is not completed because you stopped him.

[Knowlton was allowed to proceed.]

Q: During any part of the interview was she in tears?

A: No, sir.

Q: Did she sit or stand during the talk with you?

A: She stood.

Q: During any part of the interview was there any breaking of the voice, or was it steady?

A: Steady. (1: 564–65)

Although it was sometimes difficult to get to the subject, the prosecution took every opportunity to point out that Borden was remarkably levelheaded that day. Hers was not the traditional portrait of a daughter too bowed by grief to function.

The most potentially condemning narrative related to gender, however, was one that had been born in the early half of the nineteenth century. Unfortunately for Borden, it was a character that she fit almost perfectly. In the early years of medical jurisprudence, there had been few reliable tests for poison. It wasn't until the 1830s that even arsenic could be detected, let alone more exotic concoctions. As the science developed tests, more and more murders by poison were discovered—and the murderers were, in large number, women.

Although the actual number of murders probably did not rise, in the popular imagination, death by poisoning was seen as a major risk. Poison was the weapon of choice for unhappy wives. If a genteel woman *were* to commit a murder, the jury would accept poison as a weapon much more easily than an axe. The prosecution was no doubt aware of that and was ready with an argument related to Borden's visit to a drugstore the day before the murders. She had come when the shop had been crowded and was recognized by more than one person. She attempted to buy prussic acid (hydrogen cyanide) but left quietly when she was told that she needed a prescription for it. The opening statement avowed that it was no coincidence that Borden would try to purchase a deadly poison at that particular moment. Knowlton asked the jury to consider why a woman would want such a thing.

This is one of the moments when a carefully planned prosecution argument runs head on into an issue having much more to do with judges than with juries. When the prosecution called the druggist to testify, the defense moved to rule out his testimony, before he could give it, on the grounds that it was immaterial—the Bordens had not been poisoned. The jury was sent out while the lawyers argued. The prosecution claimed that the evidence was to show, along with a visit to her friend where Lizzie stated that she thought someone was trying to poison her family, her murderous frame of mind. The defense countered that it was perfectly legal to buy prussic acid; just because it could be used as a poison didn't mean that Borden was going to use it that way. The example of rat poison was used; people bought dangerous chemicals for household use all the time. After much arguing, the court allowed the jury back in to hear testimony from other witnesses (such as a druggist, a chemist, and a furrier) to determine whether prussic acid was indeed used to clean furs or whether it had some other reasonable nonmedical use. Interestingly, although all these witnesses were stumped as to any such use, the court ruled that they did not credibly establish the prosecution's point, and the drugstore clerk was not allowed to testify. What the jury must have thought—hearing all those witnesses talking about the uses of prussic acid and then never seeing the witness who could make the link to Borden—cannot be guessed. We are left only with the tantalizing hint that Borden might have been trying to commit a "feminine" murder, after all.

The prosecution attempted to dismiss Borden's gender before pursuing arguments that were still gender based. The defense, on the other hand, was careful to bring up Borden's gender directly and frequently. The assigned rhetor for arguments in this vein was Jennings. As a close friend of the family, he supposedly had special insight as to Borden's character, which he called upon when crafting his vision of her as a traditional, god-fearing, Sunday-school-teaching gentlewoman. He made sure to mention his special knowledge in his opening remarks:

> One of the victims of the murder charged in this indictment was for many years my client and my personal friend. I had known him since my boyhood. I had known his oldest daughter for the same length of time, and I want to say right here and now, if I manifest more feeling than perhaps you think necessary in making an opening statement for the defence in this case, you will ascribe it to that cause. The counsel, Mr. Foreman and gentlemen, does not cease to be a man when he becomes a lawyer. (2: 1305)

Jennings's use of his masculinity as a defense of his subsequent behaviors echoed his use of Borden's femininity as an excuse for her. Thus began the task of reconstructing agent. Borden had to be viewed by the jury as the type of person who would not kill. At the same time, the defense had to make every unknown person in the neighborhood look like the type who would. The first task was fairly easy, for Borden had a prior history of hewing to feminine stereotypes: "We shall show you that this young woman, as I have said, had apparently led an honorable, spotless life; she was a member of the church; she was interested in church matters; she was connected with various organizations for charitable work; she was ever ready to help in any good thing, in any good deed; and yet for some reason or other the government in its investigation seemed to fasten the crime upon her" (2: 1306).

As Janice Schuetz has aptly noted, Borden was more properly a woman in the mold of the "new woman" rather than that of the older, more traditional feminine narrative (Logic 65). She was unmarried but not a "spinster": She had been to Europe, had a good sense of the latest fashion, and belonged to female social clubs. She was unemployed, but not domestic; she pursued church and temperance work with diligence but did not spend much time with her own family. Readers today would probably find this normal, if not admirable, but it was still slightly suspect behavior in Fall River, which had not yet caught up with such new fashions. In fact, the prosecution used Borden's apparent self-sufficiency as a sign that there was something wrong with her.[7] In response, the defense relied on what domestic elements of her personality could be delineated. The premise was that no genteel upper-class woman would even conceive of committing a violent crime.

The defense did not allow the prosecution's description of the family scene go unchallenged. Their strategy, however, was slightly off center, in that instead of trying to show that Borden did not hate her stepmother, they attempted to show that she loved her father. Given that this was an all-male jury, such a tactic was strategic. No one on the jury was a stepmother, but everyone had at least the potential to be a father. There would be uncomfortable dissonance in even the possibility that a daughter could turn upon her male protector. That dissonance would make the jury more likely to try to make Borden fit the traditional mold.

In addition to Emma Borden's tale of family devotion, the defense added descriptions from outsiders. Each of Borden's female friends was asked about her church membership and what endeavors she pursued in connection to it. When the prosecution objected that this kind of information was immaterial, the court's reply was that since it helped show how well the witness knew the defendant, it showed competence and was allowable. Borden's character outside the family circle was used to bolster the notion that she would not suddenly be hateful inside that circle. The combination of churchgoing lady and dutiful daughter characteristics threw a shield around her character even before the arguments turned to the events of the day of the murder.

As to those events, the defense made clear attempts to show that Borden was not the unnaturally cold woman that the prosecution had painted. In an interesting move, they used only the transcript of Bridget Sullivan's testimony rather than recalling her to the stand, perhaps because she had been such a good prosecution witness earlier. They recalled the stenographer from the district court to read some of Bridget Sullivan's testimony at an earlier hearing. The exchange showed a very different Borden:

[Quoted from record]
A: She says, "come down quick. Father is dead." She was leaning against the screen door.
Q: Was the screen door open then?
A: I don't know, I could not say. She was leaning against the inside door that locks, the large door.
Q: Not the screen door but the regular door?
A: Yes, sir.
Q: How did she seem?
A: She seemed to be excited more than I ever saw her.
Q: Was she crying?
A: Yes, she was crying. (2: 1594)

So, immediately after discovering her father dead, Borden acted like a normal woman. For some reason, Sullivan had forgotten this. The defense had a great deal of such testimony read to the jury, impugning the memories or veracity of earlier witnesses. They did not rely upon those resources alone, of course. When cross-examining Dr. Seabury Bowen, the family physician who had been among the first to arrive, the defense carefully elicited from him that Borden was on the sofa, with the other ladies "fanning her and working her over" (1: 325). Eventually one of them fetched him to give Borden some medicine, first bromo-caffeine (a popular headache remedy) and later morphine, to calm her down.

This information served two purposes. First, although Bowen himself paid little attention to Borden at first, the ladies were watching her. And these women, by nature more attuned to the needs of their sex, knew that she was upset enough to need a drug. Thus, the jury heard that the characters who know women best knew that she was properly distraught.

In addition, this evidence set the stage for excusing almost all of Borden's later, unusual behaviors. She was drugged, apparently, at that incriminating inquest. Adams even tried to get Bowen to state that bromo-caffeine could cause hallucinations, but Bowen did not cooperate. Still, morphine was a pretty good excuse for being calm and low key when one's parents have been murdered. Just in case the jury still did not get the point, a friend of Borden's who went with her to the funeral reported that she cried over her father's remains in the viewing room.

The defense team worked diligently to establish that Borden's character was traditionally feminine. She was a good church member, a loving daughter, a fragile spirit, and someone who wept appropriately. This was important, for it lessened the likelihood that violence would ensue from her character. It was not enough, of course. For one thing, Borden was the only agent present that day with no alibi whatsoever. Also, being womanly did not mean that she was entirely incapable of committing the crime. The prosecution asked Dr. Draper, one of the forensics experts, whether the fatal blows could have been struck by a woman of ordinary strength. He said yes, and the defense could not get him to hedge that answer in any way. In addition, Knowlton reminded the jury that there had been plenty of female murderers in history, including a woman in Massachusetts who poisoned all of her relatives to gain an inheritance (2: 1775). Gender was a good argument, but even an all-male jury had to see that it was not a perfect excuse.

In other words, the defense did not rely on the stereotypic tactic of "she could not do it because she was a woman" but was also careful to call upon other narratives and apply them to other possible agents who were in the vicinity of the Borden house around the time of the murders. The creation of other agents, combined with their characterization of Borden, offered the jury a few alternative ways to fill in the blanks of the story.

The defense called a number of witnesses, from a neighbor who had heard someone threatening Andrew Borden months before the crime (his testimony was disallowed) to a man who saw an unfamiliar buggy tied up in front of the Borden house the morning of the murders, the driver simply sitting in it (this was allowed). In between, there were other concrete sightings of possible agents. Two male witnesses sharing a house near the Bordens' encountered a stranger sitting on the sidewalk in front of their gate the evening before the crime. Both men attempted to speak to him, and even shook him, and got no response. Each witness was asked whether there was an odor of liquor, but there apparently was none (2: 1353–59). The defense spent a lot of time getting exact details of where the man was sitting and where he was in rela-tion to the Bordens'—as though it were very important. A strange man, not drunk, yet not responding, sitting where he could see the Bordens' house, could just be a hobo, but then again, the timing was certainly coincidental.

The next day, a town doctor saw an equally strange figure on the same street: a pale young man walking very slowly, staring at his feet. "He seemed to be either agitated or extremely weak, staggering, or confused, or something of the kind" (2: 1372). The witness thought he had seen him a few days before but wasn't certain. Was it the same person who was sitting by the gate the night before? There was no telling.

A woman passing by noted that she, too, had seen a strange young man, but in a more ominous position. He was leaning against the gatepost of the Borden house. She couldn't describe him at all but knew that he was not the visiting Mr. Morse. Now the jury could envision a weird stranger wandering the neighborhood. The murders looked like the work of an insane person, and here was an agitated, wandering stranger on the scene.

A third possibility was offered by the testimony of an ice-cream peddler who was in the neighborhood that morning. He claimed that he saw a woman walking in the yard of the Borden house, perhaps even coming from the barn. He couldn't identify her but knew that she was not Bridget Sullivan. He was able to establish that he saw her at about the general time of the second murder. This could be taken as support for Borden's claim that she did indeed leave the house for a while. If it was proven otherwise, however, then what was a strange woman doing in the Borden's yard?

Here were alternative agents, at least one, and perhaps two, seen by credible witnesses. In case that wasn't enough, there was another witness, a farmer, who stated that he saw a wild stranger in the woods near his farm, four miles from downtown Fall River. Since the witness spoke only French, his testimony was translated and read:

This witness will testify that on the 16th day of August, at his farm, about four miles north of City Hall, while traveling into the woods for the purpose of cutting poles, just before he reached a turn in the road, he heard the words "poor Mrs. Borden" repeated three times, and immediately saw sitting upon a rock behind a wall and some brushwood, a man. He spoke, to the man in French twice, but received no answer. On speaking to him the second time the man took up from the ground by his side a hatchet, such as is used in shingling houses, and shook it at him. He stepped back and put his own axe up in an attitude of defence. They remained in that position some few minutes, when the man turned, leaped over a wall and disappeared in the woods. He said nothing to the witness at any time. The witness noticed upon his shirt spots of blood. He notified the police the same evening of what he had seen and heard. (2: 1455)

All the essential elements are there, mad behavior, blood, an axe, even a direct mention of a victim's name. If ever a good alternative killer could be offered, this wild man was it. Of course, as the prosecution pointed out, he appeared four miles away and twelve days after the crime. The evidence was excluded, but not until the next day, as the court wanted time to discuss the matter. Like the narrative of "Lizzie the Poisoner," "The Wild Man" was a story that the jury was told and then asked to discard, thus giving each side possession of a story told that might or might not have affected the jurors.

The primary goal of this tactic was to provide better agents to fill in the blank in the narrative of the crime. This was done partly through mitigating the scene as set by the prosecution, so that mother-hating Borden could be reborn as father-loving Borden. If the jury bought that argument, then it would be hard for them to accept that Borden, as agent, could commit a violently brutal axe murder. Even if she had gone mad, her sudden reversion back to sane, cooperative, bereaved woman in the hours afterwards would be a violation of character; the mad are not cured in an instant. On the other hand, the acts perpetrated on that day were clearly marked by savagery. The agent required would have to be a savage as well, or at least someone with no mercy. That ruled out most stereotypic women. A person from outside the family who quarreled with the patriarch, or a mad man with no motive at all, were better fits with the type of crime.

The defense kept up the subtle references to Borden's gender all the way through the testimony. This meant that Robinson, who was elected to close the case, could refer to it even as he was ostensibly discussing the circumstantial evidence. He reminded the jury that it was their duty according to their oath of office to take charge of the defendant's fate, but this charge attained new importance when it was given over to twelve men to look after a woman:

In no case except a capital case is the oath framed in that way. "Whom you shall have in charge." And Lizzie Andrew Borden, from the day when we opened this trial until this hour, has been in your charge, gentlemen. That is the oath you took. And not alone with you, Mr. Foreman, or any one of you, but with each and all of you. You have her in charge. Now has come the time when not alone her lawyers are to speak for her, not alone the judges are to watch for her protection, not alone is the learned attorney of the Commonwealth to ask no more than he ought to have, but the twelve men who sit here to try this question take the woman in their charge, and the Commonwealth says, "We intrust [sic] her to you." Now that is your duty. She is not a horse, she is not a house, she is not a parcel of land, she is not the property of anybody, but she is a free, intelligent, thinking, innocent woman, in your charge. (II 1620–21)

The lady has been entrusted to the protection of the "gentlemen" of the jury, who must decide her fate. If they accept the many descriptions of her good, Christian character, then the least that they owe her is a careful consideration of the evidence. As Robinson noted, all that was required was a reasonable doubt as to her guilt. The defense had sown all the doubt it could, from attacking physical evidence related to scene (the unlocked side door, the lack of blood on Borden), agency (the lack of a definite weapon), and purpose (defusing her motive) to providing alternate agents. All they needed was for the jury to decide that the connection between act and agent was too slender a thread upon which to hang a woman.

Although the narratives created on both sides used gender-based arguments, these were clearly not the only issues pertinent to the case.[8] Additionally, the jury had to be convinced that it was significant enough to use in a decision. Here is when it becomes clear that Borden had an additional quality that made the difference in her case: her status and family connections. After the two sides closed their arguments, it was the duty of the court to instruct the jury about rules of evidence, the issues pertinent to a verdict, and the process by which they should come to a decision on those issues. The court gave that task to Justin Dewey. As noted earlier, Dewey was a friend of Robinson, and even owed his career to a political appointment made when he was governor. Although he had this conflict of interest, Dewey could have defused suspicion by following the strict letter of the law when instructing the jury. Instead, he did something that raised eyebrows across the legal community for years to come: he argued for the defense. Only one part of Dewey's charge will be quoted here, but it is representative of the speech.

After an explanation of the difference between the role of an "essential" fact and a "helpful" fact in circumstantial cases, Dewey wished to provide examples. He briefly explained that an "essential" fact was that Borden was home that day, since she could not possibly have committed the crime were she not present. To illustrate "helpful" facts, he used two examples from the prosecution's case, and spoke at length to provide alternate explanations for them. First, he discussed the murder weapon:

> Now, take the instance of a helpful fact. The question of the relation of this handleless hatchet to the murder. It may have an important bearing upon the case, upon your judgment of the relations of the defendant to these crimes, whether the crime was done by that particular hatchet or not, but it cannot be said, and is not claimed by the government that it bears the same essential and necessary relation to the case that the matter of her presence in the house does. It is not claimed by the government but what that killing might have been done with some other instrument. (2: 1901)

After properly noting that the presence of a weapon in the house is not direct evidence, Dewey reminded the jury that the killing could have been done by some other instrument, although the prosecution had made no such concession. He then demolished a piece of evidence that the prosecution had claimed was vital, presenting the alternative explanation in great detail:

> Take another illustration. I understand the government to claim substantially that the alleged fact that the defendant made a false statement in regard to her step-mother's having received a note or letter that morning bears an essential relation to the case, bears to it the relation of an essential fact, not merely the relation of a useful fact. And so the counsel in his opening referring to that matter, charged deliberately upon the defendant that she had told a falsehood in regard to that note. In other words, that she had made statements about it which she knew at the time of making them were untrue. . . . Now what are the grounds on which the Government claims that that charge is false, knowingly false? There are three, as I understand them,—one that the man who wrote it has not been found, second that the party who brought it has not been found and third that no letter has been found, and substantially, if I understand the position correctly, upon those three grounds you are asked to find that an essential fact—a deliberate falsehood on the part of the defendant—has been established.
>
> Now what answer or reply is made to this charge? First, that the defendant had time to think of it; she was not put in a position upon the evidence where she was compelled to make that statement without any opportunity for reflection. If, as the Government claims, she had killed her step-mother some little time before, she had a period in which she could turn over the matter in her mind. She must naturally anticipate, if she knew the facts, that the question at no remote period would be asked where Mrs. Borden was, or if she knew where she was. She might reasonably and naturally expect that that question would

arise. Again, it will be urged in her behalf, What motive had she to invent a story like this? What motive? Would it not have answered every purpose to have her say, and would it not have been more natural for her to say simply, that her step-mother had gone out on an errand or to make a call? What motive had she to take upon herself the responsibility of giving utterance to this distinct and independent fact of a letter or note received with which she might be confronted and which she might afterwards find it difficult to explain, if she knew that no such thing was true? Was it a natural thing to say, situated as they were, living as they did, taking the general tenor of their ordinary life, was it a natural thing for her to invent? But it is said no letter was found. Suppose you took [sic] at the case for a moment from her stand-point, contemplate the possibility of there being another assassin than herself, might it not be a part of the plan or scheme of such a person by such a document or paper to withdraw Mrs. Borden from the house? If he afterwards came in there, came upon her, killed her, might he not have found the letter or note with her, if there was one already in the room? Might he not have a reasonable and natural wish to remove that as one possible link in tracing himself? Taking the suggestions on the one side and the other, judging the matter fairly, not assuming beforehand that the defendant is guilty, does the evidence satisfy you as reasonable men beyond reasonable doubt that these statements of the defendant in regard to that note must necessarily be false? (2: 1901–3)

He even graciously made use of the outside assassin theory, thus reinforcing the defense's position.

This pattern continued as the charge proceeded: the prosecution's argument was touched upon, the defense's discussed in great detail—always with a clear preference for the defense's explanations. He provided possible innocent reasons as to why Borden refused to testify and dismissed her statements of hatred for her stepmother as the typically overwrought dramatizing that a young girl might do:

What, according to common observation, is the habit of young women in the use of language? Is it not rather that of intense expression, whether that of admiration or dislike? Consider whether or not they do not often use words which, strictly taken, would go far beyond their real meaning. Would it be a just mode of reasoning to make use of the alleged subsequent murder to put enmity into the words and then use the words, thus charged with hostile meaning, as evidence that the defendant committed the murder? (2: 1894)

The fact that Borden was a woman in her thirties did not seem to indicate to Dewey that she might be beyond childish outbursts. The stereotypic notion that women were naturally childish and innocent was clearly a centerpiece of his argument.

After having cast doubt upon huge pieces of the prosecution's case, he reminded jurors that even the smallest doubt was grounds for acquittal. That one of the judges in the case would so clearly prefer the defense narrative no doubt carried great persuasive force. After all, one of the most basic elements embedded in legal culture in the United States is the "belief in the neutrality and objectivity of the law. If the system is ungendered, the argument goes, then the representation of gender within the system must be, by definition, neutral and objective and, thus, true" (Heinzelman 90). If Dewey was going to use Borden's gender to give her the benefit of the doubt on hostile statements about her stepmother, then it must be the right thing to do.

Thus, the gender-based arguments used by the defense were bolstered by the preferential treatment given by Dewey in his charge. If the jurors were moved emotionally by the image of Borden as dutiful daughter, Dewey had just provided them with a number of rational arguments in favor of following that emotion. The charge apparently made the task easy; in less than an hour, the jury returned a verdict of "not guilty." Later arguers have spent an entire century wrangling and have not been able to make such a clean decision.

## Conclusions

It is clear that the verdict in the Borden case represents a decision based upon narrative rationality. Since there was little or no direct empirical evidence that pointed to a specific individual, any connections to Borden, whether to show guilt or innocence, had to be woven into a drama that the jury could use to inform their decision. Indeed, any case of circumstantial evidence requires excellent storytelling on the part of the lawyers involved. Thus, the outcome of this case provides some clues as to how lawyers might proceed under similar circumstances. Although modern forensics can provide much more information to modern arguers, those dramatic connections still must be made in order for the jury to accept any interpretation of that information.

The most interesting factor in this case was that although both sides did [Not all that diff.] a great deal of storytelling based upon nineteenth-century stereotypes related to gender, they went about it in very different ways. While the defense [only expressed] frequently stated boldly that Borden's gender made her an unlikely suspect, the prosecution ostensibly ignored the issue and instead used forms of rea- [diff. Has similar] soning that tied their arguments to gender without directly mentioning it. [effects] Although the latter version would gain more political points in today's ostensibly gender-free courts, the fact that the tactic was used and rejected in the late nineteenth century is instructive. The prosecution's narrative shows the importance of maintaining believable character development in a story as well as methods of creating consistency against all odds. The Borden case was replete with evidence that brought the dramatic elements of scene to vivid life. The jury could be presented with facts related to everything from the color of a dress to what the maidservant had to eat for breakfast. There were photographs of bodies, diagrams of the layout of the house, and scientific analyses of bloodstains galore. What the evidence didn't show was anything that could directly link to Borden. There was a huge gap in the story where the role of agent should have been. The prosecution needed to close that gap by constructing Borden's character so that her agency was apparent. The simplest manner to achieve this goal would be to paint the suspect's character in a negative light and hammer away at motive, so that agent and purpose would be made crystal clear to the jury. That simple strategy was completely cut off by the circumstances surrounding the crime. Since the Bordens were a leading family in Fall River, and Lizzie Borden one of its leading lights in church and charitable causes, it was not enough for the prosecution to simply invent a plausible motive and drop it into the narrative. No jury was going to accept that an upper-class gentlewoman could turn to axe murderer and back again to lady in the space of a few hours. This would conflict with every stereotype they had about gentlewomen, and with not a few they probably held about madwomen.

Instead, the prosecution approached the identity of the agent gradually. Since the evidence concerning scene was the strongest, prosecutors used a description of scene to ground their argument. By stressing the disharmony of the Borden home, they hoped to convince the jury that it was reasonable to expect a woman reared in such a home to develop less-than-harmonious tendencies. Since auditors of a story expect the agent to be consistent with the scene, the prosecution could then use that groundwork to argue that Borden was exactly the kind of woman who might become a killer. They even took pains to address the next inconsistency that could have arisen between agent and agency. The gender stereotypes operating in forensics at the time dictated that women could kill; however, they killed in a feminine manner. Axes are not feminine weapons. In the opening address and in a few other places, the prosecution tried to create consistency by showing that Borden had tried to obtain a more feminine weapon: poison.

It was a case of scene overpowering the other elements. Since no one would sell her poison, she had to find another way. Of course, this story element was truncated by the court, but it shows that the prosecution was aware of the need to address the issue. The overall goal of using scene in this manner was to ground the story in the undisputed elements of the drama so that their more creative interpretations would better resonate with the jury. They took the more negative elements of the feminine stereotype (greed, resentment of a stepmother, passive) and attempted to prove that Borden fit that pattern better than she did the positive elements.

Apparently, it was too subtle. Not only did it fail with the jury, but later commentators on the case, quick to castigate the prosecution for making sexist arguments, ignored the prosecution's use of gendered premises. Part of the reason is that when we judge a drama, there is a tendency to expect the details of a story to line up with the element of pentad under discussion. When the defense argued character, they did it boldly and made direct connections to Borden as agent. The pattern was more traditional: "This agent is a woman, a woman could not hack her father to death, therefore this agent is innocent." The audience sees gender where it expects to see it. Since no one expects gender to be tied to scene, except perhaps in the case of a feminine "domain" like the sewing room, one does not automatically use gender to make connections between scene and agent. Still, the prosecution's resulting narrative, although unconventional, had great internal consistency, and once one accepted the notion that an odd family could produce an odd daughter, the rest of the tale could easily be interpreted exactly as the prosecution desired. Unfortunately, the most authoritative source to address the jury—Judge Dewey—used the opportunity to reconstruct the evidence in his own manner, and that makes it impossible to evaluate whether the lawyer's narratives on one side versus the other were more meaningful to the jury. Dewey's charge was a complete retelling of the story based upon his own notions of evidence, which were strongly colored by his own vision of Borden's character. Although it is clear that he was relying on gender stereotypes, his persona as the neutral voice of the law guaranteed that the jury would take his premises as "truth." He had already decided that she did not fit into the center of the drama, so the jury couldn't decide otherwise without challenging his authority.

Despite the fact that the court influenced the final result, there is still much to be learned by examining the battle between the legal teams. One thing that the use of the pentad in this case reveals is the power and flexibility of narrative elements such as gender in the crafting of tales for the jury. If the rhetor is skilled, these elements can be tied to any part of the story; which element is chosen will have a remarkable effect upon the final shape of the drama. The defense chose to use gender in the most conventional way. Feminine gender was applied directly to the image of Borden as agent. She lived up to the nineteenth-century standard of femininity well enough that she emerged as a delicate, affectionate daughter. In this drama, she was clearly innocent. The prosecution knew that the conventional featuring of agent would lose them the case. They took up the same tools but applied them first to scene, then to act, so that Borden as agent would emerge slowly. She violated the nineteenth-century standard of femininity well enough that she emerged as a cold-hearted, greedy female. In this drama, she was clearly guilty. Neither side had a radically different view of womanhood. Each was certain that the all-male jury would share their premises. The only difference was where in the story they believed those premises could be safely called upon. The more aligned with the status quo of the community, the less "artful" the narrative. Although the prosecution lost, the district attorney put together as good an alternative narrative as contemporary sensibilities would allow.

Interestingly, as time has passed, the tables have turned somewhat. At the time of the verdict, "few newspapers did anything except rejoice at the outcome" (Pearson 76). So ingrained was the conventional narrative that no one criticized its use, not even the female reporter assigned by the *New York Times* (Pearson 76). Due to cultural changes and the recognition that women are as prone to primitive impulses as men, the notion that a woman is constitutionally incapable of violent crime has been shattered. Most of the modern writers named at the beginning of the chapter found the gender argument immaterial, at best. A narrative tying human greed and jealousy directly to the motives of a female agent would be considered the "conventional" choice.

## 6. Bodies at the Crossroads: The Rise and Fall of Madame Restell

May I not suggest in conclusion, whether the incessant abuse of
me upon every possible occasion, upon the slightest pretext, or no
pretext, is not cowardly and ungentlemanly. Cowardly, because
I am a woman, and those attacking me are supposed to be men.
Cowardly, because they have an immense and crushing engine
of power, subject to their will and control, which I have not;
and ungentlemanly, because no gentleman will thus take unfair
advantage.
—"A Card from Madame Restell"

Up to this point, the principals involved in the legal cases this volume has covered have been accused of only one crime. Their cases rose to prominence rapidly and were as rapidly forgotten. Ann Lohman, alias Madame Restell, was different. Her rise and fall took over thirty years and was documented carefully—by her adversaries. "Madame Restell" was a professional abortionist.

Although she was repeatedly arrested and tried, she never once admitted that what she was doing was a crime. She was a businesswoman, she protested, supplying a much-needed service. The laws of the state of New York thought otherwise. Still, no matter how hard they pursued her, the courts were never able to close her establishment. In the nineteenth century, her name was synonymous with abortion in the United States. So much so that "Restellism" became the embodiment of the abortion controversy during that era.

Restell the character was eventually cut lose from any connection to Lohman the woman. That character was enlarged, refined, and vilified until it eventually served as a representative anecdote for the practice of abortion. Any person desiring to know the full extent of the consequences of such practices need only know her story.

In other words, the abortion controversy was embodied by a female character. During the thirty years of Madame Restell's career, one can see the continual refinement of arguments related to abortion as they were applied over and over again to that character. Abortion was the ultimate crime of womanhood, and Madame Restell embodied that crime.

This chapter explores the way the choice of Restell as a central figure framed the rhetoric of the abortion debate. After introducing the critical concepts, I will examine the rhetoric used in several of the legal battles involving Restell. Focusing on the cases merely scratches the surface, for the abortion debate evoked Restell frequently, even during times when she was not personally involved. The character of Restell lived on for decades after the death of the actual woman. The instances discussed here are specifically times when the physical body of Lohman was directly affected by the symbolic body of Restell.

## The Case of Madame Restell

The mysterious Madame Restell was the embodiment of several major currents of change in American life. Born in England, Ann Trow Sommers and her husband joined the waves of immigrants coming to New York City in the early nineteenth century. When her husband died, leaving her alone with an infant daughter to support, she joined the legion of seamstresses struggling to survive in the city. It is not clear where she got the idea of compounding contraceptive potions, but what is clear is that she made much more money selling nostrums than sewing garments.

In 1836, she met and married Charles Lohman. Lohman was a printer for the *New York Herald*. He also dabbled in publishing tracts related to contraception. Lohman was Ann's entrée into the circle of "freethinkers" who formed the core of the debate over population control, a debate typified by writers and lecturers such as Robert Dale Owen and Frances Wright.

As might be surmised, Lohman was far from shocked at his wife's profession. Indeed, he encouraged her to expand her practice. The two of them created a story of a trip to Europe to train in midwifery with a celebrated French physician named Restell. Although there is no evidence that such a trip was ever taken, the story added the appropriate exotic veneer to her persona. Ann Trow Lohman became Madame Restell.[1]

She also slowly expanded her range of services. In addition to selling abortifacients, she provided advice on contraception and kept a boardinghouse where women with inconvenient pregnancies could give birth in anonymity. For an additional fee, she would arrange for the adoption of unwanted infants. For those women whose pregnancies were too far advanced to be ended with drugs and who had no desire to participate in adoption, she offered the services of a surgical abortionist.[2]

Lohman also persuaded Restell to take a bold step: to advertise in the newspapers. At the time, it was practically unheard of for women to advertise a personal business, let alone such a controversial one. Thus, she was a sensation in more ways than one. The advertisements were discreet one- or two-line "cards" in many of the smaller newspapers, including the *Herald*. Once the *New York Times* opened its doors, she also inserted a discreet notice there: "Madame Restell, Female Physician—can be consulted upon complaints incident to females at her private residence" (January 29, 1855: 7).

The modern reader is surprised at the openness with which Restell advertised, as well as her baseless claim of being a "female physician." At the time, however, the most anyone could say was that she was unconventional. For Madame Restell also stood at the crossroads of two more developments in American culture. When she began her career, abortion was barely a crime; by the time she died, it was a felony. When she began, anyone had the right to call him- or herself a physician; by the time she died, only medical schools could bestow the right to that title.

She was initially in the right time at the right place to succeed. Not only did her own practice flourish, but her success attracted others. Eventually, the papers carried advertisements for several individuals, male and female, offering advice and "treatment" to women. Far from being a pariah, Restell found herself in the odd position of having to warn patients to "beware of imitators." So numerous where these people that the term "female physician" eventually became a well-known code word for "abortionist."

Thus, Madame Restell was the embodiment of the great American experiment. An immigrant, a female, an entrepreneur—she transformed working-class Ann Lohman into wealthy leisure-class Madame Restell. Restell and her clients were also the focus of another transformation, one that would shift the control of reproduction from the women personally involved to the men who controlled nearly every other aspect of their existence. Restell would find control of her own identity taken out of her hands. Rhetors, mostly male, working in the popular press and the courtroom once again transformed Restell, this time into an inhuman monster. By the time she died, she embodied "The Evil of the Age."

## A Professional Alliance

As has been noted in previous chapters, two professions with much potential to control women's bodies, law and medicine, were were yet to be professionalized during the nineteenth century. Often the two groups were at odds as they struggled to achieve stability and status. When the abortion question arose, however, the two groups united against a common enemy.

Abortion was an especially vexing issue for medical men, for it combined ethical and religious issues with more practical professional concerns. Contraception and abortion were moral choices but medical actions. The United States was founded in the context of Christianity. Whatever an individual's religious views were, there was tremendous social pressure to uphold the values of that faith. Respect for life was a cornerstone of the Christian faith, as it is now. What form that respect should take was less clearly defined, as it is now. A concurrent religious narrative was the mystification of and distaste for sexual activity. Indeed, according to some denominations, sex was only to be practiced when procreation was desired. Immense social pressure exerted upon members of a community insured that these tenets translated into behavioral rules.

In theory, the two narratives of respect for life and procreative sex would be enough to end abortion, since every pregnancy would have been the result of conscious choice. In practice, it is not so easy to discipline the body to follow the demands of society. As in other domains of society, the bonds of conformity were loosening. After about 1830, there was a notable shift away from religious authority; the church no longer retained "its former control over private sexual activity" (Ryan, "Power" 71). Unwanted pregnancies occurred, and onus fell squarely upon the pregnant woman. This is not the place for a discussion of the double standard for sexual behavior; suffice it to say that since women suffered the consequences of unwanted pregnancy, women were the first to seek alternatives. Thus, alongside the religious tradition that cherished childbirth, there ran a folk tradition dedicated to preventing it. Women passed down the secrets of sponges, douches, and herbal concoctions, all of varying effectiveness at contraception. When all else failed, there was the midwife, whose skills addressed both childbirth and abortion.

While the American medical profession was in its infancy, physicians tended to ignore the "unarticulated, alternative, popular morality, which supported women who had abortions" (Reagan 6). There was enough work in preventing the proliferation of untrained practitioners, many of whom posed genuine threats to public health. There was no accreditation for medical schools until 1912, so there was no standard training that a physician had undergone. As pointed out in chapter 3, there was still competition between theories and practitioners. In the decade following the establishment of the AMA, the organization began the task of consolidating power, and not merely by creating public good will. The AMA became a powerful lobbying group that worked to encode laws that controlled or eliminated competing practitioners. One of the arenas was destined to be abortion.

Restell herself bears some of the burden for attracting the attention of doctors to abortion. As noted earlier, the success of her advertising campaign attracted many imitators nationwide. What had been a dirty little secret was quickly becoming a commodity. The ranks of abortionists were filled with women, immigrants, and other "non-AMA" practitioners. Midwifes were styling themselves "female physicians" and competing with male doctors in obstetrics. In 1857, the AMA launched an official campaign to end abortion.[3]

They were joined in battle by a variety of allies within traditional religious organizations. Religious authorities had a long history of speaking against abortion for moral reasons. What the AMA brought to the table was the notion that abortion was also a medical issue. In the name of protecting women from the dangers of untrained surgeons and potentially devastating physical impairment, the organization added its weight to the debate. Their strategy was to apply pressure on state legislatures to pass laws sharply curtailing, if not completely halting, the practice of abortion. As a side effect, the power of midwives to treat their fellow women would also be curtailed. Once the laws were in place, moral, medical, and legal values would be unified. They would also be fully masculine.

In order to be successful, any group that desires to institute social change has to create broad support for its goals. The medical profession was in the awkward position of latecomer to the abortion debate. To be truly effective, the medical position had to be framed as perfectly consistent with the powerful antiabortion rhetoric that already existed. As part of the unification process, the movement needed to create a symbolic enemy, one that represented both the medical and moral evils threatening American culture. The threat had to be so powerful that its influence crossed state lines to threaten the welfare of the entire nation. That enemy was the "unschooled abortionist." This evil, shadowy figure represented all that was wrong with unregulated abortion. Unschooled abortionists had no respect for moral codes. More importantly, they also had no respect for the life and health of the mother. They spread a trail of devastation wherever they went. And the queen of them all was Madame Restell.

As the most successful practitioner in New York City, Restell came to embody the abortionist. With each change of law in the state of New York, someone would come to her door to try once more to end her practice. There would be a scandal, a hearing, possibly even a trial. Each occurrence was a public event, printed up in newspapers as respectable as the *Times* and as sensational as the *Police Gazette*. Transcripts of her trials were printed and sold as books to enlighten (or tantalize) readers. She was even included in tourist guides to New York City! As a result, Restell became the most fully documented abortionist of the nineteenth century. Her name became synonymous with abortion: writers too delicate to use the term referred obliquely to "Restellism" instead.

## Restell as Representative Anecdote

Madame Restell functioned as what Kenneth Burke would call a "representative anecdote" for the antiabortion movement, especially the medical branch of it. The rhetoric that emerged through her multiple run-ins with the law reveals that she served as a perfect embodiment of all that was evil in the practice. By using the representative anecdote concept as the lens through which to examine her role, we can see how male arguers exploited the female body even as they sought to rescue it.

Burke developed the concept by stating the psychological fact that people "seek for vocabularies that will be faithful reflections of reality. To this end, they must develop vocabularies that are selections of reality. And any selection of reality must, in certain circumstances, function as a deflection of reality" (*Grammar* 59, emphasis in the original). Humans can't possibly examine every possible phenomenon in the universe, so they decide upon a single facet. That choice naturally eliminates the rest of the universe from consideration. Nobody can account for everything.

It seems obvious. Unfortunately, Burke noted that people also forget that selection of one element is inherently a deflection from all the others, and present their sliver of insight as though it represented the entire truth. This closes off avenues of analysis, thus eliminating other universes of possible discourse. Burke's answer to what he saw as an extremely dangerous tendency was the representative anecdote. A conscious effort at analyzing the starting places of a controversy is the best antidote to mistaking one's selected part for the whole.

A representative anecdote is a narrative or image that continually reoccurs in the discussion of an issue. It is evoked as a kind of shorthand containing all the necessary rhetorical elements in a concise, easily evoked package. In order to avoid the danger of simplistic thinking, Burke asks us, as consumers of rhetoric, to examine the anecdote in a particular case in order to rediscover the elements that have been obscured.

Such an anecdote may be instantiated in a single *character* within a narrative. Some character, a single player among many, will be pulled from the pack and invested with the symbolic substance of the representative anecdote. It is the simplification of a social struggle. The tight focus on that character focuses the rhetoric. Although it is dangerously simplistic, it works well as a unifying device. A representative anecdote simultaneously frames a discourse and closes off alternative discourses. The rhetoric surrounding Restell framed the abortion controversy very neatly. In vilifying her, opponents were able to avoid a multitude of issues, from the role of men in creating the need for abortion to the economic structures that rewarded the practice. It also obscured the role of medicine in creating some of the dangers that doctors fought to eliminate.

## The Trials of Madame Restell

More surprising perhaps than how often the law pursued Restell was how long they left her alone before the first arrest. At the time she began her practice, there was a law on the books in the state of New York. That law strongly reflected the folk traditions currently in place. Tradition held that a fetus was not actually alive until "quickening"—the moment when the mother felt it moving in the womb. This roughly translated into the fourth month. An abortion prior to that time was acceptable. The law in New York, which went into effect in 1830, banned abortion after quickening and called it second degree manslaughter. Before quickening, there was no crime. After quickening, even the use of drugs was illegal.

Restell was by all accounts careful to ascertain how far a pregnancy had advanced before offering her services. If she slipped up, she risked a $100 fine and up to a year in prison. Notably, the law did allow for "therapeutic" abortion if two physicians agreed it was necessary. Thus, even this early law gave special privileges to doctors.

Only the practitioner faced penalties, not the mother who requested the service. If this omission was meant to encourage women to "confess" in order to aid prosecution, it did not work. The social stigma of requesting an abortion was apparently strong enough to keep everyone silent. As a result, there are no reliable records of how many abortions took place in New York City. There was, however, a perception among "regular" doctors seen in the medical literature that the practice of abortion was rising rapidly and becoming pervasive. Additionally worrisome was the belief that these abortions were requested not only by desperate unwed mothers but also by wives who were using it as birth control.

Although Restell had some earlier brushes with the law, it took a case that aligned with this public perception to get her into a courtroom. In 1840, a married woman named Maria Purdy lay on her deathbed, dying of tuberculosis. In her final hours, she confessed to her husband that she had gone to Restell for an abortion the year before. He went to the police. Restell was arrested, and a deathbed deposition was taken from Purdy to the effect that the abortion occured after the fourth month.

The press coverage of the case was relatively tame compared to the published booklets, editorials, and tracts that sprang to life. The basic facts of the case, as noted in the *Herald,* were fairly dry, only hinting at the public's perception of abortion. Purdy, who had a number of children, became pregnant while she was still nursing another child. She learned of Restell from a "negro wench" who had once "obtained relief" herself. For twenty dollars, Restell set her up with a man who performed the abortion. Purdy, worried about the state of her soul, wanted to confess before she died. Both Restell and Lohman were arrested, but Lohman was later released ("The Arrest").

This story introduces several interesting themes, not the least of which was that abortion was something decent married ladies found out about from black servants, who were apparently casual about the process. Since Restell called in a third-party male (not her husband) to perform surgery instead of doing it herself, she could not be charged with abortion, only for procurement. The storm of publicity that ensued was over a misdemeanor prosecution, but one would not have deduced that from the rhetoric. The discussion became hyperbolic almost immediately. The *Herald* itself moved from dismissing abortion as a low-class phenomenon to claiming that it was a rot emanating from the highest echelons:

> Madame Restell has been an accomplice with the demoralized portion of society, in violating the laws of God and man. Young unmarried females, moving in the highest circles, have applied to her for aid, and she has the evidence of the fact under their own hands. Men, who pretend to be leaders in churches, leaders of fashion, and leaders of finance in Wall Street, are connected with these extraordinary developments. Now is the time to assert the majesty of the laws, and vindicated our courts from all amputation or suspicion of winking at inequity or powerful connections. ("Madame Restell")

The trial transcript was later published by an antiabortion advocate. The introduction that was added zeroed in on Restell as evil incarnate, calling her "the monster in human shape" and accusing her of "one of the most hellish acts ever perpetrated in a Christian land" ("Trial of Madame Restell" 1). The comments portrayed Restell as a threat to the institution of marriage. The introduction directly addresses several kinds of husbands in an attempt to terrify them, as in, for example, this one aimed at sailors: "Seamen, you are going to three years wage, and have this security for the good behavior of your wife. Certain acts have certain consequences; the flow of blood proves that a blow has been given or received. Not at all: all this is at an end. Madame Restell shows your spouse that she may commit as many of adulteries as there are hours in the year without the possibility of detection" (5). For this writer, abortion was not merely murder, it was a mechanism through which women may safely mock their marriage vows. Restell insults honest women, too, provided there are any left. Why provide an abortion when the law provides the alms house for the truly destitute? By assuming that a woman lacks honor simply because she is poor, she insults the whole sex. Good women don't need her. Thus, if Restell has any customers at all, it is because there are many bad women in New York.

The theme of the abortionist as servant of evil women became popular in the press. The most colorful examples come from the pages of the *Police Gazette*, the era's equivalent of a supermarket tabloid. The editor of the *Gazette* made Restell his special target. Even when the story of the day concerned some other abortionist, a male, her name was brought in letters to the editor as one of the "hags of misery" preying upon human weakness. The *Gazette* was convinced that women were violating sexual norms right and left and using abortionists to cover their crimes, since "no mother in society (unless shielded by the secret purlieus of an abortionist's den) could dispose of her full-born offspring without inquiry and fatal investigation" ("Editorial").

Even writers in the medical profession, though more circumspect in language, echoed this attitude. One anonymous writer, claiming to be a physician, gave a fairly balanced analysis of abortion practices yet still fell into this pattern. Although he noted that the United States was sorely lacking in institutions and laws (including those aimed at fathers) that would encourage single women to choose otherwise, he stated that surgical abortion was murder, period. But then the discussion veered to married women who used abortion to avoid having children. His sympathy evaporated. There was no excuse for a married woman to dodge motherhood. He ended by claiming that "Restellism" might even encourage prostitution by removing the consequences (*Madame Restell: An Account* 24).

The discussion tells us about the general attitudes of the public during the early stages of the abortion controversy in New York. Abortionists were viewed as opportunists who prey upon human weakness. As a side effect, they enabled sexual miscreants to hide the evidence of their crimes. This in turn encouraged more sexual behavior.

Women of low morals took advantage of this opportunity and used abortion as birth control. Still, the bulk of the criticism was aimed at the enablers rather than at the anonymous low women. If the abortionists stopped, the normal biological consequences would curb promiscuity. Men were barely mentioned; they seemed to have no part in the process. The reader might be excused for thinking that pregnancy was the result of parthogenesis. The law ignored this aspect of the debate entirely; the only criminal in a post-quickening abortion was the practitioner, not the potential parents.

The Purdy case dragged on until 1842. Restell was found guilty in the initial trial, but the case was appealed to the state supreme court on the grounds that Purdy's deathbed deposition was not admissible. The court agreed that such depositions (*de bene esse*) were proper in civil suits but not criminal cases. Restell got a retrial with the deposition removed from evidence and was found not guilty.

Restell went back to work, probably suspecting that her legal battles were far from over. It is unlikely that anyone would have predicted that some of these battles would be over *not* providing abortions. Restell would soon discover that, in the eyes of the public, the abortionist was incapable of doing the right thing. Her very existence was a crime.

As noted earlier, most accounts of abortion had up to this point ignored the presence of men and minimized the reasons a woman might choose to end a pregnancy. This tendency reached an ironic peak in the *Police Gazette* of May 2, 1946. There were two lead stories in that issue. The first recounted the horrific tale of a man arrested for committing incest with two of his daughters and attempting to rape a third. In the same column, "More Work of the Abortionists" noted that several abandoned babies had been found around the city recently: "The whole of the three came doubtless from Restell's den of murder. There are no other places in the city, except the slaughterhouses of the abortionist, where a mother can be delivered of her shame and dispose of her offspring without enquiry." The disconnect between the two stories is typical, as is the mention of Restell in a story about abandoned infants, the result of *not* terminating a pregnancy.

Restell refused to perform surgical abortions after quickening. She did, however, provide boarding for the discreet delivery of a child, and would even arrange adoptions—for a fee. One would think that she would be given some credit for offering this nonlethal alternative, but it only added to her character the additional sobriquet of "baby farmer." Interestingly, it generated great sympathy for the mothers involved. When Mary Applegate filed suit for the return of her infant, she became an instant celebrity.

Applegate was a single woman who was sent from Philadelphia by her paramour for a discreet lying-in. He apparently told Restell that he wanted the child adopted but did not bother to inform Applegate. A woman Applegate believed was a wet nurse was actually an adoptive mother. She did not catch on until her return to Philadelphia, where the father unkindly told her he had washed his hands of the affair. He did, however, give her money for a train ticket back to New York to search for the child. By this time, Restell denied knowing where the infant was.

Applegate became a heroine. Restell became a villain. The father stayed safely in Philadelphia. There were demonstrations held in front of Restell's home, demanding that she find the infant and return it. Applegate's deposition was even in the *New York Medical and Surgical Reporter*, where she was cast as a hapless victim. In her deposition, she had mentioned other women who were at Restell's for lying-in; they ranged from a married woman hiding an affair to a young girl whose mother brought her in for "treatment." Applegate's testimony indicated that there were plenty of women taking advantage of the services.

The anonymous author of the *Reporter* piece used her case as a set piece to frame a new discussion: it was time for doctors to take a stand. This would be a dangerous undertaking, for "if the modest physician is heard to raise his voice against the practice of any of the popular mountebanks of the day, he is immediately accused of selfishness, and the plea of persecution is urged on the part of the Charlatan. But the time has arrived, when forbearance ceases to be a virtue" ("Editorial: Madame Restell" 158). The author proceeded from poor duped Applegate to cases of women who suffered more physically. He laid every bit of suffering at Restell's doorstep.

Although the author did not intend it, his work winds up being just as much an indictment of the medical profession. The most horrific case in the article is in a letter written by a noted "Professor of Midwifery and the Diseases of Women and Children." Mrs. M. was a young mother with two children. When she became pregnant again, she went to see Restell. Herbs having failed, she priced an abortion. Restell's fee was too high, so the woman went home and attempted to self-abort. She not only failed but produced so much scar tissue that she had to ask a physician for a cesarean section. Unfortunately for her, the doctors consulted the professor. Upon discovering the scarring, he refused to perform the surgery until she told him where it came from; when she was convinced that she was going to die, she confessed. Then the doctor performed the cesarean. The author of the letter blamed Restell for making the woman go through "twenty-nine hours" of unnecessary labor, when in merely "ten minutes" the surgery was completed. Amazingly, Restell was faulted rather than a "Professor of Midwifery" who tortured a woman for over twenty hours in order to extract a confession.

This new pattern of castigating Restell even when she did not perform abortions was part of a move to criminalize abortion under new grounds: that it was a threat to womanhood. The claim that abortionists abetted immoral behavior slowly transformed into the claim that they actively harmed "misguided" women. Whether through the physical effects of surgery or the psychic drain from giving up their babies, women who entered the abortionist's lair were doomed to suffer horribly.[4]

The choice of Restell for the centerpiece of this rhetoric is interesting. By all accounts, including Applegate's, her customers were well provided for. She had a reputation for reliability that led patients from other cities to choose her over more convenient boardinghouses. And although there were many individual cases of abortionists, including physicians, who were tried for botched surgeries, there was never such an accusation against Restell. There is no record of her being accused of directly causing the death of a woman.

Yet she eventually became the representative anecdote for the pain and suffering that untrained, unscrupulous, "irregular" physicians could cause. In focusing on Restell, antiabortion advocates were able to avoid addressing a number of embarrassing issues, including the role of men. The turning point, for Restell, was when the moral and medical narratives finally converged.

## Revenge of the "Regulars"

This convergence was over a decade in coming, but finally, in 1845, law and medicine came together. A bill to further restrict abortion was proposed to the state legislature, not by the judicial committee but by the medical committee. When it passed, it restricted the relatively permissive law of 1830. Quickening was still a marker. An abortion that occurred after quickening, or one that resulted in the death of the mother, was second degree manslaughter. But now, providing abortions or even abortifacients in *any* stage of pregnancy was a misdemeanor that would result in a mandatory one year in prison. An additional clause made the woman seeking an abortion liable as well. If a woman sought an abortion, or attempted to self-abort, she faced a $1,000 fine, or three to twelve months in prison, or both. The logic behind this additional clause was that an abortion performed by an untrained surgeon was more dangerous than childbirth. Therefore a penalty to dissuade them from taking the risk was created.

Henceforth, Restell's entire practice carried legal risks. She, like many of her contemporaries, skirted the issue of abortifacients by advertising her "menstrual pills" as a method to regulate menses, which could be delayed by other factors besides pregnancy. Since it was impossible to prove otherwise, the sale of pills and powders was rarely prosecuted. Surgical procedures of any kind, however, were now illegal.

Although the clause that punished the mother was framed as a form of protection, it functioned as a catch-22 for all pregnant women. First, it prevented any safe discussion of the issue. There were now two reasons for a woman to keep her silence: one social, one legal. Women with experience were much less likely to reveal anything that might help another woman make an informed choice. Second, knowledge of an abortion could serve as a powerful form of blackmail—anyone, male or female, could turn her in. Third, it made every woman a potential tool of the prosecution. A woman suspected of having an abortion could be threatened with prison until she confessed and agreed to turn state's evidence. This highly punishing form of protection eventually drove abortion even further underground.

However, the efficacy of the law is evidenced by how long Restell continued undisturbed after its passing. It took two years before she was charged under the new law. Even then, it was the result of her having been persuaded to go against her better judgment. When Maria Bodine was sent to Restell by an anonymous "sponsor," Restell decided that she was too far along for an abortion and suggested that the woman stay and board instead. Bodine agreed that she "would rather stay and board the time out at $5 a week, but my beau would object to the charge" (*Wonderful Trial* 6). He did indeed. He insisted on an abortion, Restell kept refusing, but finally he made her an offer she could not refuse. It should be noted that all this haggling was done through a go-between—the put-upon foreman of the father's cotton mill—with the attendant delay while he went from New York to the couple's hometown, Ramapo, a town on the New York/New Jersey border (a two-hour trip in 1845). Once the surgery was performed, Bodine claimed that she did not feel well, but she eventually returned to her job as a housemaid. She felt bad enough to consult a physician but lied to him about the abortion. Eventually, however, a Ramapo physician suspected the abortion and turned her in. She turned state's evidence. Restell was arrested. So was John McCann, the foreman who acted as procurer. Joseph P. Cook, Bodine's lover and master of the house where she was a maid, was eventually indicted, but I could find no evidence of his having been jailed at any time during the proceedings.

Thus, under the law, men did not necessarily escape the consequences of soliciting abortions. In the eyes of the public, however, it was Restell whose guilt was greatest. She was tried separately from the men, for second degree manslaughter, and her trial was covered by the press. The *Police Gazette* sent a reporter to transcribe the proceedings, which were quickly published as a commercial book. The proceedings against the men barely rated a mention, not even by the *Times*, which had a field day over Restell.

The Restell trial was framed as a contest between two women. The prosecution cast Bodine as a helpless victim whose health was permanently ruined by her experience. They made great use of physicians, several of whom spent time attempting to pinpoint how possible it was that the fetus had quickened by the time the abortion was performed. The defense cast Bodine as a loose woman and a liar. The first characterization was aimed at proving that Restell was not the person who made her ill. The second was in order to discredit her claims as to how far advanced her pregnancy really was, if indeed she was ever pregnant at all.

The strategies on both sides seem odd. After all, the law did not care whether Bodine was ill or Restell incompetent. All that mattered was whether there had been an abortion and whether it occurred before or after quickening. But the lawyers obviously believed that the jury needed to hear these arguments. More importantly, the press thought that the public at large needed to hear them. Restell's trial became an important venue for cementing two popular beliefs about abortion. First, it illustrated several of the medical claims about the dangers of abortion. Second, it emphasized that "bad" women were more likely to use the untrained abortionist.

The proceedings were published by the *Police Gazette* under the title *The Wonderful Trial of Caroline Lohmann, Alias Restell*. The editors were obviously not interested in perfect accuracy—Caroline was the name of Restell's daughter. The exciting title and parallel coverage in the weekly, however, were in keeping with the practice of legal journalism at the time. Journalists made heavy use of "theatrical metaphors to describe court proceedings" in order to "present them as a form of light entertainment" (Leps 111). The paper pulled out the stops when covering Restell. It even carried an illustration depicting her holding a winged demon munching complacently on the corpse of an infant (*Wonderful Trial* 32).

This report illustrates the power of a representative anecdote to control debate over an issue. The lawyers in the case took great liberty in their arguments, often overstepping the requirements of the law.[5] Yet there were many issues raised by witnesses that were ignored or diminished because they would have expanded the discussion into areas that did not fit the narrative of "evil untrained abortionist destroying woman." When arguers took their case beyond the borders of the law, they took it in a tightly prescribed direction.

The prosecution made it clear that this case was about womanhood. Restell was cast, from the opening argument, as a disgrace to her entire sex: "Nature is appalled, that women, the last and loveliest of her works, could so unsex herself as to perpetrate such fiend-like enormities" (*Wonderful Trial* 5). The evil is deepened because it is so unnatural. Restell is a mother herself, and thus aware of that sacred bond, yet she was willing to break it for other women. From such an evil person, only evil acts could come.

Maria Bodine's body is presented as direct evidence of the physical dangers of abortion. Her very presence is an argument. As the reporter noted, "The complainent, Maria Bodine, here came into Court to with a feeble, tottering walk, and took her seat in the chair usually occupied by witnesses. She is a young woman, about 26 years of age, middling size, and evidentially in a rapid decline of health. She was neatly dressed, and her appearance created much excitement and sympathy throughout the crowded courtroom" (5). The reporter, certainly, felt sympathy for this broken figure. The court showed delicacy, too, for Bodine was allowed to wear a veil during her testimony. It didn't hurt, either, that she fainted during her first examination and had to be carried out of court. She returned later that day. Restell's lawyer, James T. Brady, successfully demanded that the veil be removed the next day, but the image of outraged modesty was already created. Bodine was examined carefully by both sides, for at any difficult questioning she had a tendency to sicken, further proving her complete physical breakdown.

The unstated assumption was that her physical decline was directly at the hand of Restell. As a result, some odd discrepancies of evidence seemed to pass without notice. When Bodine testified as to her abortion, interestingly, she ascribed to Restell behavior that in any other arena might be described as humane and decent:

> Madam Restell attended me during the night. I remained at her house till Thursday afternoon; I had crackers and tea the first day, then afterward some vegetables and soup; on Thursday afternoon she came into the room and found me crying; she asked me what was the matter; I told her I wanted to go home, but I had no money to go with; if I wished to go, she said, she would give me money to pay my passage and to get me some refreshments; she gave me a dollar; my passage money was six shillings; she then took me down into the parlor and gave me some wine; she then said she would listen and look around to see if any officers were about; she looked out and said there were not; she said if anyone arrested or accosted me I must return to her, and I should go in a carriage; . . . she said if they [her breasts] troubled me much I must wrap them in red flannel and rub them with camphor. (7)

Far from being hauled in and out on an assembly line, Bodine stayed for several days after her abortion, which was on a Sunday. Restell slept in the room with her on Monday, allowed her to rest, fed her light meals, and did not force her to leave until she requested it. She gave her train fare (which was unlikely to be repaid), and even offered her advice on how to reduce the pain in her breasts. Although Restell was careful to remind Bodine that she was now complicit in a crime, she did not otherwise abuse her. In fact, the only person to notably mistreat her was her lover—he was two days late with his payment; the go-between ran back and forth again several times.

One might wonder, given the circumstances, how this woman's health declined so far that she could barely sit up in the witness chair. The prosecution insisted it was from the abortion. Indeed, Bodine testified that she later experienced "a great flooding" on her way to her sister's house and had to stay with her. She eventually consulted a physician and did not tell him about the abortion. She *was* ill.

The response of the defense, as framed by the "womanhood" anecdote, was to blacken Bodine's character by attributing her illness to a different proximate cause: syphilis. Bodine "had for years been accustomed to have free promiscuous intercourse with men." The defense baldly stated that Bodine was "guilty as much as the accused, and ought as much to be tried . . . Her present state of health, to which the District Attorney alluded yesterday, is caused by a long course of intemperance, a constant career of prostitution, and is the natural consequence—not of Madame Restell, but of habitual and promiscuous intercourse as a harlot—not with Mr. Cook, but with every man, every hour, or every five minutes of her life" (9). In this approach, attorney Graham went too far. Bodine had another spell in the middle of his attack. "It was with difficulty she was prevented from sinking on the floor" (9). The court was not amused and reminded Graham that her character had no relevance to whether she'd had an abortion. That slowed but did not stop the attack—her character was relevant because the defense was going to claim that Bodine was never pregnant, and that the entire case was the result of a scam having gone bad. So it came down to a fight over which woman was the least unbelievable, the abortionist or the harlot.

As a result of this focus, one interesting set of data went unnoticed. In the fight over character, a bevy of physicians were called. Their main purpose was to bolster the side they were on: Was Bodine ever pregnant? Did she show signs of an abortion? Had she likely quickened? Could those scars have been from syphilitic buboes? All these questions were expected. Along the way, however, the witnesses described the state of medical treatment in the 1840s. Could Bodine's malady be the result of "regular" medicine? Naturally, that question was never raised.

Bodine was seen by several doctors over the course of several months, and she worsened after each new hand was brought in. Some of it was Bodine's own fault. At her sister's, she told the first physician that she was having problems with her spine. He promptly treated her for that condition: "I think he gave me powders; I took to my bed; he cupped me on the back; he leeched me to my bowels; he put issues in my back" (*Wonderful Trial* 10). Cupping draws excess blood from the affected area; it works like one of the "snake bite kits" that are sold to tourists before they go camping. Leeching is literally putting leeches upon the body; they, too, draw blood. Issues are threads made of an irritant that are stitched into the skin to create open sores that will allow bad humors to "issue" from the body.

Evans, the physician, later testified that he thought she had been pregnant, and perhaps had a miscarriage, but since she did not confide in him, he merely treated her symptoms: "I cupped her on the side of her back, and side of her hip; I leeched her in the private parts; I put issues in her back. The cupping was for inflammation in the kidneys, and the issues were placed to counteract spinal irritation and the disease existing in the womb" (14). After three months of this treatment, she was worse. During this time, she was also going about her regular household duties for the Cook residence. Anemia coupled with overwork seems a reasonable explanation for Bodine's condition.

Two new physicians (brothers) were called by Cook when she did not recover. They did not for a moment believe the "spinal" story. Still, their "drops and powders" made her feel "somewhat better." Eventually, Cook refused to pay for any further treatment. Bodine had to consult a physician who worked with the poor at a public clinic. He took Bodine to his sister's to wait and reported her condition to the law.

So one doctor treated Bodine for the wrong condition. Two suspected the truth but gave her some drops for pain and kept their silence. The defense even tried to tie one of them to an extortion plot to get more money from Cook—although the evidence could be reinterpreted to show that he was simply trying to get paid for his services. The last doctor obeyed the law; his reward was to be accused by Brady of using Bodine as a pawn to prosecute Restell.

Although there is a ring of truth to that charge, it was doubtful that the jury felt too badly about a doctor who turned in a woman for committing a crime. After Brady brought it up, he dropped it. The medical profession did not look totally respectable after the litany of the actions of these men, and yet, the other physicians who were called to testify about how awful abortion was, even though they were not acquainted with Bodine, were granted full respect. Their opinions on whether one could detect an abortion several months after it occurred were treated as scientific fact. The defense used physicians, too, to try to pinpoint signs of venereal disease. The "regular" physicians had the respect of the court. The case never turned to the question of a physician's role.

The case also never questioned the role of the father. In fact, in the opening, the defense stated, "It shall be our effort neither to injure nor to disparage Mr. Cook" (21). Cook was even excused from consorting with a syphilitic woman, since he was misled about her symptoms. It is not clear what washed him clean of taking a housemaid for his mistress and being so surly about the consequences. He insisted upon an abortion because boarding would cost too much. He also wasted precious time while Bodine's pregnancy advanced, haggling over price. He failed to pay the bill on time, which made Bodine a pawn in his fight with Restell. He apparently did not reduce Bodine's household chores even though she was clearly ill. He even gave trouble to the physicians he finally called for her and neglected their bill. Bodine was reduced to going to the poorhouse to see a doctor. Although all of these details emerged during testimony, the defense refused to disparage him, preferring instead to disparage Bodine by trotting in neighbors who agreed that her reputation was bad enough that becoming Cook's mistress had not hurt it any further.

In the end, both sides circled the wagon around the defense of sacred womanhood. Abortion was a woman's issue: her crime, necessitated by her folly. The threat to a woman's health came from the unschooled abortionist—who was clearly defined as a female midwife. Men could try to help these benighted creatures see the error of their ways.

The jury made a reasonable decision, remarkable given the wild flights of rhetoric on both sides. They rejected the notion that a physician could detect quickening months after the fact and did not convict Restell of manslaughter. They also rejected the desperate narrative that claimed Bodine had faked her pregnancy and found Restell guilty of misdemeanor procurement. That charge carried a mandatory one-year prison sentence, which she served on Blackwell's Island (now Roosevelt Island).

## The Last Straw: *Comstock versus Restell*

A year on Blackwell's Island had a strong effect on Restell. She claimed that after her conviction she gave up surgical abortion, sticking instead to her pills and her boardinghouse. The advertisements that appeared in the 1850s reflect this change. She emphasized her services to "Married Ladies," and by the 1860s she billed herself as "Female Physician and Accoucheur": "Ladies who desire board and the best medical attendance during confinement, can be accommodated" (*New York Times,* September 10, 1863: 7).

Although her shift did not entirely end her legal problems, any altercations, including one more drawn-out adoption case, ended in victory if not vindication.[6] For the most part, Restell was accepted as a part of the fabric of New York City. As proof of her semi-reform, she applied for United States citizenship and was naturalized in 1854. One had to be "a person of good moral character" to be granted citizenship (Browder 107). The mayor of New York attended her daughter's wedding. She had, it seemed, finally escaped her reputation.

In reality, her troubles were merely in abeyance until the law caught up with the tenor of the times. Whatever New Yorkers thought of Restell, she had earned a national reputation that grew darker with the passage of time. She was so well known that she was included as a subject in several "guides" to the big city. One author gave her section the title "The Wickedest Woman in New York," a name that stuck. Another writer coyly referred to a "Madame___" whose "name is well known, and needs no comment" (McCabe 623).

What seemed to annoy most was the fact of Restell's wealth. She owned several lots in Manhattan, including one upon which she built a mansion. She had carriages, horses, silk gowns, and all the other appurtenances of wealth. And all because she was willing to do what poor but honest "regular" doctors "as men of honor and good citizens, as well as lovers of science" would not (McCabe 623).

McCabe is interesting because he includes in his guide to New York an entire chapter on "Child Murder" wherein he introduces what had become another thread in the argument over abortion, race: "It is an appalling truth that so many American wives are practicers of the horrible sin of 'prevention' that in certain sections of our country, the native population is either stationary or dying out" (629). Abortion was becoming part of a larger debate about the morality, or lack thereof, of the practice of birth control. The debate was once more shifting; abortion was not merely a threat to women, it was threatening the white "race" and its position in the United States. The link to birth control would greatly expand the legal weaponry of Restell's pursuers.

The race card was one of many played by moral reformer Anthony Comstock, who was practically a one-man social movement against American immorality. Comstock did not want to control only the sexual act and its consequences, he wanted to control how people thought about sex. To him, any dissemination of information related to sex, including the prevention or termination of pregnancy, was dangerous pornography. "Contraceptives allowed young people, afflicted with lust from reading pornography, to sin while affording themselves and their partners protection from disease and pregnancy" (Beisal 40).

The history of his successful career has been documented elsewhere, both by historians and journalists, who generally agree that his antipornography campaign had deleterious effects upon freedom of speech in the United States. Obviously, this chapter is concerned only with its effect upon the career of Restell. This was sensational enough at the time.

In 1873, Comstock attained the pinnacle of success when the U.S. Congress enacted the "Comstock law" on the national level. The law made it a federal offense to sell, lend, publish, or give away any information that the government deemed "obscene." It was also illegal to "cause" someone else to publish such material. This included anything related to "the prevention of conception, or for causing unlawful abortion." Telling someone where they could find such information carried a sentence of six months to five years in prison and a fine of $100 to $2,000 and court costs.

Comstock followed the passage of the legislation by embarking on a personal campaign to find and prosecute violators of the law. His methods were unusual; many of his targets claimed entrapment. He would pretend to be someone sympathetic to the cause of population control and wait until someone slipped. He "stormed the palace of Restell" in 1878. He pursued his standard pattern of misrepresentation. He visited Restell, claiming to be a married man whose wife had already given birth to many children. He was worried about her health and wondered if Restell could help him. She sold him some pills. Comstock returned the next day with a police officer and had her arrested. In her home, he found printed materials that provided birth control information as well as mysterious "instruments" with instructions for use.

So Restell was once again in court, this time for violating the Comstock law. Her strategies to avoid prosecution failed. The supreme irony was that after all their years of campaigning, the medical establishment had successfully gotten New York to outlaw abortion, and that law had nothing to do with her final capture. Restell's acts were no longer really at issue. She was targeted because of her symbolic stature. The destruction of the iconic abortionist would be a victory over abortionists everywhere.

This case, however, was markedly different from earlier cases. First, Restell was much older and had outlived most of her friends. Her husband had died and she had become estranged from her daughter (her adult grandchildren, however, came to court with her every day). She had, at least in her own mind, cleaned up her act and still faced prison. This Restell was not the confident criminal of earlier years. Second, her negative reputation was now firmly cemented in the public mind. Upon Restell's arrest, Comstock notified every paper in the state, and the feeding frenzy began. Restell was subjected to the full force of the negative publicity, without a buffer.

That the tide had turned was clear from day one. The judge at her initial hearing set bail at $10,000, an enormous sum in those days. Restell did not have the liquid funds and offered government bonds as a surety. The judge ruled that he would accept only real estate. Restell had to stay in jail until someone with enough property would put up bail.

The *New York Times,* forgetting how much advertising revenue she had once generated, crowed over the prospect of Restell in jail again. They even followed up the story with a summary of the Bodine case and Restell's sub-sequent imprisonment ("Miscellaneous"). Thus anyone who might have thought that this was only a case related to the Comstock law was quickly informed of the context. The *Brooklyn Daily Eagle* ran the story under the series title "The Wages of Sin" and noted Restell's lawyer's claim that the pills she gave Comstock were useless. But they did not elaborate. A genuine abortifacent was more interesting than a fraud.

The court's decisions and the press coverage scared away the men that Restell's lawyers had found to post bond. The judge announced that the names of the bondsmen would be made public. A reporter from the *Times* was present, and the names were indeed printed. This had the desired effect: "One man put up bail, then immediately upon finding out his name would be released said: 'Oh, the good Samaritan be blowed. I've got a wife and a family of girls, and I'll be hanged if I'm going to have my name in the papers as a bondsman for an abortionist, Christian or no Christian, Samaritan or not.' And he left the courtroom" ("Mme. Restell's Arrest"). Here is the final example of representative anecdote as a constraint upon discussion: Restell's symbolic character was such a powerful frame that it opened the door to a discussion of abortion during a trial over obscenity.

The trouble continued. On March 15, enough bondsmen were found and Restell was released. On the 16th, one of the bondsmen changed his mind and she was rearrested. Then Comstock announced that he needed to leave town and wanted the trial postponed until the 23rd. Faced with a wait in prison, Restell finally had to pay someone to serve as bondsman. The papers continued to castigate the men involved, although one, pointedly referred to as a German immigrant, held out during the entire battle ("The Case").

There was no opportunity to test the rhetorical functioning of the anecdote in this trial. On April 1, news reached the court that Restell had been found dead in her bathtub, a suicide. Since it was April Fools' Day, Comstock and company thought it was merely a tasteless joke. But it was not a joke. Restell had had enough of rhetoric and withdrew from the fight. Her death did not end her career as symbolic representative of abortion, however. The *Times* report was titled "The End of a Criminal Life." An accompanying editorial was clear: "The death of 'Mme. Restell' by her own hand is a fit ending to an odious career. The fact that such a woman should have amassed property to the value of three-quarters of the millions of dollars is a sufficiently conclusive proof of the magnitude of the ghastly trade of which she was the most notorious agent. . . . the woman who made a fortune out of child murder." Representative she was, and representative she would remain.

## Aftermath and Conclusions

In the years after her death, Restell remained a larger-than-life figure. In fact, for a while there were rumors that she had not died at all, that she had faked her suicide and left the country ("Absurd Stories"). As late as 1882, her name was evocative. When an abortionist was arrested in Illinois, the *Times* headline proclaimed her "CHICAGO'S MME. RESTELL."

The image of Restell remained a rhetorical weapon in the hands of anti-abortion advocates. One particularly powerful (and anonymous) tract was entitled *Madame Restell! Her Secret Life History From Her Birth to Her Suicide.* Subtitled "The Most Terrible Being Ever Born," the tract touched upon every major theme ever attached to her character. This Restell was a wealthy woman, having connections to the highest levels of New York society. She was coldhearted. When a sculptor was hired to carve a tombstone, she coolly laid out the body of a dead infant to illustrate her design. She was also a consummate hypocrite; she displayed a Bible in her parlor despite her profession. Before one can wonder how the author knows what Restell's parlor looks like, the rhetoric is off and running. The author states that abortion is an evil practiced by thoughtless women who would be saved by more clearly criminalizing the act:

> Oh you young and thoughtless mother, who, with your own hands, cast your offspring into the hellish maw of this fiend, and who excuse yourself with the flimsy pretexts you do, pause. Remember, in every case you deliberately commit the crime of murder, and that in the judgment day God will hold you responsible for the fearful crime, just as surely as though you went into the street and deliberately took the life of a little girl or boy who might be passing your door.(7)

Abortion is murder, period. There is no mentioning of quickening; that grace period is gone. The author states that physicians, and others with experienced eyes, can always spot a woman who has had an abortion, so there is no hiding, either. It doesn't matter whether the mother is single or married, although the author thinks a married woman without children should be "treated in the old Bible fashion. . . . with contempt" (7). It hardly needs to be said that abortion is a woman's crime; there are few mentions of men in the scenario.

Since abortion is a crime, a few women might look for other alternatives to rearing a child. Some might consider adoption. Again, the image of Restell closes that avenue. Her former practice is described thus:

> In the event of so expressing a desire, the infant could accommodatingly be *"adopted out,"* that is, they would never be troubled either with or about it.
>
> Oh, how horrible a suspicion does this cause! Were they *all* adopted? Poor little innocents! Oh, what mothers! And what relatives, who could thus bargain with the abortionist, to have the helpless little being, its veins filled with their own blood, its very features being the impress of themselves, *"adopted out?"* (22, emphasis in the original)

Adoption is evil, too; first because one does not know for sure that the child is not killed and second because it is an unnatural betrayal of "blood." The tract adds a garbled version of the Applegate story as well as other notorious adoption cases. There is also the obligatory ray of hope—in one tale a woman defies her family and keeps her child, whose presence redeems her.

In an echo of the progression of the changes in the laws of New York, the author narrows the scope of sexual activity for women by forcing them to live forever with the consequences. God made women to be mothers. Do not become a mother before marriage, and do not refuse to become a mother after marriage. If you break these rules, the law will come after you. The message is wrapped entirely in Restell's biography. The author even conjures images from her innocent youth in England, the better to illustrate her transformation to pure evil.

Not surprisingly, the author also spends time discussing the Comstock case, with lavish attention given to the imagined suicide scene. The author uses Restell to celebrate the fact that even discussing abortion or owning potential implements were at last outlawed. The Comstock law is what finally slew the dragon.

In this third phase there is some comfort. First, men are at last included in the restrictions, if only tangentially. Men can be guilty of aiding and abetting women. The author admonishes parents to teach their sons how to live a pure life. He adds that they should deal with their daughters "even more sternly," since they are the ones God is going to hold responsible.

The social implications of "Comstockery" also provide some irony. After the late 1870s, regular physicians were finding themselves on the receiving end of the law. The Comstock law had no codicil excusing physicians. In fact, it broadened control over their behavior. The Comstock law not only made abortion information illegal, it also forbade discussion of contraception and cast a wary eye upon any information related to sexuality and health, such as discussion of venereal disease. In fact, the greater proportion of Comstock's later arrests was of men who were not particularly concerned with abortion. The line between sexual information and pornography became so blurred that even scientific discussions were banned from the U.S. mail. The medical profession had gained a victory over the irregulars at the cost of their own freedom to discuss sexuality.

"Madame Restell" as imagined by the rhetoric of the nineteenth century is a good example of the uses and misuses of the representative anecdote. By framing their rhetoric around her body, antiabortion advocates could control the debate and prevent the introduction of issues that might have been too dangerous to themselves or society. The construction of Restell *deflected* attention from these other issues.

First, her sex deflected attention away from the role of male sexuality in abortion. The most salient subtext of all the discussions over the thirty years of court cases was that women had sole ownership of this crime. Focus on a male abortionist, of which there were many, would have weakened this presumption. This is not to say that men were not prosecuted, but the public debates tended either to ignore them or to introduce Restell at the slightest provocation. Only women could bear children. Thus only they could choose to murder them. And the most likely suspect in abetting those women? Another woman.

Second, because she had not been trained in a medical school, Restell could be used as an exemplar of the dangers of "irregular" medicine. This made it easier for physicians to enter into a liaison with the religious rhetoric that opposed abortion. Physicians could tie the issue of public health to the moral concerns, which opened the way for legislators to expand laws. The moral implications of regulating women's sexual behavior could be obscured behind images of sick and dying women. There were traditional physicians who practiced abortions, but these abortions were "safe" and "therapeutic." Targeting Restell made it easier to gloss over the differences between manslaughter and medicine.

Third, for better or worse, Restell was stubborn and inventive. She did not fold at the first sign of trouble. Rather, she resisted the strictures of the law and reinvented her practice with every new act of legislation. This made her a worthy enemy. Although she was certainly not the superhuman demon depicted in the rhetoric, the fact that she survived through the greater part of the century gave credence to the claim that she was the "wickedest" woman ever. It also appealed to male pride. The fact that many men over the years were unable to bring her down added insult to injury. Even Comstock admitted that this played a great part in his decision to pursue her.

The narratives spun around Restell tell us much about the growth and development of antiabortion rhetoric. There is a strongly misogynist core. Although the rhetors extolled the virtues of pure womanhood and sacred motherhood, although they passed laws with the stated purpose of preserving women's health, although they mourned for the children lost, the subtext was always that it was women, and women alone, who were the threat to these goods. Whether through ignorance or deviance, women were destroying womanhood. Although casting Restell as a vessel to contain this evil could allow rhetors to avoid attacking their own wives and daughters, the fact remained that their sex meant that they could not be trusted.

The casting of Restell as representative evil also illustrates the essentially tragic nature of the rhetoric. Once it was agreed that abortion was a detriment to society, the rhetorical focus shifted to stomping out representative practitioners. These "supply side" arguments enabled the movement to function without addressing the factors that created the demand. As history has repeatedly shown us, a rhetorical scapegoat is the simplest way to deal with flaws in the social order from within.

Antiabortion arguers accepted that their society was essentially good; if something was wrong, it had to be due to some misuse of a social element. Therefore, if some women risked death or imprisonment in order to avoid childbirth, it must be because someone was exploiting their fear of something else. The cure was to punish that exploiter, a strategy that ignores the fact that the source of the fear remained. There would be new Restells.

# 7. "You Know It When You See It": The Rhetorical Embodiment of Race and Gender in *Rhinelander v. Rhinelander*

In the fall of 1925, a scion of one of the oldest, wealthiest families of New York publicly declared that his bride of barely a month had defrauded him. She was hiding the fact that she was "colored," explained his lawyers, and had he known this he never would have married her. His wife's lawyers found this claim disingenuous. He had spent the last three years in and out of her family's home. He had seen all her relatives. More important, he had seen *her*; how could he not have known she was black?[1]

"Race" was, and still is, a problematic category that confounds attempts to define it, creating "nothing short of confusion" (Higginbotham 253). Despite its apparent grounding in a biological referent, race has no obvious objective base from which we can easily derive criteria for slotting people into racial categories. To make matters more difficult, race only sometimes refers to biological lineage. It is also used frequently to describe a complex of social and economic relationships characterizing an entire culture. As Henry Louis Gates has noted, discussions of race are instantly problemetized by the ambiguous nature of the term.

Despite the confusing manner in which "race" is used, there is an historic tendency for people to seek out the underlying biological referent in their discussions. This referent at least offers some constancy. One would think the biology would be clear enough to enable one to make simple decisions in an annulment case.

Or would it? One's first determination would be the race, according to the agreed-upon biological referents, of the bride accused of perpetrating fraud. The bride's mother, however, was "obviously" white (and English at that). Later testimony elicited that her father was a "mulatto" and did not like being branded a "Negro" by the press. Thus, the young woman had little of the biological material that comprised her legal racial category, which kept the fraud question open.

This particular debate, and the courtroom battle that ensued, forced onlookers of both races to confront a number of issues that underlaid the fabric of their social existence. Social behaviors based in tacitly agreed-upon racial categories, class distinctions, economic barriers, and sexual mores were threatened. Here, in microcosm, was the result of a process that was a national obsession in the 1920s—the transformation of white and black America into "brown" America. The discussion provides fertile ground for revealing how concepts of race and gender could come together as narrative elements rooted in white America's vision of race—both their own and the "other." Arguments created by white lawyers, aimed at a white male jury, and eventually filtered to the public by the press of both races created visions of womanhood, black, and white that came together in the body of a person who was all three simultaneously.

This chapter views the historical mutability of race by examining how racial narratives met, modified, and were modified by the sex of the principals. Clearly the issues of mixed blood as well as crossing of the boundaries of "proper" womanhood and manhood created a rhetorical melting pot from which the lawyers on each side pulled arguments in favor of their clients. This was not a clear issue of black versus white or even, after a while, of husband versus wife. There were no clear sides to label as "other" and treat accordingly. As Kenneth Burke notes, when categories blur "so that you cannot know for certain just where one ends and the other begins, you have the characteristic invitation to rhetoric" (*Rhetoric* 25).

In this trial, the rhetors were lawyers with clients to defend; they were also white males with a major stake in maintaining a hierarchy that placed themselves at the pinnacle. Neither side dared tamper with the collective norms for fear of being rejected as too threatening. Both sides peppered their arguments with references to race and gender that they hoped would serve as "bridging devices" between their clients and the jury. The defense used these devices to make "gender" the critical concept for decision making, while the accusers worked to keep "race" at the forefront. The relative success and failure of their choices reveals much about which concepts weighed more heavily with the white male audiences of the time. The verdict also offers some hope that cultural grounds can be found to balance racial stereotypes.

## The Case of *Rhinelander v. Rhinelander*

> If anything more humiliating to the prestige of white America
> than the Rhinelander case has occurred recently it has escaped our
> attention.
> —W. E. B. Du Bois

Leonard "Kip" Rhinelander had impeccable bloodlines. His family had arrived in New York in the late seventeenth century, and he could account for
every ancestor from that moment. His father was one of the richest men
in the United States. Leonard himself was identified in the *Social Register*
as a bona fide "blue blood." Unfortunately, he did not fit perfectly in the
patrician mold, for he was afflicted from boyhood with a serious stuttering
problem. Although he was by all accounts a perfectly nice and intelligent
young man, his father could never overlook the speech impediment. In 1921,
when Leonard was nineteen, his father sent him to a special boarding school
in Connecticut where doctors supervised his therapy. While at the school,
Leonard made friends with a young man who owned a new automobile. In
the time-honored tradition, they gathered a group, got in the car, and went
cruising. The car broke down in New Rochelle, New York. At the gas station,
one of the young men struck up a conversation with a pretty young girl who
was amenable to riding with them. Leonard was interested in her at first,
but later, when he met her twenty-two-year-old sister, all thoughts of other
women fled his mind.

Alice Jones had no ancestry to recommend her. Her parents had emi-
grated from England. Her father was a taxi driver. Alice herself worked as
a housekeeper at one of the resorts in the area. Her skin was a dark brown,
but depending upon whose story one believes, either Leonard did not notice
or Alice teasingly claimed that her father was Cuban. Either way, she was
pretty, charming, and evidently quite taken with Leonard.

Theirs was not exactly a whirlwind courtship. Alice and Leonard met
secretly for three years. Their sexual liaison (begun in the first year) eventually brought the relationship to the attention of Leonard's father. Philip
Rhinelander, too, followed a time-honored tradition—he packed the young
man off on a six-month cruise to the Orient, hoping distance would cool the
relationship. It did not work. One week after his return, Leonard and Alice
were married.

The couple lived happily for nearly a month. In the meantime, the local press began to hint that a Rhinelander had married a "Negress." Philip
Rhinelander hired detectives to gather concrete evidence, such as Alice's

birth certificate, and then made his move. He sent men to the Jones home to request that Leonard meet him in New York. It took a great deal of convincing, but Leonard agreed. One afternoon he got into a waiting limousine and promised to return home the next day. He never came back. A few weeks later, he filed for an annulment.

Whether Leonard Rhinelander himself was truly repelled by his wife's race can never be known for certain.[2] His reaction to the lawsuit was, however, in tune with the tenor of his time. The Rhinelander case touched sensitive nerves on two issues of significance to both black and white Americans in the early twentieth century: interracial marriage and "passing."

The issue of interracial marriage has been with this country since the Colonial era. White America's concern with interracial marriage was evidenced by the numerous antimiscegenation laws passed to forbid marriage between whites and people of other races. At one time or another until the 1960s, forty-one states or colonies had them. Several of these laws remained in effect until struck down by the Supreme Court in 1967 (*Loving v. Virginia*). When Leonard Rhinelander made his appeal, there were still twenty-nine states prohibiting intermarriage of whites and other races, athough New York was not one of them. So he could not simply "confess" to an illegal marriage and have it dissolved. He instead had to rely on the jury's belief that he would never have knowingly crossed the color line.

The African American community was divided on this issue. While some leaders, such as Mary Church Terrell, felt that marriage was a matter best left up to the individuals involved, others were less charitable. As W. E. B. Du Bois once noted about social circles in Philadelphia, "white wives have always been treated with disdain bordering on insult, and white husbands never received on any terms of social recognition" (Gatewood 179).

Both races tended to emphasize marriages between white women and black men as the major problem. When discussing mixing "between certain classes of whites and mulatto girls," noted sociologist Edward Reuter claimed, despite his own mixed blood, that it only occurred among "the lower classes of both races" (*Race Mixture* 164). The possibility that a blue-blooded white man would marry a working-class black woman was considered outrageous. If Leonard's lawyers could convince the auditors that the possibility was equally outrageous to Leonard himself, there would remain only to prove fraud on the part of his wife.

The possibility that a black woman could hide her race tied the case to the second important issue of the time, passing. The phenomenon was the result of white America's byzantine laws for determining racial categories for persons with mixed blood. By 1915, most of the United States was operating under the "one drop rule." If a person had any black ancestry at all, they were legally classified as black. As a result, a large number of individuals were legally black who otherwise showed few if any of the expected physical characteristics. In the land of Jim Crow, it was often easier to pass as white than to deal with racism on a daily basis.

Passing reached a peak during the 1920s. It was so common that one theater in Washington began to hire black bouncers in the belief that they could detect racial characteristics invisible to whites (Gatewood 337). Thus, it was not irrational to believe that Alice might have been passing when she married Leonard. This claim was marred, however, by the fact that Alice apparently never attempted to hide her race once they began to date. The white fear of passing lent credence to Rhinelander's claim among whites, although the black press was not impressed. As one editorial in *The Messenger* stated, "Of course, everybody knows that he knew that she was colored" ("Editorial: The Rhinelander Case" 388).

The conjunction of these two issues helped make the case a national sensation. From the moment Leonard filed for annulment, the press flocked to cover the story. The *New York Times* sent a full-time reporter to White Plains, where the trial took place. The proceedings made the front page of the *Times* nearly every day for over a month, kicked off only occasionally by other stories.[3] Newspapers as far removed from New York society as the Phoenix (Arizona) *Gazette* gave the story front-page status. At the courthouse, the gallery was packed with people battling for standing room only:

> Long before [the reporter] came, the courtroom was filled to capacity and the doors bolted shut. The lucky hundreds who now sat on the long rows of chairs and stood against the walls had been in their places, the reporters told me, since seven o'clock. Most of them women and most of them white, they were sitting now, dumb and placid, perfectly willing to remain motionless as wood for the resumption of the parade of emotions which they had learned, through the long days of the trial, to expect. (Markey 9)

The judge finally had to order those without seats to be ejected. The entire case was, to put it mildly, a circus.

The most prominent rhetors in the case were the counselors on either side. Leonard had retained Isaac N. Mills, a former appellate judge, and Leon R. Jacobs, the family lawyer. Alice retained Samuel F. Swinburne, a former New Rochelle city judge, and Lee Parsons Davis, a former district attorney for Westchester County. All four men were white.

The trial began with the jury selection. After the voir dire, twelve jurors were selected. All were male, white, married, and from various suburban

New York towns. On the face of it, these men would appear to be perfect for Leonard's lawyers. They were probably well acquainted with the white vision of blacks and familiar with the fears of interracial marriage based on passing. Neither set of lawyers took this presumption for granted, however. The arguments ranged widely, sometimes dwelling on issues that did not appear to be pertinent. Yet, as we shall see, each side was laying the groundwork for the jury to identify with their client.

The proceedings in the case fell into two well-defined sections. The first section developed around the plaintiff's initial claim that Alice Rhinelander had actually lied about her race to her husband. In this phase, both sides accepted Alice's "blackness" and Leonard's "whiteness" as givens. The narratives of the lawyers worked from those givens, producing narratives based on stereotypes of racial character. This phase culminated in the defense's use of rhetorical enactment, when the speaker "incarnates the argument, *is* the proof of the truth of what is said" (Campbell and Jamieson 9), to "prove" to the jury that Alice was incapable of lying.

The second phase developed after the plaintiffs were allowed to amend their plea to one of "negative" fraud. Instead of lying outright, this meant Alice had failed to tell her husband that she was black. Here, the categories of race bend into categories of gender. The plaintiffs attacked the womanly virtues of Alice and her mother. The defense used the common womanhood of Alice and her white mother to create a bridging device that attempted to create identification between the jurors and Alice.[4]

## Part 1: The Enactment of Race

> [I]f Rhinelander had used this girl as a concubine or prostitute, white America would have raised no word of protest; . . . It is when he legally and decently marries the girl that Hell breaks loose and literally tears the pair apart. Magnificent Nordic morality!
> —W. E. B. Du Bois

At the start of the trial, both sides accepted that the legal definition of race was a given, and that by this definition, Alice was black. Despite this common starting place, the plaintiffs spent a good deal of time reading the legal evidence into the file, planting the seeds for a later discussion of her character. Alice had once denied to reporters that she was black (when she and Leonard were still together); now she admitted she had "some negro blood in her veins" ("Rhinelander's Wife Admits" 14). Thus she had been known to lie, if not to Leonard. The legal documents were clear: her father's immigration certificate was marked "colored" and Alice's birth certificate categorized her as "black." When Mills added these to the record, he pointedly noted that Alice was four years older that Leonard: she was an older woman. Mills also took the time to mention that he had sent someone to England to check out her father but was unable to find a birth certificate for him in England. Was there something to hide? Leonard's birth certificate was also offered up to show that he was white, although that had never been at issue.

With that question settled, the two sides created their competing narratives. Although no one ever stated it directly, both sides used stereotypic notions of race. The plaintiffs portrayed Alice as a sexually aggressive woman who lured the younger, more innocent Leonard into an unfortunate liaison. The defense cast Alice as a girl whose innocence arose from her lack of social standing, thus making her emotions exploitable by the wealthy, more sophisticated Leonard. In the end, the defense clinched their argument by "proving" that Alice could not have lied about her race.

The narrative created by the plaintiffs had a great deal of currency in the culture of the 1920s. In this decade, a number of popular novels were published about interracial romance. In them, "there is a sickening trail of lust, an immature white youth and a young mulatto woman, tempting and being tempted" (Shannon 33). They usually ended tragically. The plaintiffs recreated this story for the jury and offered them a chance to change the ending by freeing Leonard before his mistake marred his life forever and conferred "undying disgrace on the family by an alliance with colored blood" ("Calls" 8).

The plaintiff's narrative of the "inexperienced boy and a woman several years older than he" began in the opening statement. Leonard, because he was "tongue-tied," suffered "mental backwardness." He was thus easy prey for Alice, a woman who had been "the mistress of another man" ("Calls" 8). Their claims were bolstered during the trial by testimony from various people, including a governess, the family minister, and the therapist who ran Leonard's special school. Leonard's character emerged in terms that must have been embarrassing for his blue-blooded family, yet it served the purpose of the narrative, which tried to establish that he was a boy easily manipulated. This characterization was repeated in the *Times* by a reporter's description of an unprepossessing Leonard: "There was an expression of bewilderment in his eyes, which peered through heavy glasses, and an intense effort at concentration. When he attempted to speak it was usually with violent physical effort, which showed in his tense muscles. His hands clasped and unclasped over his knees, and then words would suddenly shoot forth, spasmodically, brokenly, sometimes only in a rapid mumble in which his meaning was indistinguishable" ("Rhinelander Tells Story" 1).

Alice, on the other hand, was described as looking unconcerned about the proceeding, except when she occasionally bent her "dark head" to her handkerchief. Her ensemble, consisting of a "tigth [*sic*] fitting tan gown, black silk stockings and black pumps" highlighted her sexual charms ("Rhinelander Tells Story" 8). The reporter was obviously playing to the narrative's characterization of her.

The implicit proof of Alice's sexual aggressiveness lay in the white vision of black womanhood. As Patricia Collins notes, one of the "controlling images" of black women within the white male system is "the Jezebel, whore, or sexually aggressive woman" (77). This myth served to control black women by controlling images of her sexuality. If every "black woman was, by definition, a slut . . . to assault her and exploit her sexually was not reprehensible" (Lerner 163). Alice was black, therefore she had to be the instigator of the sexual liaison with Leonard.

With her natural tendency for sexual looseness a given, Alice's every move could be construed as strategic. "There were several stages in this woman's attack on the boy" ("Calls" 8). To prove her designs were shady from the start, the plaintiff's lawyers obtained from Leonard all the love letters Alice had written him during their courtship and had them read into the record over a period of four days. The letters were "pleading, cajoling, threatening, suggesting" and "aroused pity and anger and disgust" ("Rhinelander Tells of Baring" 1). Their purpose was clear: as the *Times* subheading noted, "Illiterate Love Notes Put Before Jury to Show Negress Wooed Him" ("Rhinelander Tells of Baring" 1). Every line Alice wrote was framed within the racial stereotype, so not a word could be construed as innocent.

By modern standards, the letters are tame, but at the time some of them were considered racy enough that the judge barred all underage citizens from the courtroom and asked the women in the audience to leave (they stayed). On the surface, they told a story of adolescent love that would be familiar to the audience. Alice's tactics were quite basic, as when she would make a point of telling Leonard about the other men who wanted to date her—turned down, of course: "There was a nice young chap, came hear [*sic*] the other day, of Mrs. Hubbard's, and he wanted me to make a date with him. I said no, I had one what I really cared a lot for" ("Loved" 8). She also told him whenever her loyalty made her turn down a chance for fun. She claimed once that Al Jolson, who was "some flirt with the girls," had made flirtatious conversation with her at the resort hotel where she was a maid, and that she gave up a chance to party with Irving Berlin: "Well my darling talk about men up hear. All a girl wants. Berlin the musical fellow has gotten a camp right next to us. He is a swell chap, and lots of actors hear" ("Told Rhinelander" 1).

All these statements came back to haunt her, for the plaintiffs actually called Jolson to the stand to testify that he had never met her and Berlin issued a denial. Thus, even a little self-aggrandizement became evidence that she was plotting to ensnare Leonard. When she disingenuously pretended not to want a gift that she was fishing for, she was branded as greedy. When she put popular song lyrics into her letters without attribution, she was scrutinized as a plagiarist ("Rhinelander Verses" 6). The overall impression the plaintiffs tried to create was of a woman who would have no scruples about lying about her race if it was necessary to win herself a rich husband. Most damning of the letters was the one in which she revealed to Leonard that she was not a virgin: "Len dear, I often think, I am awful soary [*sic*], I wished I knew you before I knew that Al Rose you would have gotten a pure girl, but darling I have been truthful, to tell you how I stood, also shown you in letter black and white, because I always want you to trust me, around other men" ("Rhinelander Tells of Baring" 10).

One would think that this letter, wherein Alice confesses to the one thing she was convinced might stand between them, would speak for her honesty. In the racist framing of her character, however, all it does is reveal her superior sexual experience and brand her as another man's mistress. This framing holds that "all black women were incapable of fidelity and sexually loose" (hooks 61). Even the newspaper reports that admitted Alice sounded sincerely in love did not defend her from charges against her morals.

Leonard was called to the stand several times to augment the letters with his version of the story. He claimed that most of their sexual escapades were her idea. He also claimed that both Alice and her father had at least once lied to him about their race. From the testimony, it appears that Alice only mentioned the matter once. She was telling Leonard a story and within it implied that her father was a Spaniard: "She told me she had become acquainted with a Harvard man in the Adirondacks and he asked Alice, 'What are you?' and Alice said, 'I'm of Spanish extraction.'" ("Loved Rhinelander" 8). Again, stereotypes found in real life made his story more believable, for one of the most common forms of passing among darker-skinned blacks was to adapt "Spanish, Portuguese, or other Latin names that explained their color and features well enough" (Williamson 100–101). Leonard claims that he took the implication of the story at face value.

Alice's family was viewed as more obviously involved in a cover-up. For example, when one of Alice's sisters married a black man, her father took it as a disgrace upon the family, "telling me [Leonard] they were not colored, they were English" ("Loved Rhinelander" 8). Since Alice's other sister had married a white man, Leonard might be forgiven for becoming confused, but he again took the statement as proof Alice was white. There were no other witnesses to these statements, but Alice's character had been drawn so as to make them believable. Black people wanted to pass and did so by claiming foreign blood. The Jones family could be expected to try the same tactic. English extraction did not explain their dark features as well as Spanish, but Leonard was not sophisticated enough to question the explanations. In other words, in the plaintiff's narrative, Alice's race makes it impossible for her to be genuinely in love with Leonard. She was only following her natural inclination to use sexuality as a way to climb the socioeconomic ladder. There might have been sexual passion, but it was used by her as a tool to gain the prize: a rich white husband.

Alice's defenders knew that they had to challenge these negative characterizations in order to redeem her. They first made it clear that in their version of the story, this "son of wealth enters a home to get a girl, and it is not enough that he gets her, but because papa becomes cross he must drag her in the slime as well, crush not her alone, but her whole family" ("Rhinelander's Wife Admits" 14). Where the plaintiffs created an untried boy and a Jezebel, the defense created a little girl and a bounder: "If they start calling this girl black in that way, referring to her character, I'll show who is the pot calling the kettle black" ("Rhinelander's Wife Admits" 14).

At the same time as they refuted the plaintiff's racist narrative, they drew upon another stereotypic element of race to create a different outcome. By calling upon accepted generalizations about the physiological features of blackness, they set the stage for a grandstand play of enactment to prove that Alice, regardless of what the jury thought of her character, could not lie. The attack on Leonard's character was twofold. The first move was to prove that Leonard was not as backwards as the plaintiffs claimed: "They say she led this innocent youth to the Marie Antoinette Hotel, but he knew enough to sign the register" ("Rhinelander's Wife Admits" 14). The second move was to call upon a white stereotype—that "magnificent Nordic morality" referred to by Du Bois, to show that Leonard was violating all principles of decent manliness.

Their initial moves were what might be expected. When Leonard's therapist testified to his mental state, Davis brought out the doctor's journal to show that since meeting Alice, Leonard stammered less and was more responsive. Perhaps Alice was actually good for him? The doctor also admitted that Leonard occasionally was able to take the social initiative at school: "So he was the life of the party and talked without stammering?. . . . Yes" ("Rhinelander's Wife Admits" 14). The defense also refuted the claim that Alice was the aggressor. Under questioning, Rhinelander admitted that the hotel was his idea, and that Alice had at first refused to go until he argued with her for "about twenty minutes" ("Rhinelander Tells of Baring" 12). Rhinelander was also attacked for giving his wife's personal love letters to his lawyers, a horrible betrayal that no red-blooded man would countenance. The *Times* reported the pivotal moment as follows:

> "You promised this little girl to keep them safe?" said Davis, turning to his client, who sat weeping into her handkerchief.
>
> "Yes."
>
> "But for your own benefit you agreed to let them be read?"
>
> "Yes, on the advice of counsel."
>
> "You are a man," demanded Davis, his head thrust forward. "And a gentleman?"
>
> There was a long pause, and when the answer, "I try to be," came from reluctant lips there was a titter in the room.
>
> "And yet for your own benefit you were willing to break this sacred promise. And you still consider yourself a man," Davis said with sarcasm. ("Rhinelander Tells of Baring" 10)

Leonard's reputation was tarnished, but he was firm in his claim that using the letters was his lawyers' idea and that he believed he had no other recourse. Since this might have weakened the attack on his character, one more tactic was added. On November 18, the defense decided to have a couple of letters from Leonard entered into the record, letters that Davis referred to as "filth" ("Rhinelander Says He Pursued" 4). Alice, it seems, had had enough of hearing her own letters read. Using the letters as leverage, they grilled Leonard until he admitted that *he* had less-than-pristine motives. He wanted to have sex with Alice well before he had even considered marrying her, and did his best to achieve that goal.

Alice, on the other hand, was nothing but "ladylike" until Leonard worked on her ("Rhinelander Says He Pursued" 4). As a black woman, Alice was, of course, more subject to sexual passion than a white one, but the pointed question for Leonard was "What did you do to play on that sex urge in Alice?" ("Rhinelander Says He Pursued" 4). This was an important moment, for here Alice was transformed from villainess to victim. As a scion of an important family, Leonard, more than anyone, should have been aware of the requirements of proper manhood. If he truly believed that Alice was white, how could he possibly have treated her so shabbily? Asked Davis, "What is the worse deception, to lead a girl to believe you want to marry her and take that which is most precious to a woman, or for her to say she is white and not colored?" Leonard's reply, not surprisingly, was, "The latter" ("Rhinelander Says He Pursued" 4).

Just in case there were jury members who agreed with him, the defense had a second narrative, one based on another set of stereotypes. For this, the lawyers depended not upon secondhand evidence, but upon a direct rhetorical strategy of enactment. As Davis stated, "He knew what the Jones family was . . . if he didn't he was not suffering from mental weakness, but from blindness" ("Rhinelander Wife Admits" 14).

Again, enactment is when the speaker embodies the argument. In this case, the claim was that black racial characteristics are so obvious that a person can tell by looking whether a person is white or black. That claim was not out of line with common beliefs. In fact, it was so prevalent that a "scientific" study was finally done in 1932 to categorize the physical effects of mixed blood. The most important traits were "swarthy skin, frizzly hair, and heavy features" (Williamson 126). There was no scientific evidence to go on in 1925, but the defense was counting on the belief that one could "know it when he saw it."

Obviously, in cases of mixed blood, some of those features might be obscured. The defense eliminated this possibility by beginning with Alice's family, starting with members who were fully black, working their way to her father, and finally to Alice. Thus, the jury was predisposed by the time Alice made her own most compelling argument. The *Times* at first referred to the strategy as "comedy" ("Rhinelander Says He Pursued" 4). The defense made family member after family member stand before Leonard and asked him whether that person looked black. Since the Jones family was of mixed blood, the defense began with Robert Brooks, Alice's brother-in-law, whom Markey of the *New Yorker* characterized as "an honest Virginia Negro" (9). Then sister Emily, who was "undeniably of colored blood" stood ("Rhinelander Says He Pursued" 4). Leonard had claimed that he never wanted any connection with persons of colored blood, yet he visited the Brooks frequently and even played poker with their friends.

The second sister, Grace, was asked to stand. The *Times* reporter, at least, considered her to be "unmistakably of colored blood" ("Rhinelander Says He Pursued" 4). Finally, Mr. Jones himself stood up. He, too, was deemed an "unmistakable Negro" by the *Times* reporter ("Rhinelander Suit Suddenly Halted") and as "palpably Negroid, despite his aquiline nose" by Markey (9). This categorization might serve as evidence that the strategy was working, for Mills was of the opinion that Jones's "features were all those of a Caucasian," but his perception was not shared ("Jones Interrupts" 3). Leonard stated that Jones had claimed to be "an Englishman with the jaundice." Since Leonard had known Jones for three years, Davis asked, "Didn't it strike you he had had that jaundice for some time?" When pressed, Leonard admitted, "He looks darker to me now" ("Rhinelander Suit Halted" 9). He did not back down when it came to Alice, however. While admitting she was "very dark," he insisted that her skin was not "any darker than the arms of women I have seen in Havana" ("Rhinelander Wilts" 6).

When faced with the Jones family in court, Leonard admitted that most of its members looked black. Yet he insisted that Alice did not look black. This set the stage for the final ploy of the defense, a classic use of enactment to convince the jury that anyone would recognize Alice as black. It is arguably one of the more shameful moments in the courtroom, but it was extremely effective.

> Mrs. Rhinelander was told to go into the jury room, where before the jury and a lawyer from each side she bared her body to the waist. She was crying as she was led into the room, and crying as she left it. . . . Rhinelander, also in the room, seemed reluctant to look at his wife, but Mr. Davis insisted. When they returned to the court room Mr. Davis asked:
> "Your wife's body is the same shade as when you saw her in the Marie Antoinette?"
> "Yes," said Rhinelander.
> "That's all," said Mr. Davis, and the long cross-examination was over. ("Rhinelander's Wife Cries" 3).

It did not matter whether Alice really did embody her race, what mattered was whether the jury believed it. The defense had led up to the moment carefully by introducing her family until a predisposition had been created. Then they asked Alice to show the jury what her husband saw in the bedroom. The vision was planted: Alice could not possibly have lied about her race, for her own body would have given her away. This strategy had its price; the next day Alice was too distraught to appear in court. The plaintiffs suggested that this was a ploy to avoid having to testify right after Leonard, ignoring the fact that she had just made the most eloquent testimony of all.

The success of the enactment is evidenced by the fact that the very next day the plaintiffs entered a request to amend their charges. Instead of affirmative fraud, which required proof that Alice lied to Leonard, they wished to charge negative fraud, which required proof only that Alice had never said she was black. The defense exploded: "First they say she said too much, and now they say she said nothing" ("Rhinelander Asks" 3). Despite strenuous objections from the defense, the judge allowed the amendment. This set the stage for the second phase of the trial.

## Part 2: Gender as a Bridging Device

When the trial resumed after the change of plea, the defense complained that their plan for the case had been severely disrupted. The proceedings, however, revealed that they still had a few weapons. Although the narratives thus far had played with notions of gender, such as the attack on Leonard's lack of gentlemanly virtue or the implication that black women were sexually aggressive, gender had not been central to the issue of whether Alice had lied. It probably was not central to the issue of whether Alice withheld the truth, either, except that the plaintiffs decided to use sexual "dishonesty" as a point of attack upon several witnesses, including Alice's mother. The defense took the point and made rhetorical hay from it, using gender as a bridging device to change the focus of the case from black/white to man/woman.

Kenneth Burke has noted that rhetoric can be used as a device for "transcending social estrangement" (*Rhetoric* 208). He terms the use of such devices "courtship," a metaphor quite appropriate for the Rhinelander case. Although Burke's example is a poem about a woman/goddess lowering herself to love a male/mortal, it can hold equally true for a narrative about a man/white/blue blood who "lowers" himself to love a woman/black/maid. As mentioned in chapter 2, a bridging device is a symbol that shares substantive elements of more than one social category, creating those "areas of ambiguity" from which one can transform meaning (*Attitudes* 224).

The racial makeup of the parties involved in the Rhinelander case became ambiguous quickly and not just because of the mixed blood of the Jones family. Leonard, although white, was not a clear symbolic embodiment of his race, given his physical disabilities and lack of gentlemanly virtue. One thing that was clear, however, was that Alice and her mother were incontrovertibly women while their foes were men. Alice's mother was clearly white, the same race as the jury. In the movement from ambiguous to clear positions arose fertile ground for rhetorical transcendence.

At first it did not seem that a bridging device would be necessary. The defense had a slate of witnesses to nail Leonard down tightly as to what he did and did not know and when he knew it. A reporter testified that when she cornered him after the marriage, Leonard admitted his wife was black but asked her to keep it quiet. In other words, he knew before his father supposedly swooped down and told him. It did not, however, prove he knew before he married her. For that point in the timetable, the defense had a firsthand witness: the Rhinelander chauffeur. The driver who who took him to the couple's trysts testified that he was appalled at who Leonard was dating and asked him outright, "I said, 'Don't you know her father is a colored man?' And he said, 'I don't give a damn if he is.'" ("Says Rhinelander Knew" 3). Alice did not have to tell Leonard anything, he had been told.

The response of the plaintiffs was representative of how they handled much of the rest of the case. When they could not shake his story, they had read into the record that the driver was paying support for an illegitimate child and was certainly no one to judge Leonard's sexual behavior ("Mrs. Rhinelander"). The technique of questioning the morals of a witness was also used on Alice's mother Elizabeth. Mrs. George Jones took the stand for the defense to testify that she had never heard Alice or Leonard discuss race in her home.[5] She was not prepared for what would happen on cross-examination. Suddenly, she was under attack on several points. First, she was asked to recall what she was doing thirty-five years ago in England. The plaintiffs had discovered a discrepancy in the birth certificate of her eldest child: Alice's eldest sister had been born out of wedlock, and George Jones was not the father. He had married Elizabeth and raised the child as his own. The details of her indiscretion were painfully pulled from her, ostensibly to evaluate "whether this woman guarded, as you contended, these young people" ("Says Rhinelander Knew" 3). Naturally, a woman who could not guard her own virtue was not fit to guard her daughter's.

Remarkably, this was an accusation made by the plaintiffs. She had to defend her ability as a mother to protect her daughter's virtue. Leonard had confessed to occasionally lying about going on trips with Alice in the company of other adults when their real goal was a hotel room. The defense had used this to show that Leonard was not as innocent as he had claimed. The plaintiffs used it as a tool to attack Mrs. Jones. Why hadn't she suspected something was up? Didn't she worry? Didn't she check? Alice was once gone for two days, yet neither she nor her husband called the Missing Persons Bureau. By the end of the cross-examination, it had become *her* fault that the youngsters were lying to her. The defense did some repair during the reexamination, bringing up that she had been only eighteen years old at the birth of her first child. It was also noted that although George Jones knew the truth, the children were learning it at the same moment as the rest of the world.

When court resumed after Thanksgiving, the plaintiffs got their first warning that attacking Alice's mother might not have been a good idea. The defense announced that it had decided not to call Alice to the stand. She was still upset about having to show her body to strangers. The manner in which the plaintiffs treated her mother had convinced the defense that she would only be subjected to a similar ordeal: "It struck me that it was just about time the world was through with the slime of this case. . . . Would you have us sit here and watch them drag this girl in the sewer?" ("Mrs. Rhinelander" 12).

Davis quickly assumed the role of protector, conveniently forgetting that Alice still had a father: "I am the only one to stand between this young girl and absolute ruin" ("Mrs. Rhinelander" 12). Over the next few days, and

throughout his summation, Davis hammered at gender roles in an attempt
to separate Alice and Leonard from their racial categories. In so doing, he
created a "perspective by incongruity" that showed the jury who was really living up to the standards set by whites. Perspective by incongruity is
a method for " extending the use of a term by taking it from the context in
which it was habitually used and applying it to another" (Burke, *Permanence*
79). In this case, constructions usually reserved by whites for their own race
were shown to be applicable to someone ostensibly belonging to the "other."
It was a fitting strategy, for it "is designed to 'remoralize' by accurately nam-
ing a situation already demoralized by inaccuracy" (Burke, *Attitudes* 309).
Gender "remoralized" everyone to the extent that the principles came to
embody important symbolic aspects of both races.

First, the plaintiffs were characterized as violators of white masculine roles.
Instead of protectors of womanhood and defenders of the family, they acted
as fiends, destroying not only the Jones family but the eldest daughter who
was suddenly branded illegitimate: "My God . . . How can the Rhinelanders
ever forgive themselves? They allowed their senior counsel to disgrace this
mother, to disgrace another mother and her five children—for what? For
nothing!" ("Mrs. Rhinelander" 12). Leonard Rhinelander was no gentleman,
for he ruined Alice, then "was willing to bare her past that she got from him
to win this lawsuit" ("Rhinelander Jury" 3). Philip Rhinelander was no better,
hiring investigators to unearth private love letters and expose their content
to the public. Davis reserved his deepest disgust for Mills. It was Mills who
cross-examined Elizabeth Jones and forced her to reveal her shame. As Davis put it, "I don't know of what death by burning is to be preferred to the
living death which Judge Mills has brought to this old woman. . . . I'd rather
be burned at the stake than as a 75 year old man stand before her and tear
from her that secret of her eighteen year old girlhood. This is a living death"
("Mrs. Rhinelander" 12).

George Jones embodies the more manly virtues. When Elizabeth became
pregnant with another man's child, he married her and raised the child as
his own. He could have shamed her; instead he saved her. Davis here made
his most blatant statement of the symbolic point: "Many a white heart beats
under a dark skin" ("Mrs. Rhinelander" 12). The women are portrayed as
victims of a conspiracy to destroy "every scrap of respectability that a woman
loves most" ("Mrs. Rhinelander" 12).

While the focus was on Alice and her mother, even her sisters were not safe.
One sister was branded illegitimate. Another saw her interracial marriage
discussed in the daily papers. Elizabeth was a dedicated "little woman" who
made sacrifices for her daughters only to have Mills question her every move

("Mrs. Rhinelander"). She worked all her life to hold her family together only to see that family destroyed. Most importantly for the narrative, this family was modeled upon the traditional working-class white family. After all, they were English in spirit, no matter what one thought of their bodies.

As a daughter of that class, Alice was especially vulnerable. Davis paints her as a victim of the gender roles of her class rather than of her race. She was a simple housemaid while her traducer was a scion of a wealthy family. His superior social standing completely outweighed the difference in their ages. If the conspiracy succeeded, Alice would belong to neither race: "she will walk out of court shunned by the colored race and shunned by the white race" ("Rhinelander Jury" 3). The jury bore the burden of deciding whether this woman was to become a complete outcast.

In his summation of the plaintiff's position, Mills pointedly ignored these issues in favor of characterizations he thought would carry more weight with the jury. Initially, he deflected some ill will toward Leonard by emphasizing the role his father had played in rearing the boy as an outcast. It was Philip Rhinelander, by violating his role as a father, who made Leonard less of a man. Leonard is thus as much a victim of role violation in this debacle as is Alice. After this initial sortie, however, he focused on the women. He stayed within the realm of racial stereotypes, peppered with direct appeals to racism.

In his favor, it must be said that Mills backpedaled mightily in his attacks on Elizabeth Jones. He did it in such a racist manner, however, that the modern reader shudders. Of course Mrs. Jones was a good mother who wanted the best for her daughters; that is exactly why she schemed so mightily to acquire white husbands for them. If that white man also happened to be rich, so much the better. Leonard was, in effect, the brass ring on the merry-go-round. Mrs. Jones behaved exactly as could be expected.

Alice, for her part, was understandably upset, but that was her own fault for daring to reach too high. Mills vacillated between the sexual/unsophisticated stereotypes as he described her deliberate seduction of Leonard and her inability to appreciate the social outlandishness of her position. In the end, she was painted as too shallow to be hurt by the proceedings: "After that indecent exhibition in the jury room, she shed tears, . . . And they were genuine tears, for what woman would not weep after such thing. But with the buoyancy of her race she will regain her spirits. She will rally when the scandal passes. Let her gain a husband of her own race and find happiness with him as did her sister, Emily, who without vaulting ambition wed within her own color and kind" ("Lays" 3).

The narrative of fatherless boy seduced by social-climbing woman was framed by direct appeals to the racism of the jury. Marriage to a black woman was cast as a fate worse than death, and Mills counted on the jury to believe this and to save the boy's life. He opened by appealing to the jury's fatherly instincts, stating that there "is not a father among you—and I tried to fill this jury box with fathers—who would not rather see his son in a casket then wedded to this mulatto woman" ("Lays" 3). He ended with a plea for mercy more suited to a capital case than to an annulment: "You should have no hesitation in giving this young man a chance to live, a chance to redeem himself. I am through. I leave this young man, 22 years old, in your hands. Relieve him from this horrid, unnatural, absurd and terrible union. I pray you grant him deliverance" ("Jones Interrupts" 3).

The jury was left with two narratives, one that appealed directly to race-based narratives about the evils of race mixing and one that appealed instead to gender-based concepts of womanhood and family. Importantly, the latter narrative had been deliberately wrenched away from the gender characterizations that these white men might have held about black women and placed squarely into characterizations that they might have held about white women.

The jury deliberated for twelve hours. It was leaked that for a time jurors were deadlocked ten votes to two, but in the end, the jury unanimously found in favor of Alice Rhinelander. The annulment was denied. If Leonard wanted to separate from Alice, he would have to divorce her. When interviewed afterward, one juror stated that "race prejudice didn't enter into the case at all" and that it was decided as "a case between a man and a woman." A second juror agreed. Only one juror hinted that "if we had voted according to our hearts the verdict might have been different" ("Rhinelander Loses" 27).[6]

## Conclusions

> The brilliant defense of this case in question and the fair
> mindedness of judges and juries are to be thanked for the outcome,
> but it leaves many morals to ponder. And not the least of these
> concerns the hazards of young and attractive Negro girls who are
> not uncommonly looked upon as safe prey.
> —"Rhinelander Suit," *Opportunity* editorial

The strategies used in the Rhinelander case graphically demonstrate the extent to which judgments of racial categories are subject to rhetorical manipulation. The results of these manipulations provide important lessons about the rhetoric of race and gender.

The evaluation of Alice's body, ostensibly as empirical a demonstration of race as could possibly exist, made use of rhetorical stereotypes to alter the jury's perception of where she belonged. By identifying her with stereotypes held by whites about blacks and then literally placing her alongside a racial "spectrum," the defense team turned a woman who was technically three-quarters white into an icon of the black body. She suddenly enacted her race so well that her "blackness" would overwhelm any statements she might have made to the contrary. All the physical attributes accepted as "givens" for racial categorization were turned on their ears. Whereas the first half of the trial revolved around a woman defined by her race, the second showed a black person defined as white through her gender. In this case, Elizabeth Jones served as a bridging device. Through her womanhood, a bridge could be built from her whiteness to Alice's blackness, allowing Alice to be evaluated according to ideals of white womanhood and making her an icon of her sex. From there, it was a matter of defining crimes against womanhood as more salient that crimes against a white male who was obviously less than "white" in his heart.

This strategy was a masterful way to allow the jury to vote in favor of an individual, Alice, despite her ostensible membership in a suspect class. By dialectically wrenching her from the category of race to the supposedly equally obvious category of gender, it was possible for the white male participants to avoid the injustice demanded by the social structure without dismantling that structure, which was, after all, the basis of their social and economic power. The success of this strategy is heartening, for it shows that it is possible for a common ground of symbolic qualities shared by two races to overcome racist stereotypes. By all the stereotypes we hold about whites in the 1920s, typified by Mills's racist appeals, the jury should have been more than willing to consign Alice to ruination because of her race. The use of gender to create identification allowed them to break through their stereotypic notions and see the case as a defense of womanhood, regardless of race. The hope engendered by this strategy is tempered by the fact that the participants were freed of these notions in only one specific case. The racist categories were not dismantled, although their place in the hierarchy was significantly reduced. The gender stereotypes used were no more enlightened than the racial ones, and they, too, remained intact.

Finally, it is important to note that the gender stereotypes used were only effective because they appealed to the values of the dominant group: Alice and her father were ennobled because they met white expectations, not because black gender expectations were to be admired. This strategy attempted to erase racial barriers by making everybody white.

Despite the caveats, there is much to be learned from studying techniques through which to shift our perceptions of categories within a social hierarchy. If, as Burke often implies, hierarchies are inevitable, then our best hope for fomenting social change is to unearth the classes of terms that comprise our hierarchies and reveal from whence they derive their rhetorical power. This effort is a possible way to "systematically extend the range of rhetoric, if one studies the persuasiveness of false or inadequate terms which may not be directly imposed upon us from without by some skillful speaker, but which we impose upon ourselves, in varying degrees of deliberateness and unawareness, through motives indeterminately self protective and/or suicidal" (*Rhetoric* 35).

If human culture will persist in ordering terms, the least a rhetorical critic can do is search for ways to make "false or inadequate" terms less damaging, either by redefining the terms themselves or, as in this case, reorganizing their place in the hierarchy. "Race" is so easily destabilized that it must be treated as a contested term, its meaning shifting with the rhetorical strategies summoned by the rhetor. Only by knowing what race means to a specific rhetorical community can we create bridging devices of our own, ones that may enable us to find common ground for understanding and appreciating "others," each group on its own terms.

# Conclusion

*Womanhood as Narrative*

## Plus ça change

In the search for a common thread uniting the use of gendered narratives in legal arguments, one eventually comes to the conclusion that the only surety is that there was no surety. The overarching narrative framework that dictated feminine roles was a clear as any rhetorical construction could be, yet that clarity provided no safe formula that could be used by an individual—female or male—to guarantee a particular outcome.

In the courtroom, the evaluation of human behavior was made under strict rules of law and evidence created by males who maintained that the facts were "ungendered." These rules were ancient, venerable, and embedded in the culture of the Anglo-American legal system. Of all the rhetorical strategies that occurred, questioning these suppositions and procedures did not; one does not expect men who were the product of their times to consider the rhetorical impact of legal procedures as they might be applied centuries later.

The sacredness with which these procedures were endowed made later efforts to alter the rules extremely difficult. Even today, a belief in the purity of the law helps to maintain the idea that gendered narratives have no effect upon legal decision making. Feminist legal scholars attribute a great deal of trouble to the denial of the existence of gender-based narratives: "Women's disempowerment is a function of the culturally embedded belief in the neutrality and objectivity of the law. If the system is ungendered, the argument goes, then the representation of gender within the system must be, by definition, neutral and objective and, thus, true" (Heinzelman 90).

Rhetorical scholars recognize that in the realm of practical decision making, the "facts" can only be given voice by human actors who are products of their particular cultural milieu. The present volume is aimed at demonstrating how that voice was created by the predominantly male agents of the nineteenth century. If the echoes of those voices occasionally have an uncomfortably contemporary ring, it is further evidence of the staying power of these narratives in American culture.

Those echoes are evidence that the popular concepts that infused the legal arena still influence public and private decisions concerning the role of women in contemporary society. In order to demonstrate this, I will begin with a summary of the insights presented in each case analysis and follow with a discussion of the implications of the narrative for modern advocates.

## Common Threads

Although they cover a wide range of possible "crimes" spread over a century of legal history, the cases in this volume exhibit some underlying insights for students of rhetoric and popular culture. Despite the premise that the law was unisex—that murder is murder and madness is madness whatever the principals' sex—gendered narratives were still major tools in the lawyers' arsenal. These men were well aware that, regardless of the law, juries still required rhetorical appeals. These appeals were partly grounded in the law and partly in the cultural narratives that imbued their lives.

Of course, those lives were male. The frequent juror confusion over whether or when to take womanhood under consideration reveals the pitfalls of excluding one sex entirely from the legal discussion of gender roles. The resulting lack of information concerning issues classified as "feminine" hampered juries in decision making. In addition, the mystery of womanhood sometimes allowed male rhetors to use women's bodies as battlegrounds. Often, a woman's circumstances were exploited by men to argue for their own interests. Since male jurors found women's lives mysterious, a skilled rhetor could capitalize on stereotypes that men had without having to consider what a woman may actually have known. Physicians and lawyers could freely argue that their side "understood" women best in their attempts to gain legal control over female bodies. Women became "womanhood" on a regular basis, and defense of womanhood occasionally justified horrific behavior.

Lawyers were not necessarily guilty parties in this exploitation. The narratives related to the feminine character have been demonstrated to have had a strong effect on American culture. No rhetor is culture free. One clear result of the metaphor of "separate spheres" was that men were *expected* to be as ignorant of the realities of women's lives as women presumably were of men's. Entire universes of knowledge and experience were denied to the men whose job it was to construct interpretations of events. Thus, there was not much information other than stereotypes upon which to make decisions. These stereotypes, since they were unlikely to come from experience, had to be gleaned from another source: thus, the wholesale use of characterizations and plotlines lifted from the popular media of the day.

Reliance upon masculine constructions as guides to womanhood was not limited to the law. The separation of sexes was also firmly established in another venerable masculine establishment, medicine. The medical profession was in a state of upheaval in the nineteenth century; therefore, when it attempted to cement its authority, it spoke with much volume and force. Challenges were not taken lightly. This volume touches upon several unfortunate examples where the challenge was taken up in the middle of a woman's life-or-death legal battle. Her case could cease to be about *her* and instead become focused on who had the right to speak *for* her. In these cases, the medical emphasis upon the body meant that a woman's body was her own worst enemy.

The most obvious physicians to take their stand over a woman's body were the "mad doctors," representatives of the burgeoning field of psychiatry. Elizabeth Parsons Ware Packard was perhaps the first woman to successfully take control of her body in the face of medical opposition. Ironically, her victory made psychiatrists fight harder for control of women's bodies, which probably made trials and commitment hearings more difficult for other women. In the ensuing years, physicians made certain that their interests were represented. As the reader may recall, the leading physician to be defeated by Packard made sure that his opinions were included in the Lincoln case.

Mary Lincoln arguably suffered from a mental imbalance; most of the arguing in her case concerned degree. Yet the medical opinions offered in her case still demonstrated that it was Lincoln's female body that determined her fate. According to the cult of domesticity, Mary Lincoln personified womanhood at its peak of perfection. These virtues, however, were spiritual rather than physical. Her imprisonment was based upon the "objective" observation of her behavior. By focusing only upon Lincoln's body in specific, the arguers were able to avoid discussion of whether the roles imposed upon women in general might be a catch-22.

The case of Mary Harris was the archetypal battle of law and the medical profession. It has long been a truism that the medical profession believed that women's fates were determined by their female bodies (Smith-Rosenberg, *Disorderly Conduct*). The Harris case shows that the medical narrative also rang true with cultural narratives held by a jury of laymen.

Despite the number of medical victories, it should be emphasized that some of these cases showed that it was possible to overturn these dominant narrative. In fact, by simply adding a female voice to the legal arena, sometimes jurors come to completely different decisions. After freeing herself, Packard became a tireless advocate for legal reform by raising her voice in the legislature, which seemed to be willing to hear a woman's arguments. Sidestepping the court in order to reach a different "jury" could have results that moved back into the court. For example, Mary Lincoln's two trials were differentiated by the inclusion of a woman's perspective in the second. Myra Bradwell, barred from the courtroom because of her sex, was able to apply her legal training and her practical knowledge of women's lives in the popular press. She almost singlehandedly won Lincoln a new trial. There a group of "objective" males reversed the decision of a previous group of "objective" males. Had it not been for her "feminine" reinterpretation of what disordered females needed to recover, Lincoln would have spent the rest of her days in an asylum.

Bradwell's success is also a testament to the power of narrative to cross fields of argument. Bradwell used the popular press to create a tide of sentiment that forced the court to reevaluate Lincoln's case. A woman's point of view was not allowed into the case directly, but a narrative read by the male decision makers (and perhaps their wives) could get certain important elements imported into the arguments.

Of course, that transference of narrative was a two-edged sword. As Lizzie Borden discovered, when there was no other evidence to be had, the men in charge of her case used the fact that she did not behave like a typical overemotional female as proof that she was a potential murderer. If a woman does not love her stepmother and does not weep at the death of her father, then there is something clearly wrong with her character. Because these stereotypes were based on fictitious, rather than real, relationships, it was equally simple for the men in charge of her defense to redefine them as the natural responses of a frail woman overwhelmed by shock. Interpretations of the concrete evidence that might have been useful, such as the correct dress for morning visits, the proper care of furs, or the best way to dispose of ruined fabric, were in women's sphere. The arguers sanctioned by the court were out of their element.

Although the determination of mental competence or whether a crime has been committed are clearly vital in a court of law, the close relationship of popular and legal narrative also affected women who never entered a court-room. As the century progressed, physicians cemented their control over women's bodies through the legislation of abortion. Throughout this period, rhetors turned again and again to the body of Ann Lohman, a.k.a. Madame Restell. As Lincoln before her, Lohman became a physical embodiment of a complex system of beliefs about womanhood. And, as usual, arguing about her enabled the males in the legal system to avoid addressing the role of men in perpetuating these beliefs and behaviors. Hiding behind a woman's body was not merely a tactic for a villain in a melodrama.

It was not always a safe tactic, however. For a woman's body is not "woman-hood." "Woman" is a rhetorical concept, and is as such subject to any number of transformations. In fact, on rare occasions the rhetoric will outweigh the body in the minds of the jury members. Symbolic manipulation once served to transform a black woman into a white woman. Despite the fact that the jury in the Rheinlander case looked directly at Alice Rhinelander's body and agreed that she was a member of one racial group, her lawyers were able to convince them that she was the embodiment of another. Given that the case arose during the height of American fears of race mixing, this transformation was all the more remarkable.

In every case discussed, the tenets of womanhood served as transforma-tive tools. Is the tendency toward violence different between the sexes? Are women closer to madness than men? Are there crimes that only women can commit? The answer to this question is, at best, "sometimes." These cases demonstrated that the answer to these "factual" questions depends heavily upon the rhetorical tactics of the arguer and the cultural materials that are brought to bear upon a case.

## *Plus c'est la même chose*

Although the cases here might be from an era long past, they have much to say about the present. One might be inclined to note that the nineteenth century was clearly a modernist culture, where grand narratives about gender and sex roles could easily be imposed upon the populace and norms of feminine behavior more directly enforced. In today's postmodern welter of simultane-ous narratives communicated in dozens of technological avenues undreamed of by antebellum storytellers, surely a few outdated cultural norms enforcing the destiny of the female body would have much less power to oppress.

However, the heralded death of the grand narrative seems premature. As social norms begin to shift and change and new gender narratives seek to exploit those uncertainties, those in the culture resistant to change turn right back to the courts to enforce the old narratives. The law is one powerful arena in which narrative is, to borrow a term from popular culture, "not quite dead yet." The court has traditionally been both a target and a major actor in the pursuit of social change.

Obviously, the predominance of male actors in the legal system helped to contort representations of women into the odd one-sided narrative that the cases in this book have demonstrated. But what about today—is gender less salient in the courtroom since women are an inescapable part of the system? Definitely not. If anything, it is more important than ever. As late arrivals on the legal scene, women are the inheritors of a centuries-old construct of themselves that they had no role in constructing. That means they face a constant battle to reframe the law to dismantle the destructive elements of the womanhood narrative.

In addition, many other groups historically disenfranchised from the law because of race, class, sexual orientation, or physical condition of the body have begun to take on the task of addressing their concerns. One sure symptom of the postmodern condition is the increasing number of individuals with multiple identities and loyalties who must face the court with one "legal" identity imposed upon them. Women have more than gender to worry about and must work on multiple fronts.

The insights gained from examining the strictly male construction of the female sex (and a few women who turned it against them) are extremely useful to those who must now tackle more diverse forms of narrative. It is clear that when an interpretation of any story is a matter of life or death, it is vital that multiple experiences of that story are represented. Many of the decisions made in our examples were made in the absence of the segment of the population most relevant to the case. Sometimes the introduction of another point of view makes all the difference.

Today, access to the experience of other classes of individuals is improved, but particpation still falls short. Although sex and race are no longer impediments de jure to participation in the legal system, they are still part of the matrix of impediments de facto, along with economics, class, and culture. The more diverse the narrators, the more comprehensive the narrative, and the more open to alternative interpretations. Obviously, these interpretations must be made within the context of the law, therefore the importance of ensuring that there are also diverse voices within the legal profession.[1]

This particular "story" of the role of gender in decision making also elicits questions for those scholars interested in women's history, feminist and otherwise. The narrative elements unearthed in the stories recapitulate the same stereotypic characterizations of what it means for a female to embody womanhood. Interestingly, they also resonate with Welter's claim that popular literature was molding an image of "true womanhood" that influenced decision making in other arenas. Although Welter's work is not the touchstone for antebellum scholars that it once was, the motifs she discovered are rediscovered again and again by feminists in a strategy of transformation that is itself rhetorical in nature.

Most recently, the construction of womanhood has begun to inform scholarship in the arena of sexual politics. Philosophers Linda Hirshman and Jane Larson begin their discussion of modern sex law with the direct claim that the "sexual politics of the present cannot be understood without understanding where the present came from, because many sexual arrangements . . . are the products of history" (3). This claim is no surprise; what is interesting is what occurs during their promised historical discussion. Beginning with de Tocqueville's foundational claim that one of the most admirable aspects of American society was its attitude toward its women, they trace that attitude across time, searching for their own set of narrative elements. The result of that search is a grand narrative they termed the "republic of virtue." "What we call the republic of virtue other historians describe as the Cult of True Womanhood or the ideology of domesticity. American society before the Civil War glorified domesticity as women's arena of achievement and fulfillment and romanticized the companionate family. Sentimental novels, popular magazines, religious tracts and sermons, public lectures, and advice books counseled both women and men on the duties and responsibilities of their roles in this emerging social order" (89). The authors discuss the core virtues of domesticity, piety, and so forth in much the same terms as those who went before. The narrative of womanhood, renamed to stress its ties to Americanism (rather than Welter's Marxism) and relieved of the somewhat paranoid element of a male conspiracy, becomes the core element in the construction of modern sex law.

In fact, Hirshman believes that this narrative is still so ingrained in American society that it affects the personal decisions of modern women. In a later work that has raised many eyebrows and no small ire in feminist circles, Hirshman claims that feminism's failure to dismantle the true womanhood narrative was one of the greatest mistakes of the feminist movement (Hirshman). Liberal feminism made great strides politically, but in an effort to become acceptable to the mainstream, its leaders took great pains to deny that feminism was antifeminine. Unfortunately, remaining feminine means not questioning the character traits assigned by the womanhood narrative. Hirshman's research revealed that one of the greatest stumbling blocks to progress was old-fashioned domesticity. The belief that woman's "natural" state is to make a lovely home and raise perfect children still influences the career decisions of well-educated young women. What they think is their free choice, says Hirshman, is actually constrained by centuries of social pressure. When asked by a reporter what is wrong with a woman choosing to quit working to raise her children, she replied with some asperity: "Don't you think it's a little weird that it's only women who make this choice?" (Tyre).

Given her background in philosophy, it is not surprising that her solution to the problem is for women to revert to another narrative—the classical notion of virtue and the "good"—to frame their decisions. This, unfortunately, means that she would substitute a sexist popular narrative with a sexist elite narrative. Neither of these options sounds useful to a woman making life-changing decisions from moment to moment.[2]

On the other hand, a rhetorical perspective on this issue would hold that narratives are malleable. Through the process of symbolic transformation, it might be possible to reshape and redefine aspects of sex roles and shake them loose from sexualized bodies. The male lawyers in this study had clear (if temporary) success at taking a narrative framed around white middle-class women and molding it to serve their legal goals. Imagine what a woman, with her greater stake in the outcome, might be able to achieve.

Whatever one might think about the existence of a woman's sphere, its political motives, or whether narratives in the popular culture should have had an effect on the lives of women, the fact remains that the narratives influence decision making in concrete situations. Whatever the reality might be, the interpretation of that reality is made as a result of argument, and often the rhetorical efforts of some of well-trained legal minds. Rhetorical scholars are well placed to offer women's history insights into the argumentative strategies that make some cultural beliefs salient to human actors and others less so. Although the courts are an excellent laboratory for testing these strategies, they are not the only, nor even the most prominent arena of rhetorical framing and reframing.

If the myth of the gender-free courtroom does not prevent communicators from dragging gender into the argument, imagine the use of such narratives in fields that do not pretend to be unbiased. More rhetorical studies of the persuasive texts related to gender will further the call made by Kerber nearly a decade ago "to understand that gender itself is a rhetorical construction" ("Introduction" 5).

Beyond that immediate practical focus, there is a similar call, made over six decades ago, to expand our knowledge of symbolic transformations in general. It has long been known by rhetoricians that the power of symbols to alter human perception is great enough that audiences can be persuaded to dismiss the evidence of their own eyes. Indeed, if there is a single insight common to all the cases covered in this collection, it is that gender expectations are almost completely disconnected from the realities of the human body. At the same time, these rhetorical forces are pervasive. Even in an arena that explicitly attempts to limit discussion to concrete facts, the skilled communicator can draw upon gendered images from other realms. These images can be incorporated into narratives in such a way that the audience might be completely unaware of their presence even as they make important decisions guided by the narrative.

The power of such rhetoric is part of the nature of symbols. As long as human beings must use symbols to communicate, then the manipulation of those symbols is inherent in every act of communication. There is no escape. This uncomfortable truism is particularly troubling in the courtroom, because the legal system is completely devoted to the unbiased examination of evidence. Great lengths are taken, from the jury selection process to the rules of evidence, to eliminate any outside influences that might "taint" an interpretation.

However, there is no "outside" of our symbolic nature. Lawyers, judges, and juries are human beings. Although legal training certainly gives rhetors access to specialized rules and premises for arguments, it cannot eliminate the rules and premises of the broader culture. Juries can be instructed on how to come to a verdict but not on how to discard the experiences of a lifetime should they conflict with those instructions. Like it or not, the law is stuck with rhetoric.

This volume has attempted to demonstrate that the application of a coherent rhetorical theory to a number of texts across time reveals typical strategies of symbolic transformation that can be applied to a narrative structure. These strategies have an impressive ability to turn the force of a narrative toward the service of "justice" or "injustice." That effect depends to a great extent upon the rhetor that calls it forth. The inclusion of a woman rhetor in an argument field can tip the scales, especially if that woman understands the power of transformation.

Kenneth Burke created critical tools through which to apply rhetorical transformations in a more positive direction: "Thus we 'win' by subtly changing the rules of the game—and by a mere trick of bookkeeping, like accountants for big utility corporations, we make 'assets' out of 'liabilities.' And can we, in our humbleness, do better than apply in our own way the wise devices of these leviathans, thereby 'democratizing' a salvation device as we encourage it to filter from the top down?" (*Attitudes* 171).

Although Burke's favorite examples involved economic theories and political campaigns, one can see his principles operating in these narratives related to gender. Gender is a linguistically created concept unbound from physical sex. One can be "masculine" or "feminine" regardless of one's genetic composition. The concept of true womanhood created a set of defining characteristics that were divorced from the physical requirements of the day-to-day life of the middle-class white woman.

The social order had begun a symbolic construction of genteel dependency, but the teleology of the narrative demanded that eventually the characterological elements must reach a symbolically perfect form. No woman living in the real world could hope to achieve feminine perfection, nor would doing so be guaranteed to make her life perfect. Men might like to contemplate the perfectly dependent, loving, innocent, domestic feminine icon, but it was another thing to have to live with such a woman.

The inherent teleology of true womanhood would not be immediately evident to society for a number of reasons—not the least of which was that there were not many "perfected" women around. Still, the symbolic progression toward perfection set up the social constraints that limited a woman's choices. Most women were bound to strive for true womanhood and bound to fail. The powerful remnants of true womanhood still affect women's choices, to the point where defending domesticity leads back into the legislature and the courts.[3] In order to expand the cultural repertoire for such women, the narrative has to be altered to embrace other possibilities for successful femininity.

The task is not easy, but rhetoricians can at least provide some tools from which social agents might choose. There are some impressive rhetorical "accountants" operating in the United States, and not just within the court system. It is important to pay attention to how they operate before our society finds itself facing an accounting of its own.

# Notes

## Introduction

1. An excellent summary of the debate over domesticity can be found in Kerber, "Separate Spheres."

2. Depending upon the case, era, and law of a particular state, the number and kind of person considered a peer will vary. Jurors were invariably male, however. Utah was the first state to allow women on juries, in 1898. There was no federal law securing defendants' right to have women on their jury lists until 1975. See Kerber, *No Constitutional Right.*

## Chapter 2. Framing Madness in the Sanity Trial of Elizabeth Parsons Ware Packard

1. In the initial stage of the trial, the plaintiff was the state of Illinois and Reverend Packard was the defendant. When the trial shifted to the matter of Elizabeth Packard's sanity, she became the individual being accused. Therefore I will refer to Reverend Packard and his lawyers' narrative as accusatory and to Packard and her lawyers' as defensive.

## Chapter 3. The Mad Doctors Meet McNaughton: The Battle for Narrative Supremacy in the Trial of Mary Harris

1. One has to wonder what Louisa Devlin knew or suspected about Burroughs that would lead her to devise such a complicated scheme once she decided that the mystery letter was in his handwriting.

2. Burroughs testified that Harris showed up the day before the wedding and that he put her off because he believed she was trying to extort money for the letters. Harris claimed she came the day of the wedding and had no idea Judson Burroughs was marrying.

3. The District of Columbia did not differentiate degrees of homicide.

4. The main text for this analysis is Clephane's *Official Report of the Trial of Mary*

*Harris.* The trial was also covered extensively in the *New York Times*, who sent their own stenographer once they realized how sensational the case was becoming. In order to further investigate the discussion of the case within the medical profession, I also surveyed letters to the editor in various other newspapers as well as articles in the *Journal of Insanity*, which was the professional organ of the burgeoning specialty of psychiatry.

5. It was not until 1912 that the Federation of State Medical Boards was established to create an accreditation standard for medical schools. See the AMA history at http://www .ama-assn.org/ama/pub/category/1854.html.

6. The prosecutors were the district attorney, Edward C. Carrington, and his assistant Nathaniel Wilson. Harris had four defense lawyers in addition to Bradley, all working pro bono. They were Daniel Voorhees, Judge James Hughes, William Fendall, and Judge Charles Mason. Voorhees was a congressman from Indiana and Hughes was a former congressman from the same state. The rest of the team were experienced lawyers with federal court experience. See Spiegel and Suskind for a summary of their careers. The prosecution was well "outgunned." All quotations of the trial are taken from the *Official Report* unless otherwise indicated.

7. Despite the pervasiveness of the concept of the "frail femininity" and hysteria in the United States, the application of that concept was not universal. Women of color were excluded from the narrative, as well as working-class white women. See Briggs for the details of this exclusion.

8. Wilson and Carrington apparently divided their duties. Wilson asked polite questions and stuck to the legal definition of insanity. Carrington became the "bad cop" who impugned Harris's motives and the characters of those around her.

9. He was examined by Hughes.

10. It is worth noting that the subject of menstruation was always handled obliquely. The polite term for mental disorders related to menstruation was "paroxysmal insanity." References to "paroxysms" and "periodic disturbances" were made, but nobody used the word *menstruation* itself. Female witnesses were asked whether Harris was "sick" or "unwell" on a particular date. So delicate were the physicians that no one asked Harris to her face whether she was having her menstrual period at the time of the murder: Dr. Nichols wrote her a note that she read when she was alone. Then she wrote a note back that answered in the affirmative (*Official Report* 74).

11. The quotation is cited from the official transcript (*Official Report*), p. 121. The court reporter admitted that his notes were lost and that he had to use the *New York Times* report's transcript for Wilson's argument. Wilson agreed that the report was substantially correct.

12. Ray's speech is reproduced in the *American Journal of Insanity* 23 (1866): 263–79.

13. After staying with her parents for a decent interval, Harris returned to Baltimore to rejoin the Devlins. While she was gone, however, some changes took place. Louisa Devlin was engaged to be married. Harris attempted to take a carving knife to the new fiancé. Louisa Collins (née Devlin) eventually took Harris to D.C. and asked Bradley to deal with her. Bradley signed the commitment papers. In a bizarre coda, Bradley married Harris in 1883, soon after his eighty-first birthday. Harris was forty-two. Bradley continued as the oldest practicing lawyer in the District of Columbia until his death in 1887. It is not clear

whether Harris had stopped having manic episodes ("J. H. Bradley Marries," "A Romance of the Court").

## Chapter 4. "True Womanhood" and Perfect Madness: The Sanity Trial of Mary Todd Lincoln

1. The newsletter was called the *Chicago Legal News*. Bradwell was finally admitted to the Illinois bar in 1890. The legislature decided to make admittance retroactive to the year she took the exam, thus making her "America's First Woman Lawyer" despite the fact that she had not been allowed to practice until well after women in other states. She died in 1894. For a complete biography, see Jane Friedman, *America's First*.

2. Texts reviewed in this case begin with court documents and private papers donated to historical researchers by the last living descendant of Mary and Abraham Lincoln (Neely and McMurty). Although he apparently destroyed many other family records, Robert Todd Lincoln kept every single document connected to his mother's case, and these remained undisturbed until discovered by his grandson. Also available for scrutiny in other historical archives are reports of both hearings as presented in the *Chicago Daily Tribune* and *Chicago Times*, as well as stories "planted" by Bradwell in several places. She even arranged for reporters to visit Lincoln and give "unbiased" reports as to her mental state.

3. Other first ladies were ridiculed for pursuing similar interests. Nancy Reagan consulted an astrologer regularly. Hillary Rodham Clinton purportedly sought the advice of Eleanor Roosevelt through means of a "channeler"—the current term for a medium. That channeler, Jean Houston, has written several books, which can be found on her Web site at http://www.jeanhouston.org/.

## Chapter 5. Womanhood as Asset and Liability: Lizzie Andrew Borden

1. Since there are multiple Bordens referred to in the case, I have taken the liberty of referring to them by their first names.

2. This was determined by noting differences between the two bodies in the amount of coagulated blood and the amount of food digested from breakfast.

3. This does not entirely free her from suspicion. There is a conspiracy theory that has Lizzie killing Abby while Bridget establishes her alibi. Then Emma supposedly kills Andrew while Lizzie cleans up.

4. Massachusetts law required that three judges be present in a capital murder case. The third judge, Caleb Blodgett, was apparently not controversial. In addition to Robinson, Lizzie was represented by Andrew Jennings, the Borden family lawyer. These two were aided by Melvin Adams, chosen by Jennings for his skill at cross-examination. On the prosecution sat Knowlton, aided by William Moody. Although Moody had a good reputation, this was his first murder trial. An excellent genealogically oriented volume by Hoffman traces the various careers and connections of nearly all the principals in the Borden case, including the professional relationships of the lawyers (*Yesterday in Old Fall River*).

5. Burke introduces the pentad in *A Grammar of Motives* and discusses ratios on pp. 3–20.

6. The official report of the murder trial (Frank Burt, ed., *The Trial of Lizzie A. Borden*) is available on microfilm at the Boston Public Library. The *New York Times* also covered the trial. More technologically inclined readers can find complete transcripts of the official record of the trial, as well as other digitized documents, at http://lizzieandrewborden .com. This chapter cites the digitized version of the transcript, which was made from the original documents by Harry E. Widdows for the Lizze Borden Society in 2001. Due to the poor quality of the originals, Widdows had to type and proofread the entire document by hand, so I have cross-checked any portions quoted directly in this chapter with other available editions in case he made transcription errors. There are many edited volumes collecting the various documents, and several are cited in the bibliography. The reader is warned, however, that most editors selected for inclusion the documents that best proved their claim as to who was guilty of the crime. In order to get a reading of the entire trial, one has to consult multiple editions.

7. Fall River was not especially parochial in this instance. In the 1890s, the medical establishment questioned the femininity of the "new women" to the point of branding them potential lesbians (Smith-Rosenberg, *Disorderly Conduct* 265). Interestingly, in later years, Borden was accused of a scandalous lesbian relationship with an actress.

8. One additional issue not explicitly about sex but with gendered implications was the question of how Lizzie could have committed the murders without getting blood on her clothing. Assuming that Bridget Sullivan's testimony was accurate, she saw Lizzie in between the two murders and noticed nothing out of the ordinary. In order to kill Abby, appear to Andrew and Bridget in a clean dress, then kill Andrew, and finally appear to Bridget and the neighbors in another clean dress, Lizzie would have had to change clothes twice—no mean feat for a woman wearing the complicated clothing of the era before zippers and Velcro. The testimony about dress in the trial touches upon gender in an amusing manner. Since it was a serious question whether Lizzie had handed police the clothing she was really wearing that morning, nearly every witness was asked to describe what she had been wearing. The male witnesses had a difficult time when asked whether a dress was blue or blue and white, whether it looked like silk or cotton, and whether it had a striped, diamond, or "sprig" pattern on it. When one female witness said a dress looked like Bedford cord, she was asked what material it was made of by the male lawyer. Her mystified reply was that Bedford cord was made of Bedford cord (corduroy). The women sometimes had to explain it to the jury.

## Chapter 6. Bodies at the Crossroads: The Rise and Fall of Madame Restell

1. Since the rhetoric was aimed at defining the public persona of Restell rather than the private Ann Trow Lohman, this chapter will refer to her by her professional pseudonym.

2. Witnesses differed as to who actually performed the surgery. Some claimed Restell herself, while others reported that she brought in a male (never identified) who might

have been a physician. It did not matter once the law changed to make even abetting an abortion illegal.

3. Although the AMA's campaign was inspired by professional issues, this does not mean that individual physicians were not also concerned about abortion for moral reasons. The profession was divided—some "regular" doctors performed abortions. There was debate on all sides within the medical literature. The AMA, however, pursued an antiabortion agenda.

4. This was not the only adoption to haunt Restell. Later, another woman who had agreed to surrender her infant but then changed her mind sued Restell to find and return it. The infant was born in 1855. The mother filed her suit in 1857 and the case dragged through the courts until 1862. The child was never recovered. The irony in this case was that the state justice who eventually ordered Restell to produce the child ruled that the mother was not fit to rear it, either, and hinted that he would put it in a foster home.

5. The state was represented by District Attorney John McKeon, Joseph B. Phillips, and Ogden Hoffman. Restell was represented by James T. Brady and David Graham. Brady had a successful practice specializing in "moral" issues (especially divorce). He once successfully defended four murderers in one week ("Brady, James T.," in *Appleton's Cyclopedia of American Biography,* ed. James Grant [New York: D. Appleton and Co., 1888–1889]).

6. Restell was arrested many times, but did not have another full trial for decades. Witnesses died, disappeared, or simply changed their minds. This chapter does not address cases that were interrupted. These are often interesting: in one ironic case, a woman went to Restell to request an abortion but changed her mind. She went to the police, who arrested Restell for procurement. Since there had been no abortion, the charges were dropped. The woman died in childbirth.

## Chapter 7. *"You Know It When You See It":* *The Rhetorical Embodiment of Race and Gender in* Rhinelander v. Rhinelander

1. When dealing with the rhetoric of race it is difficult to walk the fine line between being true to one's historical subjects and showing sensitivity to contemporary concerns. At the time of the Rhinelander case, "Negro" was considered by both races to be the polite term for those of African American descent. This is not acceptable today. Some of the witnesses in the case referred to themselves as "colored"—also no longer acceptable—as, to them, it was preferable to being "Negro." "Afro-American" was a suspect term in the black community in the early part of the century, not the least because lighter-skinned blacks were suspected of using it to differentiate themselves from those with darker skin (for an interesting discussion of the color factor, see Gatewood). The author does not wish to violate the truth of the discourse by editing any of its terminology and hopes the reader will not take offense. Here the terms "black" and "white" will be used to denote race when not quoting primary sources.

2. Philip Rhinelander was never called to testify about convincing his son to pursue annulment, so we will never know exactly what changed Leonard's position.

3. The *New York Times* coverage is the primary source of textual material. Every day,

the paper ran a multipage story. First, the reporters would summarize the day's proceedings for the casual reader (the nature of these summaries is in itself instructive). Then it reproduced verbatim testimony for the reader who wished to follow the trial closely. It speaks to the importance of the case that the nation's "newspaper of record" allotted so much front-page space to the trial. An important speech by the president, for example, knocked the Rhinelanders off the front page, but when the dowager queen of England died, her obituary and funeral coverage had to share space with the trial.

4. Unless otherwise indicated, all quotations from the case are from the *New York Times*. I cross-checked those stories extensively. Two other newspapers of the era, the *Herald* and the *Daily News,* were also extensively consulted. The case generated appeals from appellate court to the state supreme court, and those records and decisions are publicly available. Although verbatim testimony was not reproduced, the lawyers' main arguments were recapped along with their new appeals. Those accounts are consistent with the *Times* (*Rhinelander v. Rhinelander,* 219 A.D. 189; 219 N.Y.S. 548, Jan. 4, 1927; also *Rhinelander v. Rhinelander,* 245 N.Y. 510; 157 N.E. 838, Mar. 29, 1927). The defense lawyer also had some trouble getting paid (*Rhinelander v. Rhinelander,* 219 A.D. 722; 219 N.Y.S. 902, Jan. 1927). The final word, for those interested in following the case to its bitter end, is *In re Rhinelander,* 264 A.D. 607; 36 N.Y.S.2d 105, July 6, 1942. The author also consulted a number of other New York newspapers and magazines to check for inconsistencies.

5. Her given name was Elizabeth. As was typical of that era, the *Times* did not use a first name other than "Mrs. George."

6. Although our rhetorical case study ends here, the Rhinelander story continued for years. As soon as the verdict was in, Leonard was off to Reno for a "quickie" divorce while his lawyers appealed the annulment verdict on the grounds that Alice hadn't testified. Alice responded by suing Philip Rhinelander for alienation of affection. Leonard agreed to return to New York for a normal divorce if Alice would drop her lawsuit. The eventual settlement provided Alice with a lump sum plus alimony payments. Alice moved to Paris. Oddly, when Leonard died, Philip continued to make payments to Alice until his own death. At that time, Alice sued to have the payments continued from the estate. This time, she lost.

## Conclusion

1. The Supreme Court agrees to some extent, at least regarding the use of race as a factor in law school admissions. Preserving a diversity of trained legal professionals is still viewed by the court as necessary. See *Grutter v. Bollinger* 539 U.S. (2003).

2. In fact, some of her advice seems to mirror traditional "masculinity." For example, she exhorts young women to seek as mates men who are much younger than themselves. Presumably that would reduce the pressure to stop working. It is a strategy that has been employed by males for centuries to obtain the proper sort of "wife."

3. The current furor over the "defense of marriage" is one example. Defining "marriage" as "one man married to one woman" does more than disenfranchise gays and lesbians. It also reifies the notion that the two sexes have specific roles that cannot be interchanged. Same-sex couples would have to decide which partner was the "woman" in order to assure that someone would love and nurture the children while the assigned "man" took on traditional economic duties.

# References

"Absurd Stories about Mme. Restell." *New York Times*, Apr. 4, 1878: 8.

American Medical Association. *Timelines of AMA History* June 2, 2001 [accessed Oct. 15, 2004]. Available from http://www.ama-assn.org/ama/pub/category/1854.html.

Andrews, Joseph (defendant). *An Account of the Trial of Joseph Andrews for Piracy and Murder*. New York: n.p., 1769.

*Ann Lohmann, Alias Madame Restell, v. the People*, 1 N.Y. 379 (1848).

"Another Chapter of Supposed Infant Murder." *National Police Gazette*, Feb. 7, 1846: 197.

"The Arrest of Madame Restell." *New York Herald*, Mar. 24, 1841: 2.

Association of Medical Superintendents of American Institutions for the Insane. "Proceedings of the Annual Meeting." *American Journal of Insanity* 20 (1863): 60–107.

Ausband, Stephen C. *Myth and Meaning, Myth and Order*. Macon, Ga.: Mercer University Press, 1983.

Baker, Jean H. *Mary Todd Lincoln: A Biography*. New York: W. W. Norton, 1987.

Barker-Benfield, G. J. *The Horrors of the Half-Known Life: Male Attitudes toward Women and Sexuality in Nineteenth-Century America*. New York: Harper Colophon Books, 1977.

Basch, Norma. *In the Eyes of the Law: Women, Marriage, and Property in Nineteenth-Century New York*. Ithaca, N.Y.: Cornell University Press, 1982.

Baym, Nina. *Woman's Fiction: A Guide to Novels by and about Women in America, 1820–1870*. Ithaca, N.Y.: Cornell University Press, 1978.

Beck, Theodric R., and John B. Beck. *Elements of Medical Jurisprudence*. Albany: Packard and Van Benthuysen, 1835.

Beisal, Nicola. *Imperiled Innocents: Anthony Comstock and Family Reproduction in Victorian America*. Princeton, N.J.: Princeton University Press, 1997.

Bennett, D. M. *Anthony Comstock: His Career of Cruelty and Crime*. New York: D. M. Bennett, 1878.

Bennett, W. Lance. "Storytelling in Criminal Trials: A Model of Social Judgment." *Quarterly Journal of Speech* 64 (1978): 1–22.

Bennett, W. Lance, and Martha S. Feldman. *Reconstructing Reality in the Courtroom: Justice and Judgment in American Culture.* Crime, Law, and Deviance Series. New Brunswick, N.J.: Rutgers University Press, 1981.

Berg, Barbara. *The Rembered Gate: Origins of American Feminism.* New York: Oxford University Press, 1978.

Bjork, Daniel. *The Victorian Flight: Russell Conwell and the Crisis of American Individualism.* Washington, D.C.: University Press of America, 1978.

Black, Edwin. *Rhetorical Questions: Studies of Public Discourse.* Chicago: University of Chicago Press, 1992.

Bloom, Stephen. "Prozac for PMS." *Salon* (2000) http://www.salon.com/health/feature/2000/07/18/pms/ (accessed July 21, 2003).

*Bradwell v. Illinois,* 16 Wallace 130 (1873).

Braude, Ann. *Radical Spirits: Spiritualism and Women's Rights in Nineteenth-Century America.* Boston: Beacon Press, 1989.

Bremmer, Robert. Introduction to *Traps for the Young* by Anthony Comstock. Cambridge: Belknap, 1967.

Briggs, Laura. "The Race of Hysteria: 'Overcivilization' and the 'Savage' Woman in Late Nineteenth-Century Obstetrics and Gynecology." *American Quarterly* 52, no. 2 (2000): 246–73.

Brodie, Janet Farrell. *Contraception and Abortion in Nineteenth-Century America.* Ithaca: Cornell University Press, 1994.

Brooks, Peter, and Paul Gewirtz, eds. *Law's Stories.* New Haven: Yale University Press, 1996.

Broun, Heywood, and Margaret Leech. *Anthony Comstick: Roundsman of the Lord.* New York: Literary Guild, 1927.

Browder, Clifford. *The Wickedest Woman in New York.* Hamden, Conn.: Archon Books, 1988.

Brown, Arnold R. *Lizzie Borden: The Legend, the Truth, the Final Chapter.* New York: Dell, 1991.

Browne, Stephen. "'Like Gory Spectres': Representing Slavery in Theodore Weld's American Slavery as It Is." *Quarterly Journal of Speech* 80 (1994): 277–92.

Brummett, Barry. "Burke's Representative Anecdote as a Method in Media Criticism." *Critical Studies in Mass Communication* 1 (1984): 161–76.

———. "The Representative Anecdote as a Burkean Method, Applied to Evangelical Rhetoric." *Southern Speech Journal* 50 (Fall 1984): 1–23.

Bryan, Patricia L., and Thomas Wolf. *Midnight Assassin: Murder in America's Heartland.* Chapel Hill, N.C.: Algonquin Books, 2005.

Burke, Kenneth. *Attitudes toward History.* Berkeley: University of California Press, 1984.

———. *Counterstatement.* Berkeley: University of California Press, 1968.

———. *A Grammar of Motives.* Berkeley: University of California Press, 1962.

———. *Language as Symbolic Action.* Berkeley: University of California Press, 1966.

———. *Permanence and Change.* Berkeley: University of California Press, 1984.

———. *Philosophy of Literary Form.* Berkeley: University of California Press, 1973.

———. *The Rhetoric of Motives.* Berkeley: University of California Press, 1969.

Burr, Agnes Rush. *Russell H. Conwell and His Work*. Philadelphia: John C. Winston, 1926.

Burt, Frank, ed. *The Trial of Lizzie A. Borden. Upon an Indictment Charging Her with the Murders of Abby Durfee Borden and Andrew Jackson Borden. Before the Superior Court for the County of Bristol*. Boston: 1893. Boston Public Library Microform, http://lizzieandrewborden.com (accessed Aug. 29, 2005).

"Calls Rhinelander Dupe of Girl He Wed." *New York Times*, Nov. 10, 1925: 1, 8.

Campbell, Karlyn Kohrs. "Style and Content in Rhetoric of Early Afro-American Feminists." *Quarterly Journal of Speech* 72 (1986): 434–45.

Campbell, Karlyn Kohrs, and Kathleen Hall Jamieson. Introduction to *Form and Genre: Shaping Rhetorical Action*. Falls Church, Va.: Speech Communication Association, 1978.

"A Card from Madame Restell—Classified Ad." *New York Daily Times*, Aug. 21, 1856: 8.

Carlson, A. Cheree. "Limitations on the Comic Frame: Some Witty American Women of the Nineteenth Century." *Quarterly Journal of Speech* 74 (1988): 310–22.

———. "Narrative as the Philosopher's Stone: How Russell H. Conwell Changed Lead into Diamonds." *Western Journal of Speech Communication* 53 (Fall 1989): 342–55.

———. "The Role of Character in Public Moral Argument: Henry Ward Beecher and the Brooklyn Scandal." *Quarterly Journal of Speech* 77 (1991): 38–52.

———. "'You Know It When You See It': The Rhetorical Hierarchy of Race and Gender in Rhinelander v. Rhinelander." *Quarterly Journal of Speech* 85 (1999): 111–28.

"The Case of Madame Restell." *New York Times*, Feb. 16, 1878: 3.

"The Case of Madame Restell: Examination in a Police Court." *New York Times*, Feb. 24, 1878: 5.

"The Case of Madame Restell: Flight of Miss Grant, the Complaintant." *Brooklyn Eagle*, Mar. 3, 1854: 2.

"The Child Murderess." *National Police Gazette*, Feb. 28, 1846 (1): 220.

Clephane, James O., ed. *Official Report of the Trial of Mary Harris for the Murder of Adoniram J. Burroughs*. Washington, D.C.: W. H. & O. H. Morrison, 1865.

Cloud, Dana. "The Limits of Interpretation: Ambivalence and Stereotype in *Spenser for Hire*." *Critical Studies in Mass Communication* 9, no. 4 (1992): 311–24.

"Clouded Reason: Trial of Mrs. Abraham Lincoln for Insanity." *Chicago Tribune*, May 20, 1875: 1.

Cogan, Frances B. *All American Girl*. Athens: University of Georgia Press, 1989.

Collins, Patricia Hill. *Black Feminist Thought*. Boston: Unwin Hyman, 1990.

Condit, Celeste Michelle. *Decoding Abortion Rhetoric*. Urbana: University of Illinois Press, 1990.

———. "Democracy and Civil Rights: The Universalizing Influence of Public Argumentation." *Communication Monographs* 54 (1987): 1–18.

Conrad, Charles. "Agon and Rhetorical Form: The Essence of 'Old Feminist' Rhetoric." *Quarterly Journal of Speech* 32 (1981): 45–53.

Crable, Bryan. "Burke's Perspective on Perspectives: Grounding Dramatism in the Representative Anecdote." *Quarterly Journal of Speech* 86, no. 3 (2000): 318–33.

Davis, Charles G. *The Conduct of the Law in the Borden Case*. Boston: Boston Daily Advertiser, 1894.

Dewey, Richard. "The Jury Law for Commitment of the Insane in Illinois (1867–1893)." *American Journal of Insanity* 69, no. 3 (1913): 571–84.

Dickinson, Emily. *Poems by Emily Dickinson*. Boston: Little, Brown, 1896.

Du Bois, W. E. B. "Opinion of W. E. B. Dubois." *Crisis*, Jan. 1926: 112.

"Editorial." *Police Gazette*, Mar. 7, 1846, vol. 1: 228.

"Editorial: Madame Restell and Some of Her Dupes." *New York Medical and Surgical Reporter* (1846): 158–65.

"Editorial: The Rhinelander Case." *Messenger* (Jan. 1925): 388.

Ekirch, Arthur A., Jr. *Progressivism in America: A Study of the Era from Theodore Roosevelt to Woodrow Wilson*. New York: New Viewpoints, 1974.

Eliade, Mircea. *The Myth of the Eternal Return; or, Cosmos and History*. Princeton, N.J.: Princeton University Press, 1971.

"The End of a Criminal Life." *New York Times*, Apr. 2, 1878: 1.

Evans, W. A. *Mrs. Abraham Lincoln: A Study of Her Personality*. New York: Knopf, 1932.

"The Evil of the Age." *New York Times*, Aug. 23, 1857: 6.

Ferguson, Robert. "Untold Stories in the Law." In *Law's Stories*, edited by Peter Brooks and Paul Gewirtz, 84–98. New Haven: Yale University Press, 1996.

Fields, Barbara J. "Ideology and Race in American History." In *Region, Race, and Reconstruction*, edited by J. Morgan Kousser and James M. McPherson. New York: Oxford University Press, 1982.

Fisher, Walter R. *Human Communication as Narration: Toward a Philosophy of Reason, Value, and Action*, Studies in Rhetoric/Communication. Columbia: University of South Carolina Press, 1987.

———. "Narration as a Human Communication Paradigm: The Case of Public Moral Argument." *Communication Monographs* 51 (1984): 1–22.

Freedman, Lawrence Zelic, ed. *By Reason of Insanity: Essays on Psychiatry and the Law*. Wilmington, Del.: Scholarly Resources, 1983.

Friedman, Jane M. *America's First Woman Lawyer*. Buffalo, N.Y.: Prometheus Books, 1993.

———. "Myra Bradwell: On Defying the Creator and Becoming a Lawyer." *Valparaiso University Law Review* 28 (Summer 1994): 1287–1304.

Friedman, Susan Stanford. "Guest Editor's Remarks." *Journal of Narrative Technique* 20 (Spring 1990): 87–88.

Fullinwider, S. P. "Insanity as the Loss of Self: The Moral Insanity Controversy." *Bulletin of the History of Medicine* 49, no. 1 (1975): 87–101.

Gates, Henry Louis, Jr. *"Race," Writing, and Difference*. Chicago: University of Chicago Press, 1986.

Gatewood, Willard B. *Aristocrats of Color: The Black Elite, 1880–1990*. Bloomington: Indiana University Press, 1990.

Gehring, Mary Louise. "Russell H. Conwell: American Orator." *Southern Speech Communication Journal* 20 (Winter 1954): 117–24.

Geller, Jeffrey L., Johnathon Erlen, Neil S. Kaye, and William H. Fisher. "Feigned Insanity in Nineteenth-Century America: Tactics, Trials, and Truth." *Behavioral Sciences and the Law* 8 (1990): 3–26.

"Gerry Spence's Trial Lawyers College." http://www.triallawyerscollege.com/ (accessed July 14, 2006).

Gewirtz, Paul. "Narrative and Rhetoric in the Law." In *Law's Stories*, edited by Peter Brooks and Paul Gewirtz, 2–13. New Haven: Yale, 1996.

Gilman, Sander. "Black Bodies, White Bodies: Toward an Iconography of Female Sexuality in Late Nineteenth-Century Art, Medicine, and Literature." *Critical Inquiry* 12 (Fall 1985): 204–42.

Glaspell, Susan. "A Jury of Her Peers." In *The Best Short Stories of 1917*, edited by Edward J. O'Brien, 256–82. Boston: Small, Maynard, 1918.

Goldberg, David Theo. "Racism and Rationality: The Need for a New Critique." *Philosophy of the Social Sciences* 20, no. 3 (1990): 317–50.

———. "The Semantics of Race." *Ethnic and Racial Studies* 15, no. 4 (1992): 543–69.

Grant, James., ed. *Appleton's Cyclopedia of American Biography*. New York: D. Appleton and Co., 1888–1889.

"Grant-Shackford Trial." *New York Daily Times*, Mar. 3, 1854: 2.

*Grutter v. Bollinger et al.*, 539 US 306 (2003).

Hall, Stuart. "Signification, Representation, Ideology: Althusser and the Post-Structuralist Debates." *Critical Studies in Mass Comunication* 2 (1985): 91–114.

Hammond, William A. *Spiritualism and Allied Causes and Conditions of Nervous Derangement*. New York: G. P. Putnam's Sons, 1876.

Hariman, Robert, ed. *Popular Trials: Rhetoric, Mass Media, and the Law*. Tuscaloosa: University of Alabama Press, 1990.

Harris, Richard. *Hints on Advocacy*. St. Louis: William H. Stevenson, 1881.

Harris, T. M. *The Assasination of Lincoln: A History of the Great Conspiracy*. 1892; reprint, Bowie, Md.: Heritage Books, 1989.

Hart, Roderick P. *The Political Pulpit*. West Lafayette, Ind.: Purdue University Press, 1977.

Hartman, Mary S. *Victorian Murderesses*. New York: Schocken Books, 1977.

Hartog, Hendrick. "Mrs. Packard on Dependency." *Yale Journal of Law and Humanities* 1, no. 79 (1988): 79–103.

———. "Pigs and Positivism." *Wisconsin Law Review* 899, no. 4 (1985): 899–935.

Heinzelman, Susan Sage. "Women's Petty Treason: Feminism, Narrative, and the Law." *Journal of Narrative Technique* 20, no. 2 (1990): 89–106.

Heinzelman, Susan Sage, and Zipporah Batshaw Wiseman, eds. *Representing Women: Law, Literature, and Feminism*. Durham, N.C.: Duke University Press, 1994.

Higginbotham, Evelyn Brooks. "African-American Women's History and the Metalanguage of Race." *Signs* 17 (Winter 1992): 251–74.

Himelhoch, Myra Samuels, and Arthur H. Shaffer. "Elizabeth Packard: Nineteenth-Century Crusader for the Rights of Mental Patients." *Journal of American Studies* 13 (1979): 343–75.

Hirshman, Linda R. *Get to Work: A Manifesto for Women of the World*. New York: Viking, 2006.

Hirshman, Linda R., and Jane E. Larson. *Hard Bargains: The Politics of Sex*. Cary, N.C.: Oxford University Press, 1999.

Hoffman, Paul Dennis. *Yesterday in Old Fall River*. Durham, N.C.: Carolina Academic Press, 2000.

hooks, bell. *Ain't I a Woman: Black Women and Feminism*. Boston: South End Press, 1981.

Hughes, John Starrett. *In the Law's Darkness: Issac Ray and the Medical Jurisprudence of Insanity in Nineteenth Century America*. Linden Studies in Legal History. New York: Oceana Publications, 1986.

"J. H. Bradley Marries Mary Harris." *New York Times*, Nov. 4, 1883: 9.

Jackson, Bernard. *Law, Fact, and Narrative Coherence*. Chippenham, U.K.: Deborah Charles Publications, 1988.

Jacoby, Susan. *Wild Justice: The Evolution of Revenge*. New York: Harper and Row, 1983.

Jamieson, Kathleen Hall. *Eloquence in an Electronic Age: The Transformation of Political Speechmaking*. New York: Oxford University Press, 1988.

Johnson, William R. *Schooled Lawyers: A Study in the Clash of Professional Cultures*. New York: New York University Press, 1978.

"Jones Interrupts Rhinelander Trial." *New York Times*, Dec. 4, 1925: 3.

Kammen, Michael. *People of Paradox*. Ithaca: Cornell University Press, 1990.

Keller, Allan. *Scandalous Lady*. New York: Athenium, 1981.

Kelley, Mary. *Private Woman, Public Stage: Literary Domesticity in Nineteenth-Century America*. New York: Oxford University Press, 1984.

Kent, David. *Forty Whacks: New Evidence in the Life and Legend of Lizzie Borden*. Emmaus, Pa.: Yankee Books, 1992.

Kerber, Linda K. "Introduction: Gender and the New Women's History." In *Women's America: Refocusing the Past*, edited by Linda K. Kerber and Jane Sharon DeHart, 3–23. New York: Oxford University Press, 1995.

———. *No Constitutional Right to Be Ladies: Women and the Obligations of Citizenship*. New York: Hill and Wang, 1998.

———. "Separate Spheres, Female Worlds, Women's Place: The Rhetoric of Women's History." *Journal of American History* 75, no. 1 (1988): 9–39.

Kerber, Linda K., and Jane Sharon DeHart, eds. *Women's America: Refocusing the Past*. New York: Oxford University Press, 1995.

Kirkwood, William G. "Parables as Metaphors and Examples." *Quarterly Journal of Speech* 71 (1985): 422–40.

Lamott, Kenneth. *Who Killed Mr. Crittenden?* New York: David McKay, 1963.

"Law Intelligence." *New York Times*, Apr. 23, 1858: 5.

"Lays Son's Plight to Rhinelander Sr." *New York Times*, Dec. 3, 1925: 3.

Leitch, Thomas M. *What Stories Are: Narrative Theory and Interpretation*. University Park: Pennsylvania State University Press, 1986.

Leps, Marie-Christine. *Apprehending the Criminal: The Production of Deviance in Nineteenth Century Discourse*. Durham, N.C.: Duke University Press, 1992.

Lerner, Gerda, ed. *Black Women in White America*. New York: Vintage Books, 1973.

"Letter to Editor." *National Police Gazette*, Nov. 8, 1845: 92.

Lincoln, Victoria. *A Private Disgrace: Lizzie Borden by Daylight*. New York: G. P. Putnam's Sons, 1967.

Lohman, Ann. "A Card." *New York Times*, June 15, 1855: 8.

"Loved Rhinelander, Wife's Letters Say." *New York Times*, Nov. 13, 1925: 1–2.

*Loving v. Virginia*. 388 US 1 (1967).

Lowndes, Marie Belloc. *Lizzie Borden: A Study in Conjecture*. New York: Longmans, Green, 1939.

Lustgarten, Edgar. *Verdict in Dispute*. New York: Charles Scribner's Sons, 1950.

Lutes, Jean Louise. "Into the Madhouse with Nellie Bly: Girl Stunt Reporting in Late Nineteenth-Century America." *American Quarterly* 54, no. 2 (2002): 217–53.

"Madame Restell." *New York Herald*, Mar. 26, 1841: 2.

*Madame Restell: An Account of Her Life and Horrible Practices*. New York: Charles Smith, 1847.

"Madame Restell: Female Physician." *New York Times*, Jan. 29, 1855: 7.

*Madame Restell! Her Secret Life History from Her Birth to Her Suicide*. New York: n.p., 1890.

Markey, Morris. "A Day in the Country." *New Yorker*, Nov. 28, 1925: 9.

Martin, Edward Winslow. *The Secrets of the Great City*. Philadelphia: Jones Brothers, 1868.

"Mary Harris Goes Home—the Devlins to Baltimore." *New York Times*, July 21, 1865: 1.

Maynard, Nettie Colburn. *Was Abraham Lincoln a Spiritualist?* Philadelphia: Rufus C. Hartranft, 1891.

McCabe, James D. *Lights and Shadows of New York Life*. Philadelphia: National Publishing, 1872.

"Miscellaneous City News." *New York Times*, Feb. 12, 1878: 8.

"Miss Harris Acquitted." *New York Times*, July 20, 1865: 1.

Mitchell, W. J. Thomas. *On Narrative*. Chicago: University of Chicago Press, 1981.

"Mme. Restell." *New York Times*, Sept. 3, 1871: 8.

"Mme. Restell in Court." *New York Times*, Dec. 28, 1866: 2.

"Mme. Restell in Trouble: A Baby Missing." *New York Times*, July 20, 1862: 6.

"Mme. Restell's Arrest." *New York Times*, Feb. 14, 1878: 8.

Mohr, James C. *Abortion in America: The Origins and Evolution of National Policy, 1800–1900*. New York: Oxford, 1978.

———. *Doctors and the Law*. New York: Oxford University Press, 1993.

Moore, Stephen R. "The Great Trial of Mrs. Elizabeth P. W. Packard." In *Marital Power Exemplified in Mrs. Packard's Trial*, edited by E. P. W. Packard. Hartford, Conn.: published by the authoress, 1866.

"More Work of the Abortionists." *National Police Gazette*, May 2, 1846: 293.

Morris, Virginia. *Double Jeopardy: Women Who Kill in Victorian Fiction*. Lexington: University Press of Kentucky, 1990.

"Mrs. President Lincoln." *Chicago Daily Tribune*, June 16, 1876: 8.

"Mrs. Rhinelander Fails to Testify." *New York Times*, Dec. 1, 1925: 12.

Nakayama, Thomas K., and Robert L. Kriezek. "Whiteness: A Strategic Rhetoric." *Quarterly Journal of Speech* 81, no. 3 (1995): 291–309.

Neely, Mark E., and R. Gerald McMurtry. *The Insanity File: The Case of Mary Todd Lincoln*. Carbondale: Southern Ilinois University Press, 1986.

Newby, I. A. *Jim Crow's Defense: Anti-Negro Thought in America, 1900–1930*. Baton Rouge: Louisiana State University Press, 1965.

Omi, Michael, and Howard Winant. *Racial Formation in the United States*. New York: Routledge, 1986.

Ono, Kent. "Communicating Prejudice in the Media: Upending Racial Categories in Doubles." In *Communicating Prejudice*, edited by Michael Hecht, 206–20. Thousand Oaks, Calif.: Sage, 1998.

Packard, Elizabeth P. W. *Modern Persecution, or Insane Asylums Unveiled*. 1875; reprint, New York: Arno Press, 1973.

Papashvily, Helen Waite. *All the Happy Endings*. New York: Harper and Bros., 1956.

Parigot, James. "Letter to the Editor." *New York Times*, July 28, 1865: 4.

Pascoe, Peggy. "Miscegenation Law, Court Cases, and Ideologies of 'Race' in Twentieth-Century America." *Journal of American History* 83, no. June (1996): 44–69.

———. "Race, Gender, and Intercultural Relations: The Case of Interracial Marriage." *Frontiers* 12 (1991): 5–16.

Pattee, Fred Lewis. *The Feminine Fifties*. Port Washington, N.Y.: Kennikat Press, 1966.

Pearson, Edward, ed. *Trial of Lizzie Borden*. Garden City, N.Y.: Doubleday, 1937.

*The People v. Madam Restell, Alias Ann Lohman*, 3 Hill 289 (1842).

"Progress of the Trial of Miss Harris." *New York Times*, July 12, 1865: 1, 2.

Radin, Edward D. *Lizzie Borden: The Untold Story*. New York: Simon and Schuster, 1961.

Randall, Ruth Painter. *Mary Lincoln: Biography of a Marriage*. Boston: Little, Brown, 1953.

Ray, Isaac. "The Insanity of Women Produced by Desertion or Seduction." *American Journal of Insanity* 23, no. 2 (1866): 263–79.

———. *A Treatise on the Medical Jurisprudence of Insanity*. 1838; Reprint, New York: Da Capo Books, 1983.

Reagan, Leslie J. *When Abortion Was a Crime: Women, Medicine, and Law in the United States, 1867–1973*. Berkeley: University of California Press, 1997.

"The Recent Case of Alleged Abortion: Complaint Dismissed." *New York Times*, Sept. 25, 1856: 1.

"Restell, the Female Abortionist." *National Police Gazette*, Mar. 13, 1847: 212.

"The Restell and Grant Case." *New York Daily Times*, Mar. 3, 1854: 4.

"The Restell Case." *New York Times*, Apr. 23, 1858: 5.

"The Restell Felony Case." *New York Daily Times (1851–1857)*, Feb. 16, 1854: 8; ProQuest Historical Newspapers.

"Restell's Charnel House." *National Police Gazette*, Feb. 28, 1846: 219.

Reuter, Edward Byron. *The Mulatto in the United States*. 1918; reprint, New York: Johnson Reprint, 1970.

———. *Race Mixture: Studies in Intermarriage and Miscegenation*. New York: Whittlesey House, 1931.

*Rhinelander, In re*. Supreme Court of New York, Appellate Division, Second Dept. 264 AD. 607; 36 N.Y.S. 2d 105, no. 6 July (1942): no number in original.

"Rhinelander Asks to Amend Charge." *New York Times*, Nov. 25, 1925: 3.

"Rhinelander Jury Reaches a Decision after Twelve Hours." *New York Times*, Dec. 5, 1925: 1, 12.

"Rhinelander Jury Warned by Defense." *New York Times*, Dec. 2, 1925: 3.

"Rhinelander Loses; No Fraud Is Found; Wife Will Sue Now." *New York Times*, Dec. 6, 1925: 1, 27.

"Rhinelander Says He Pursued Girl." *New York Times*, Nov. 18, 1925: 4.

"Rhinelander Suit." *Opportunity*, Jan. 1926: 4–5.

"Rhinelander Suit Suddenly Halted." *New York Times*, Nov. 20, 1925: 9.

"Rhinelander Suit to Go on, Says Mills." *New York Times*, Nov. 21, 1925: 1, 4.

"Rhinelander Suit under Negotiation." *New York Times*, Nov. 22, 1925: 1, 20.

"Rhinelander Tells of Baring Letters." *New York Times*, Nov. 17, 1925: 1, 10.

"Rhinelander Tells Story of Courtship." *New York Times*, Nov. 12, 1925: 1, 12.

"Rhinelander Verses Familiar to Stage." *New York Times*, Nov. 19, 1925: 6.

*Rhinelander v. Rhinelander*, 219 N.Y.S. 548 (1927).

*Rhinelander v. Rhinelander*, 157 N.E. 838 (1927).

"Rhinelander Wilts; Gets Adjournment." *New York Times*, Nov. 19, 1925: 6.

"Rhinelander's Wife Admits Negro Blood." *New York Times*, Nov. 11, 1925: 1, 14.

"Rhinelander's Wife Cries under Ordeal." *New York Times*, Nov. 24, 1925: 3.

"Rhinelander's Wife Now Planning Suit." *New York Times*, Nov. 28, 1925: 23.

Roberts, Mary Louise. "True Womanhood Revisited." *Journal of Women's History* 14, no. 1 (2002): 150–55.

Robinson, Daniel. *Strange Beasts and Idle Humors: The Insanity Defense from Antiquity to the Present*. Cambridge, Mass.: Harvard University Press, 1996.

"A Romance of the Court: Marriage of an Aged Attorney to His Fair Client." *Washington Post*, Nov. 3, 1883: 1.

Rosenberg, Charles. "Sexuality, Class, and Role in Nineteenth-Century America." *American Quarterly* 25 (1973): 131–53.

Rosenberg, Charles E. *The Trial of the Assassin Guiteau: Psychiatry and Law in the Guilded Age*. Chicago: University of Chicago Press, 1968.

Ross, Rodney A. "Mary Todd Lincoln, Patient at Bellevue Place, Batavia." *Journal of the Illinois State Historical Society* 63 (1970): 5–34.

Ryan, Mary P. *The Empire of the Mother: American Writing about Domesticity, 1830 to 1860*. New York: Haworth Press, 1982.

———. "The Power of Women's Networks: A Case Study of Female Moral Reform in Antebellum America," *Feminist Studies*, 5, no. 1 (1979): 68–85.

———. *Womanhood in America*. New York: Franklin Watts, 1983.

Sacks, Eva. "Representing Miscegenation Law." *Raritan* 8, no. 2 (1988): 39–69.

Sandburg, Carl. *Mary Lincoln: Wife and Widow*. New York: Harcourt, Brace, 1932.

Sapinsley, Barbara. *The Private War of Mrs. Packard*. New York: Paragon House, 1991.

Sarat, Austin. "Rhetoric and Remembrance: Trials, Transcription, and the Politics of Critical Reading." *Legal Studies Forum* 23 (1999): 355–79.

"Says Rhinelander Knew of Girl's Race." *New York Times*, Nov. 26, 1925: 3.

Schuetz, Janice. *The Logic of Women on Trial*. Carbondale: Southern Illinois University Press, 1994.

Schuetz, Janice, and Kathryn Snedaker. *Communication and Litigation*. Carbondale: Southern Illinois University Press, 1988.

"The Seduction in High Life." *New York Daily Times*, Feb 14, 1854: 1.

"The Shackford and Restell Case." *New York Daily Times*, Feb. 23, 1854: 8.

Shannon, A. H. *The Racial Integrity of the American Negro* [1925], edited by John D. Smith. Vol. 8, *Anti-Black Thought, 1863–1925*. New York: Garland, 1993.

Showalter, Elaine. *The Female Malady: Women, Madness, and English Culture*. New York: Pantheon Books, 1985.

Sklar, Kathryn Kish. *Catharine Beecher: A Study in American Domesticity*. New Haven: Yale University Press, 1973.

Small, Helen. *Love's Madness: Medicine, the Novel, and Female Insanity 1800–1865*. Oxford: Clarendon Press, 1996.

Smith, B. H. "Narrative Versions, Narrative Theories." In *On Narrative*, edited by W. J. T. Mitchell. Chicago: University of Chicago Press, 1981.

Smith-Rosenberg, Carroll. *Disorderly Conduct: Visions of Gender in Victorian America*. New York: Alfred A. Knopf, 1985.

———. "Puberty to Menopause: The Cycle of Femininity in Nineteenth-Century America." In *Clio's Consciousness Raised*, edited by Mary S. Hartmann and Lois Banner, 23–37. New York: Harper and Row, 1974.

Smith-Rosenberg, Carroll, and Charles Rosenberg. "The Female Animal: Medical and Biological Views of Woman and Her Role in Nineteenth-Century America." *Journal of American History* 60 (1973): 332–56.

Spiegel, Allen D., and Peter B. Suskind. "A Paroxysmal Insanity Plea in an 1865 Murder Trial." *Journal of Legal Medicine* 16 (1995): 585–606.

Spiering, Frank. *Lizzie*. New York: Random House, 1984.

Storer, Horatio Robinson. *The Causation, Course, and Treatment of Reflex Insanity in Women*. 1871; reprint, New York: Arno Press, 1972.

Stormer, Nathan. "In Living Memory: Abortion as Cultural Amnesia." *Quarterly Journal of Speech* 88, no. 3 (2002): 265–83.

"Told Rhinelander He Had Many Rivals." *New York Times*, Nov. 14., 1925: 1, 2.

*Trial of Madame Restell, Alias Ann Lohmann*. New York: n.p., 1841.

"The Trial of Miss Mary Harris." *New York Times*, July 9, 1865: 8.

Turner, Justin G., and Linda Levitt Turner. *Mary Todd Lincoln: Her Life and Letters*. New York: Alfred A. Knopf, 1972.

Tyre, Peg. "Managing Mommies." *Newsweek*, June 19, 2006: 10.

Vincinus, Martha. *Suffer and Be Still: Women in the Victorian Age*. Bloomington: Indiana University Press, 1973.

"Wages of Sin." *Brooklyn Eagle*, Feb. 25, 1878: 4.

Wasserstrom, William. *Heiress of All the Ages: Sex and Sentiment in the Genteel Tradition*. Minneapolis: University of Minnesota Press, 1959.

Weisberg, Robert. "Proclaiming Trials as Narratives: Premises and Pretenses." In *Law's Stories*, edited by Peter Brooks and Paul Gewirtz, 61–83. New Haven: Yale University Press, 1996.

Welter, Barbara. *Dimity Convictions: The American Woman in the Nineteenth Century*. Athens: Ohio University Press, 1976.

Wess, Robert. *Kenneth Burke: Rhetoric, Subjectivity, Postmoderism*. Cambridge: Cambridge University Press, 1996.

Wetlaufer, Gerald B. "Rhetoric and Its Denial in Legal Discourse." *Virginia Law Review* 76, no. 8 (1990): 1545–97.

White, James Boyd. *Heracles' Bow: Essays on the Rhetoric and Poetics of the Law*. Madison: University of Wisconsin Press, 1985.

———. *The Legal Imagination*. Chicago: University of Chicago Press, 1973.

Wiesenthal, Chris. *Figuring Madness in Nineteenth-Century Fiction*. New York: St. Martin's, 1997.

"Wife Admits Negro Blood during Trial." *Phoenix Gazette*, Nov. 10, 1925: 1.

Wilkie, Franc. "Reason Restored." *Chicago Times*, Aug. 24, 1875: 5.

Williamson, Joe. *New People: Miscegenation and Mulattoes in the United States*. New York: Free Press, 1980.

*Wonderful Trial of Caroline Lohman, Alias Restell*. New York: National Police Gazette, 1847.

Wright, Sarah. "Scientists Patent Prozac Use for PMS." MIT News Office, 1997, http://web .mit.edu/newsoffice/tt/1997/ju116/prozac.html (accessed July 23, 2003).

"Your Small Change Wanted." *New York Times*, July 1, 1865: 1.

# Index

A. CHEREE CARLSON is a professor in the Department of
Communication at Arizona State University, where she is also
affiliated with the women's studies program. Her articles have
appeared in publications such as the *Quarterly Journal of Speech*
and *Journal of American Culture.*

The University of Illinois Press
is a founding member of the
Association of American University Presses.

---

University of Illinois Press
1325 South Oak Street
Champaign, IL 61820-6903
www.press.uillinois.edu